garden
design

▶ This minimalist garden employs strong hard-landscaping and design features. Perfect for a low-maintenance garden used for entertaining.

versa. (See pages 224–227 for more information.)

Then you need to ask how you intend to use your garden and what your general situation is. If you have a young family it will be going against the grain to have a rambling cottage garden or an immaculate lawn; if you have little time to spare there is no point in developing the kind of garden that needs constant attention... and so on. If you want to use the space for living, perhaps as an area for entertaining friends, dining, or even practicing sport, rather than gardening, there are lots of ways of doing this too.

If you inherit a ready-made garden don't be in too much of a hurry to dig it up and start from scratch. Instead, live with it for a while to see what it has to offer in each season. And when redesigning, aim to retain any good plants or features and make the most of the garden's advantages. To see what plants thrive in your area observe other people's gardens and to get design ideas visit gardens that are open to the public and note effects that you like and how they are achieved.

▶ Many different materials can link the garden to the home—reclaimed railroad ties and gravel are a good combination for steps.

◀ The geometric lines of this formally planned herb garden are softened as the many different varieties begin to grow and billow out.

General design principles

Certain general principles apply with almost any garden. The materials you use for paths, hard areas, walls or fences, and screening, and for defining beds where applicable, should be in keeping with

those of the house, and the garden should relate well to the house. It often helps to have a hard surface—from gravel or pebbles, bricks, stone slabs, or even concrete—linking the house with the garden proper. Don't overstep the limitations of the plot and try to cram in more than will happily fit, and do select your plants to suit any constraints imposed by the nature of the soil and the garden's situation.

To make visual adjustments to the plot, use curves to disguise awkward shapes, open areas to make narrow parts of the plot seem wider, and thickly planted areas to narrow down a wide part. If a plot is long and narrow divide it crosswise to make a series of well-shaped areas leading on from each other.

▲ *You can liven up a simple family scheme with wacky furniture such as these sunflower-inspired tables and stools—perfect for young children.*

Safety and convenience of use are important considerations in any garden to be used for leisure, especially by families or older or disabled people. Potential danger spots include changes of level or direction, which should all be gradual if there is any question of special safety needs, and hard surfaces, which should have good grip and not be slippery after rain. Anything that looks as though it could be used needs to be as strong as it looks. This includes posts which a child might climb or an older person lean on to rest, garden seats, which may need to be constructed so that they are easy to get up from by someone elderly, and fences, which may need to be strong enough to be hit by a football or run into by a bicycle. Water is an attraction in any garden but how to use it needs be considered with care as open water can be a danger where children are playing. A well-designed moving water feature, however small, is a delight for everyone who uses the garden for relaxation. Paths and openings should be wide enough, where possible, for two people to walk side by side, and certainly need to be wide enough for one person and a wheelbarrow. If a path leads alongside a border you need to allow extra width for the plants to spill over the edge of the border or the path will be lost in no time. A curving path can look even better if it curves around something such as a beautiful shrub, while a focal point, whether an ornamental tree or shrub, a stone birdbath, a piece of sculpture or a fountain can give the eye something to rest on and give a path something to lead up to.

Using color

Color is an essential element of the garden design, and although it will partly be a question of personal taste there are a few general rules about the effect that colors have—used singly, as a backdrop, or in combination.

Green—There are more shades of green than all other colors put together and it forms an essential buffer and backdrop to colors throughout the garden. Used on its own, it can be clipped and elegant, or lush and jungly, a calm and subtle range of forms, or exotic blend of glossy leaves.

Pink—Pink may be rich and dramatic as in the purple pinks and hot magentas, soft and gentle as in the middle range of rose-pinks, or pale and sugary. It is best set against blues and purples.

Red—Hot reds are exciting and dramatic, but too much will give you the jitters, so tone them down with lots of surrounding, cool green. Exciting contrasts can be made with true blue and scarlet red or bright yellow.

Blue—True sky blue is one of the rarest of nature's colors, but there are numerous other blues ranging from cold, icy pale blue through lavenders to deepest violet. Blues in shade create a somber mood, but look cheery and fresh if combined with yellow in spring. Darker shades suit strong summer light.

◄ *Less can be more. This garden relies on well placed natural materials—rocks, gravel, and grasses—to create a calming impression.*

Yellow—Yellows, like reds, are warm and inviting, but some are very strong and even brassy, so use these in moderation, with lots of green.

White—This is the most difficult color to use well and white gardens can easily look either insipid or like a pile of dirty washing. But a white garden can also be sophisticated and elegant, especially if lots of architectural, green, large-leaved plants are used to create a lush backdrop. A good rule is to use only warm whites—those with pink or yellow in them, or cool whites—those containing a hint of blue or green. Don't mix them.

Making your design

While you are bound to want to make adjustments as the garden develops, having an overall plan to start with is important, especially where expensive materials and hard construction work will be involved, or when using budget-breaking plants that don't like being dug up and replanted. Start by making a rough plan of your plot, noting any good and bad points, such as shady and sunny, dry or damp areas, good and bad views, good shrubs or trees that you'd like to retain and the direction of the wind.

Use copies of this to map out rough ideas about planning and planting. Then, when you are ready, take the garden's measurements carefully and work out your final plan to scale on squared paper, marking out both position and eventual size of plants you intend to use and the position of all the construction features such as paved areas, steps, and garden divisions. We hope that this book will help by providing some ready-made solutions to a variety of real-life plots whose owners all have very different ideas about what they want from a garden. Seeing how these designs are made up, the plants our designer chose, practical projects for planting or building, and the alternative schemes that can be devised for the same plot should give you lots of ideas to borrow when you are planning your own garden.

◄ *If you want a garden full of flowers, give some attention and preplanning to how well the range of colors work together.*

water gardens

Water adds an exciting extra dimension to even the tiniest garden. It reflects light, changing clouds, clear blue sky, or nearby plants. A limpid pool creates a feeling of space while flowing water is refreshing to listen to and fascinating to watch, especially when lit at night. Whether still or moving, water attracts a whole range of wildlife—small mammals, frogs and toads, birds, butterflies, dragonflies, and other insects, many of which are beneficial to the garden.

pond and bog garden

If you make a pond the dominant feature in the garden everything else can be designed to acknowledge it. All you will need is somewhere to sit and watch the water and a pathway from which you can observe the life of the pond at close quarters and enjoy all it has to offer.

Guidelines to design

Placing a pond requires some planning. First, a pond needs light and shelter. If the place for sitting and looking at it can be sited with the light falling from behind, it will enhance the pond experience. Once filled, the pond will be kept topped up by the natural rainfall in all but the driest weather, so water supply is not vital. Choose an area not too close to the house and without overhanging trees—fall leaves will decay in the water and make it smelly and shade will cause algae and slime to gather on the water. Full sun is also to be avoided, except for a water lily pond, as this too encourages excessive growth of algae.

The best possible site is a hollow or in a low level of the garden where you'd expect water might collect naturally. Make sure, however, that this is not a frost pocket where plants will fail to thrive, and not a place where the water table will rise higher than the lining of the pond. This will cause the liner to balloon in the middle and you will have an unwanted "hippo" in your pond.

Style and size of pond

When it comes to choosing a garden pond, natural and informal are the key words for all but the grandest or most formal gardens. Make your pond as appropriately large as you can afford. Not only does it look better, but also the bigger the surface

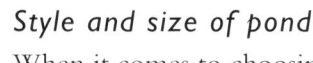

◄ *Moisture-loving plants for a bog or pond garden grow rapidly and are easy to maintain; they soon provide a lush, almost tropical look.*

◀ *Make sure you plant some marginal aquatics in the shallow reaches of the pond to soften the edges where it meets the bank.*

If you plan to stock fish, your pond needs to be at least 90cm/3ft deep at the center, in case the surface freezes in winter and so that the fish can hide away from predators. It's a bad idea to introduce ornamental "koi" carp to a natural pond. They need a high quality filtration system and impeccably clean water with plenty of depth. And they also need protection from herons, which, although beautiful birds, will wade in and enjoy delicious takeouts at your expense.

Wood and stone are natural companions to water, and decking in treated timber can extend over the pond so that you can stand above the water. A means of crossing the water, usually best located at the neck of the pond, can be used to add to the sense of flow and link the two sides of the pond visually as well as physically.

area the less likely it is to suffer from unwanted algae. Keep curves generous and unfussy and avoid a complete circle, which, like squares and rectangles, is suitable only for a formal setting. A kidney shape with a generously proportioned inner curve will look good and allow you to observe pond activity more easily. Modern flexible liners, used with a cushioning layer of underlay, are the best materials for such ponds.

Digging out will create a lot of spoil that you will have to cope with. Rather than disposing of it, you may prefer to landscape the rest of the garden, and use the spoil from the pond to create undulations. Save any fertile topsoil for the planted areas whatever you do.

▶ *This beautiful pond and water feature emulates a mountain stream. The margins are densely filled with bog and pond plants.*

Finishing details

Edge at least half of the pond with a damp garden, or bog area, where moisture-loving plants can grow and soften the outline. They will also provide shelter for wildlife. Include a shelf for marginal plants and a gently sloping shingle beach for small animals to climb in and out of the water. If possible allow for grass to run right to the edge of part of the pond, for a natural look.

designer's pond and bog garden

A constantly damp garden is often the result of badly drained surface water. There may be a heavy clay subsoil preventing drainage, or a hard, compacted surface where the soil has not been cultivated for many years, or the garden may be sited in a hollow which gathers the run-off rainwater from surrounding higher ground.

▲ *A predominantly damp site is ideal for bog plants, most of which are lushly dramatic and will shelter a range of amphibian wildlife.*

GARDEN DATA

location:	New Jersey
climate:	mild
soil type:	wet clay, slightly acid
direction:	east
aspect:	overlooks woodland

Design brief

This is a small garden with a high water table, which makes it difficult to site a pond. In consistently wet weather the pressure from held ground water will cause a pond liner to billow up like a hippo. However, the owners of the garden would like to encourage wildlife and are keen to make the most of their boggy ground. We need to bear in mind that the level of moisture will vary at different times of the year as the water table rises and falls.

Design solution

The answer is to go with the flow! We designed the garden informally, along curvy, natural lines, using timber ties for the decking and bridge, and log rounds to form stepping stones in the grassy path.

The planting is equally informal and concentrates on several big, dramatic feature plants, interspersed with moisture-loving perennials and grasses. The larger plants form natural

–/ 3.5 m x 7 m / 43 ft x 23 ft –

barriers so that the whole garden cannot be seen from any one vantage point. The secrecy and intimacy that this kind of planting creates also provides hideaways for small and timid wild creatures.

▲ Log rounds used as
stepping stones.

iris

▲ Some irises
require a
wet situation.

plank bridge

water butt

◀ A simple plank
over the pond.

▶ A recycled water tank
houses a small lily.

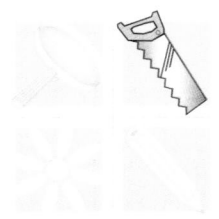

practical projects

▲ Primula vialii *is a hardy perennial.*

A bog—or damp—garden is easily made using flexible lining material and makes a lovely, informal water feature. Bog areas can link a pond to the rest of the garden but they can also form a feature in their own right.

Bogs in nature aren't a feature of open, sunny places, so you need to site this kind of garden thoughtfully. If you haven't made a pond near which a damp garden will be sited, the most natural looking place will be in a hollow (existing or dug out) in a low-lying part of the garden, preferably where there is some shade.

You are aiming to create an area that is constantly moist, yet where there is enough movement of air through the soil to prevent it from becoming stagnant and provide plant roots with oxygen. When constructed next to a pond the bog garden will absorb some overspill water, but if it is self-contained you will need to top it up in dry weather.

All you do is to make a hollow of a suitable depth and shape and line it with perforated pond liner. A bottom layer of gravel will help drainage, while clean soil and a gravel top-dressing form the planting medium.

▼ *This cross-section shows how a bog garden can be created using simple materials. This will enable damp-loving plants to flourish.*

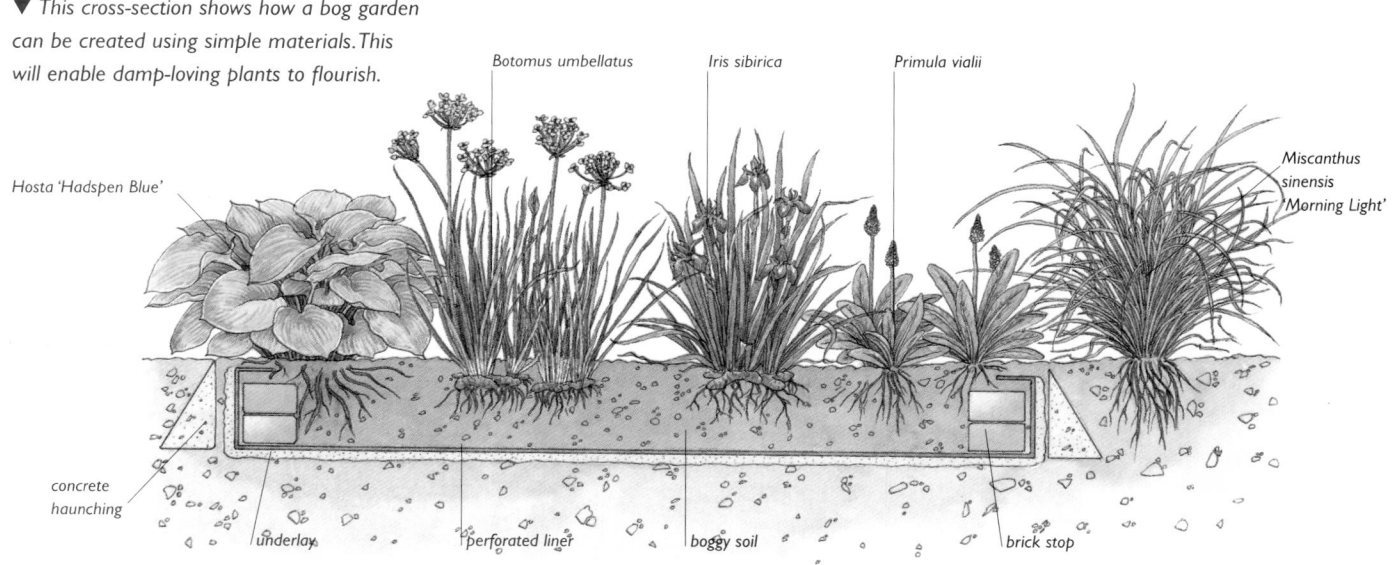

Botomus umbellatus

Iris sibirica

Primula vialii

Hosta 'Hadspen Blue'

Miscanthus sinensis 'Morning Light'

concrete haunching

underlay

perforated liner

boggy soil

brick stop

gargoyle, decorative mask, or a length of bamboo.

Moving-water features are often fixed to a wall, and therefore relatively safe even when there are young children about, but you should always bear safety in mind if you have a young family. If this is not a consideration, and you would rather have a still and silent feature for calm, serene contemplation, it is very easy to produce a miniature water lily pond in a watertight container. If you do this, however, don't even think about adding even the smallest fish (the water could get much too hot in summer, and will freeze in winter). Ground-level features such as fountains or millstones spilling onto

▶ The stone Buddha adds to the mood of contemplation created by the gentle sound of flowing water and simple planting.

pebbles may be safe for children as there is no depth of water, but even the smallest pool and fountain, with any water depth however shallow, would be inadvisable for unattended young children.

Discreet charms

Sometimes discretion is the better part of fixed water features. They are at home in shady positions, where they can gather moss. The sound should be restful not irritating, and not annoying to the neighbors. It becomes more muffled as the depth

of water in the receptacle increases: a depth of 25cm/10in or more creates a restful splash. The rate of flow and the height from which the water falls are also important (the faster and the higher, the noisier). Water falling onto stones creates a soothing splashing sound quite different from the sound of water on water. The wider the delivery pipe, the more restful the gurgle.

Adjusting the flow valve on the pump enables you to vary the rate of water flow. Make sure that the valve is accessible so that you can experiment until you get the visual effect—and sound—exactly to your taste. Art lies in concealment—the pump must not be visible, and preferably should not be audible.

◀ This contemporary water feature comprises a series of stones. The sharp concrete edges are softened by the use of lilies and grasses.

designer's water feature garden

Patios and terraces can often seem devoid of interest. One way of enlivening the space is to add a small, self-contained water feature. This will provide the soft and refreshing sound of water during lazy summer lunches al fresco and a theatrical night-time feature when carefully lit.

▲ At present, the home and garden do not fully integrate. A water feature on the terrace echoes the stream along the boundary.

GARDEN DATA

location:	Connecticut
climate:	cold/windy
soil type:	light clay
direction:	west facing
aspect:	sloping to trees

Design brief

This imposing 19th-century home has a substantial width of terrace along the two sides of the house facing the garden. The garden slopes down and away from the house and so there is no feeling of the house nestling in its setting. The problem was to find a way of linking the building with the garden below.

Design solution

A stream runs along the far boundary at the bottom of the site and this provided the clue as to how to link house and garden. A water feature integral to the terrace would bring a natural element to the hard landscaping and echo the wilder parts of the garden below. The owners love to entertain and much of the level terrace space is taken up with tables and seating for large parties. An existing old brick wall at one end of the main terrace offered an ideal support for a wall-mounted fountain which would trickle into a reclaimed

– 6m x 3m//18ft x 10ft –

stone trough. This was set in stone chippings among random sized crazy paving identical in color and texture to the slabs on the existing terrace. By matching colors and textures we were able to move from formal terrace to informal water feature with the minimum of work and cost. The fountain is softened by the planting of large ferns, perennials, hostas and grasses, and aquatic plants.

▲ Water spouts out of a mounted lion's head into a reclaimed stone trough.

▲ Waterproofed wooden barrels as containers offer further scope for water plants.

▲ Asplenium ferns appreciate the moist, shady, cool conditions found beside water.

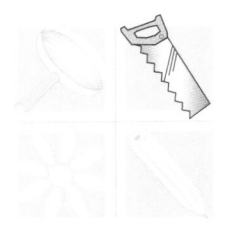

practical projects

▲ *A reproduction antique drinking fountain is an ideal feature for an enclosed courtyard garden, nestling among climbing plants.*

DESIGNER'S TIPS

• If you raise your submersible pump by standing it on bricks you are less likely to suck debris into it.

• Either bring in your pump during the winter, or make sure that you use it for at least an hour once a week to keep it in good order.

• If you have a pump with a filter clean this out regularly.

• **ALWAYS CALL A QUALIFIED ELECTRICIAN TO INSTALL A PUMP.**

Water features look sophisticated but are relatively simple to install. They can be bought complete and ready made or you can buy a submersible pump and devise something of your own imagining, with water from a wall spout or welling from the ground.

Small water features

Water features must be beautiful of course, but for most of us they also need to be simple to install and maintain. The understated is more successful than the overambitious and the design should suit the surroundings in scale and style.

Naturally you need access to an electricity supply, with a length of armored cable and a waterproof connector to connect to the pump. The cable from the supply, protected with armored sleeving, must be safely buried at least 60cm/2ft below the soil surface, and you should always use a Ground-Fault Interrupter (GFI), circuit breaker, fitted to the socket, to cause the circuit to cut out if anything goes wrong. The pump should be completely submerged and connected to the water feature with flexible plastic piping.

A 24-volt pump should be satisfactory for a small feature, with a transformer to adapt the mains supply. This lives inside the house.

▲ *This traditional wall fountain is in a classical style, and would certainly add interest to any terrace or patio.*

▶ *A bubble fountain erupts from the center of an old mill wheel surrounded by cobbles that conceal the reservoir.*

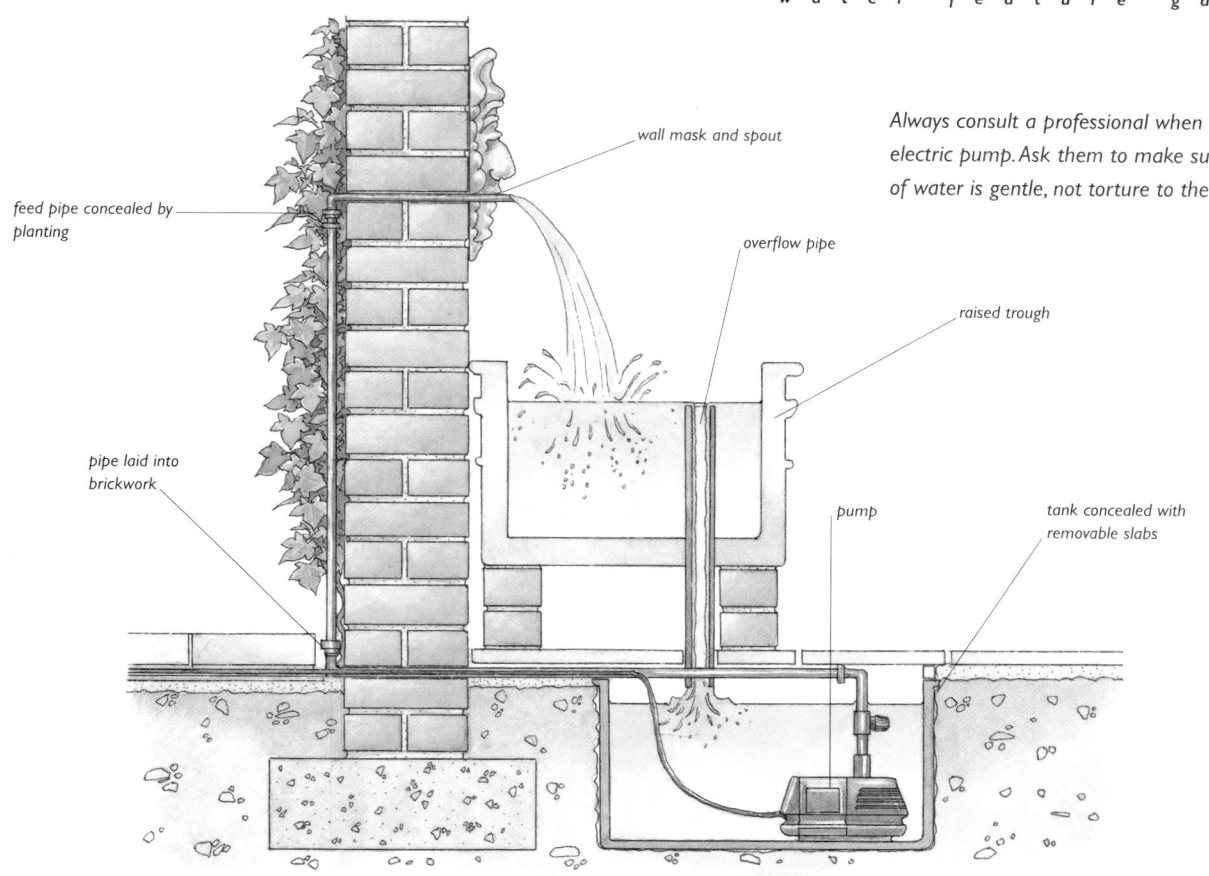

wall mask and spout

feed pipe concealed by planting

overflow pipe

raised trough

pipe laid into brickwork

pump

tank concealed with removable slabs

Always consult a professional when installing an electric pump. Ask them to make sure the flow of water is gentle, not torture to the ear.

water plants and planting

Lush and green are usually the keynotes for planting around a water feature, with ferns and mossy-looking plants enjoying the cool moisture. Exceptions apply to a water bubble, fountain, or rill in a sunny courtyard or on the patio, where pots of spiky and exotic hot-weather plants provide a tropical mood.

Cool schemes

Since few plants like to be disturbed by constantly moving water most planting is done next to the water feature, although leaves and flowers will soften the edges. Shape of foliage and habit of growth are all-important, and you'll be surprised how many shades of green there are for color contrasts. Including a few evergreens such as hellebores, will make sure there is interest throughout the winter months.

◄ Asplenium scolopendrium *'Crispum'*

▼ Helleborus orientalis

WATER PLANTS

Ferns

Ferns make fronds of green, large or small, smooth or crimped, broad or narrow, beside the water. You may be able to grow smaller ones in a crevice in a wall.

Adiantum capillus-veneris (maidenhair fern)—fine, wiry stems with delicate, shell-like leaves; good in shady waterside crevices
ht and sp 15–30cm/6–12in

Asplenium scolopendrium (spleenwort or hart's tongue fern)—tapering, slightly leathery, wavy-edged fronds of bright apple-green (evergreen)
ht and sp 60cm/2ft

A. s. 'Crispum'—densely growing, upright, very frilled, apple-green fronds (evergreen)
ht and sp 60cm/2ft

A.s. Marginatum Group—(various upright and frilly-edged hart's tongue ferns, some with tooth-edged fronds)
ht 35cm/14in
sp 45cm/18in

Dryopteris affinis (golden male fern)—tall stalks have golden brown scales and the unfurling fronds are yellowish green, turning deep green (often evergreen)
ht and sp to 80cm/32in

D. erythrosora—smaller, deciduous variety with reddish coloring
ht 60cm/2ft
sp 38cm/15in

D. filix-mas (male fern)—very tall, clump-forming variety with mid-green foliage
ht and sp to 1.2m/4ft

Phegopteris connectilis (narrow beech fern)—low-growing, pale-green, bracken-like fern in light yellowish green, for acid soils
ht 20–25cm/8–10in
sp 30cm/12in

Polystichum setiferum (hedge fern)—soft, waving fronds of mid-green for dappled shade (evergreen)
ht 60cm–1.2m/2–4ft
sp 45–90cm/18–36in

Woodsia polystichoides (hollyfern)—small, pale green fern, native of rocky places and ideal for moist, but constantly draining, areas such as in a wall by a

spout (needs shelter/protection from frost)
ht and sp 20cm/8in

Water lilies for a tiny pond

Water lilies (*Nymphaea* cultivars) thrive in still water and a sunny spot. Several are small enough for a miniature pond in a barrel.

N. tetragona 'Helvola'—clear yellow, star-shaped flowers; tiny, maroon-mottled leaves

N. 'Pygmaea Rubra'—rose-pink flowers, deepening to blood red; copper-green leaves

N. 'Sulphurea'—bright yellow flowers raised well above the surface; brown-marked leaves

N. 'Daubeny'—starry blue, yellow-stamened, scented flowers; pointed, olive-green leaves (needs min. 21°C/70°F water temperature summer and 10°C/50°F winter)

Other plants at home beside the water

Arum lily (*Zantedeschia aethiopica*)—white spathes on erect, fleshy stems and broad, smooth, tapering leaves
ht 45–90cm/18–36in
sp to 60cm/2ft

Astilbe (*Astilbe*)—feathery plumes of flowers in red, cream, and pink; good varieties include *Astilbe* 'Bridal Veil' (syn. 'Brautschleier') (creamy white), 'Fanal' (deep crimson), 'Sprite' (shell pink)

▲ Hosta *'Tokudama'*

and *A. chinensis* var. *pumila* (dwarf, reddish pink),
ht and sp 20–90cm/8–36in

Bleeding heart (*Dicentra spectabilis*)—hanging lockets of pink or white, feathery foliage (see page 240)

Candelabra primroses (*Primula* species)—erect stems of tapering or drumhead flowerheads; good varieties include *P. japonica*, *P. pulverulenta*, *P. secundiflora*, *P. vialii*
ht to 45–90cm/18–36in
sp 45–60cm/18–24in

Hellebores (*Helleborus* x *ballardiae* 'December Dawn', and varieties of *H. niger* and *H. orientalis*)—nodding, cup-shaped flowers in plum or white, some pink-stained or with pretty markings
ht and sp to 30cm/12in

Meadowsweet (*Filipendula*)—fuzzy, deeply scented flowers in creamy white, red, and pink; good varieties include *F. rubra* (red stems, peach-pink flowers), *F.r.* 'Venusta' (rose-pink flowers—both these can be very tall), *F. ulmaria* (creamy white—smaller)
ht 60cm–1m/2ft–3ft or more

Hostas (*Hosta* cultivars)—shade-loving plants with broad, attractive leaves and heads of tubular, bell-shaped flowers (see page 115)

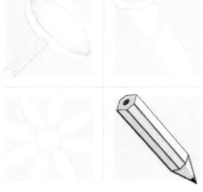

design alternatives

SKETCHES

Here are some alternative schemes our designer penciled for our water garden. They follow simple, classical lines using traditional materials such as brick, terracotta, and stone, to complement the central water feature.

brick wall approx 1.5m/5ft high with brick or tile coping

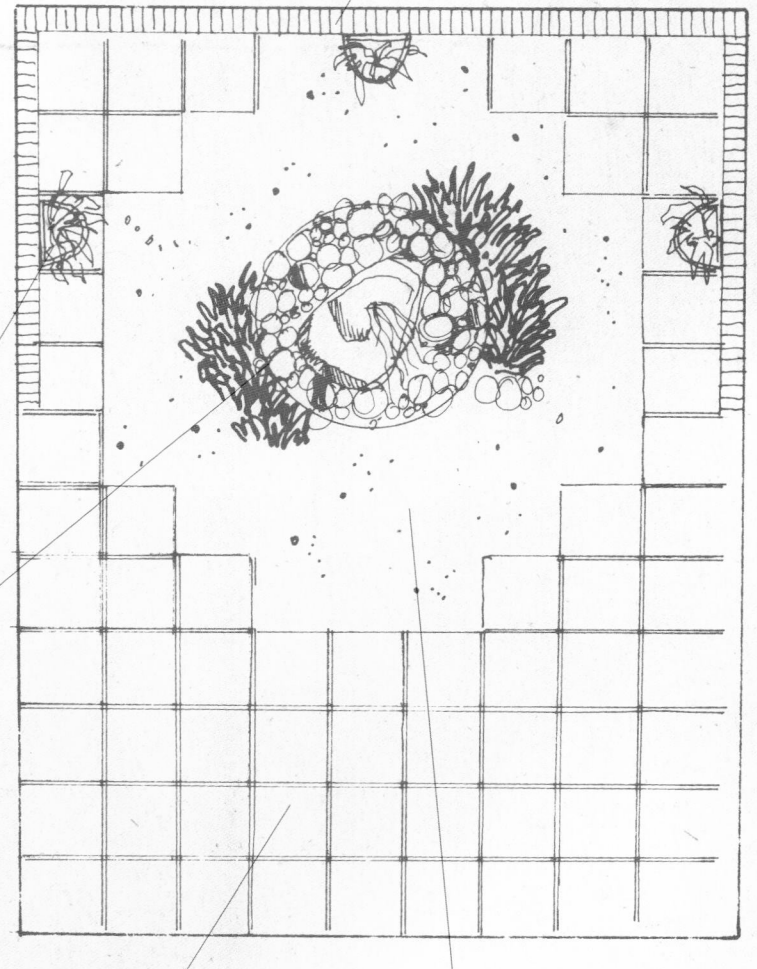

hanging clay or ceramic planters (purchased), all matching, fixed to wall

pierced boulder water feature (purchased), over pebble base, with planting or irises or grasses to soften edges

terracotta tiles

20mm/¾in angular stone chippings over weedproof membrane

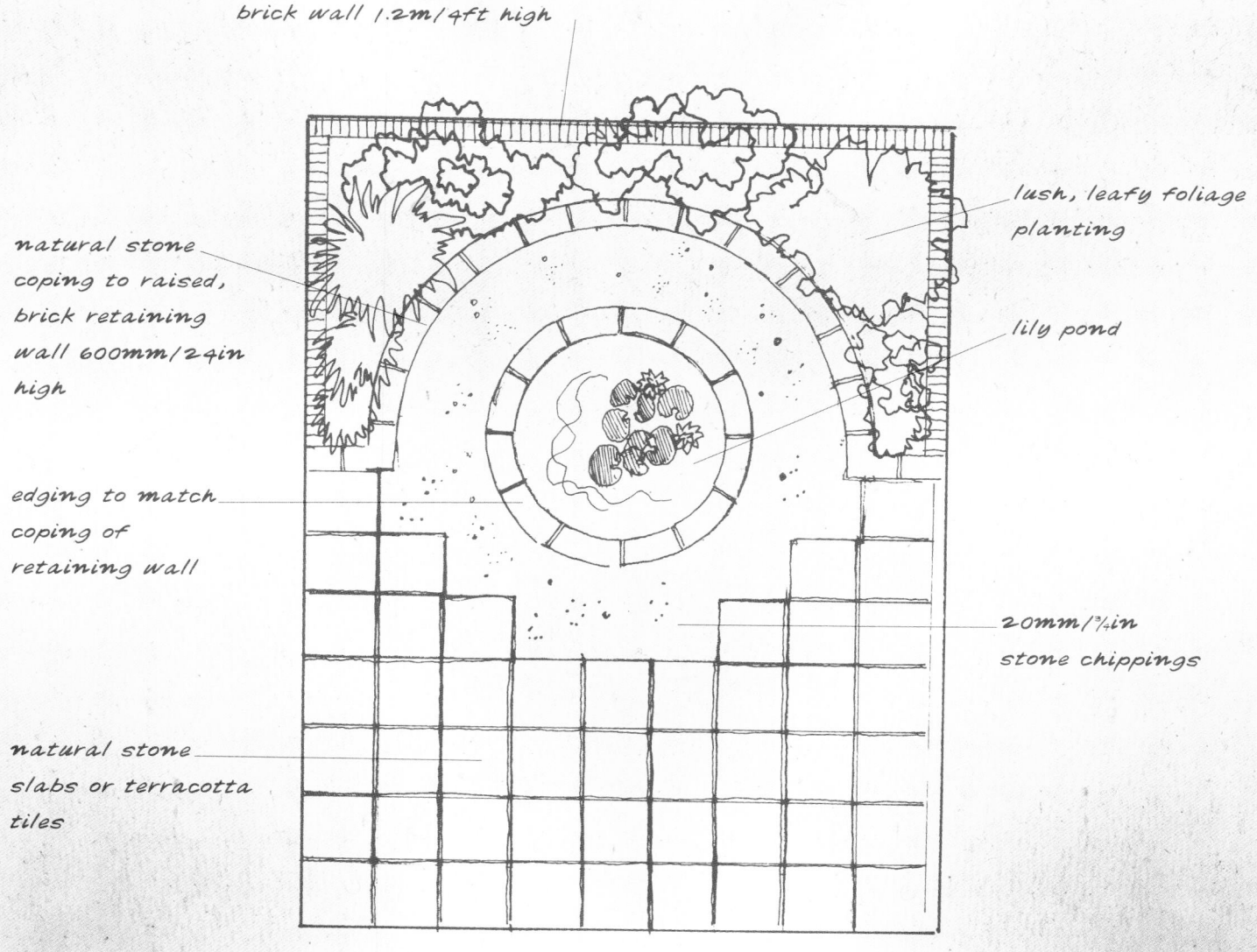

brick wall 1.2m/4ft high

lush, leafy foliage planting

natural stone coping to raised, brick retaining wall 600mm/24in high

lily pond

edging to match coping of retaining wall

20mm/³⁄₄in stone chippings

natural stone slabs or terracotta tiles

traditional gardens

The gardens in this section are inspired by some traditional garden classics. They all give the impression of being in harmony with nature or with their built surroundings, and of having an unchanging quality of stillness about them. They are places to sit, places to admire plants and the way they mix and mingle, and also places to enjoy cultivating plants as an occupation.

cottage garden

A cottage garden doesn't have to be in the country, but a small plot with a compact design is a key ingredient. In a cottage garden vegetables, flowers, and fruits are jumbled up together so that the effect is of a haze of myriad colors, textures, and scents with plants allowed to self-seed at random.

▲ *In a cottage garden a wide range of plants— from flowers and herbs to fruits and vegetables—are grown closely together.*

An idyll from the past

The real cottage garden of old was far removed from our romantic visions of today in which flowering plants loll over winding paths attracting bees and butterflies; for the plot around a cottage in the past had to be put to good use. Plants were grown for food, for medicine, and for practical purposes such as dyeing and keeping away fleas and lice or scenting household linen to disguise the smell of mildew. Flowering plants on the whole had a practical function as well as providing visual delight. The crammed appearance of the garden resulted from the need to get as much use as possible out of a small plot.

Modern cottage gardeners can adapt this idea by growing a variety of fruits, herbs, and vegetables among the flowers and by making use of every bit of space, including the vertical. The look is not for those who prefer order. In it plants jostle against their neighbors with not a patch of bare earth in sight. Informality is the key

to this style. The would-be cottage gardener needs to be warned, however, that this look is deceptive. Creating, and even more so maintaining, a successful garden in the cottage style is hard work.

The informality of appearance belies the art and work involved. But if you want to learn to love your plants and have the time, a cottage garden may be the garden for you.

Essentials

It doesn't matter if your house is not a cottage, but ideally the garden should be compact. The surroundings are important. Boundaries in particular need to be in keeping with the style of the garden. True cottagers were gardening gleaners and used what came to hand and so simplicity of materials is best. A wattle or hurdle fence for example is more in keeping than something complicated or metallic, and picket fencing, recycled pallets, or even chestnut paling can lend the right informal tone.

◄ *Filling your borders with traditional plants that suit your soil and situation is the ideal way to create the cottage garden look.*

A good hedge also makes an attractive boundary for this style of garden. For higher hedges a natural look can be achieved using native plants such as hawthorn and blackthorn. Robust shrub roses such as the rugosa roses will make thick flowery hedges with red hips in the fall and winter. Hornbeam or hazel make good deciduous hedges and hazel poles can be used as plant supports. Holly in the hedge makes the garden more interesting in winter, as do low dividing hedges of box, another evergreen. Lavender, rosemary, or roses grown as a low to medium hedge defining areas within the garden will give flowers and scents as well as structure. Climbing plants such as honeysuckle or rambling roses can be used to add flowery confusion to a fence or hedge.

Maintenance

To maintain your cottage garden you will need to be adept with a hoe, for plants and weeds will seed themselves in the spaces. Don't be too ruthless in removing seedlings however, as some self-sown annuals will add their authentic cottage garden charm. It also pays to collect ripe seed from annuals and biennials such as poppies, pot marigolds, and foxgloves so that you can sow them in your chosen places.

Planning and design

Many of the things you grow will need your attention during the summer, and it's as well to allow

▶ *This ancient stone seat makes a perfect resting place in which to appreciate the scents, sights, and sounds of a cottage garden.*

yourself a few stepping places between the apparently closely knit plants so that you can deadhead a rose, pick your currants, goose-berries, or pole beans, adjust the supports and apply the hoe, as well as occasionally, in most summers, water a thirsty phlox or spray a mildewed michaelmas daisy.

In planning your own cottage garden, bear in mind that such gardens, while charming and colorful in spring and summer, can look dull in winter without evergreens to provide interest and color. The essentially unstructured look, with winding paths and informal planting, also needs to include some structural elements if it's not to look a mess.

designer's cottage garden

The cottage garden evolved as a means of growing as many flowers, vegetables, fruits, and herbs as possible in a small space. Everything is jumbled up together, so this style is not for the tidy minded. Cottage gardens are colorful and charming, especially in the spring and summer when they come into their own.

▲ *The established hedges are worth maintaining in this otherwise under-exploited country plot.*

GARDEN DATA

location:	▦ Ohio
climate:	▦ mild
soil type:	▦ chalk/clay
direction:	▦ west facing
aspect:	▦ open downland

The brief

This small, west-facing, country garden has great views of open farmland and often spectacular sunsets. It already has useful, dense, boundary hedges to protect from cold winds and the garden has plenty of sun, but the border beneath the hedge on the south side stays shady and cool until the afternoon. The owners love the idea of a traditional flower garden mixed with a few vegetables. They are young and fit and don't mind the physical work entailed in managing their new plot.

The design solution

We stripped the existing turf, used a nonresidual spray to kill germinating weed seedlings and then dug in loads of ecocompost to enrich the soil. To make life easier we then covered the entire surface of the garden, except for the patio, with a layer of washed pea gravel, allowing for curving paths to connect different areas. The shingle will help to keep weeds

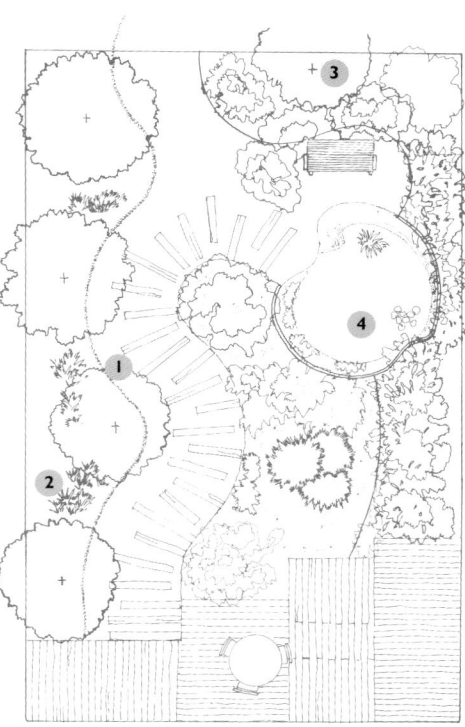

– *20m x 9m/65ft x 28ft* –

down and they will be easier to remove. No cottage garden should be without at least one fruit tree and for additional structure we included hazel wigwams to support climbing annuals and vegetables. A small wildlife pond is a surprise element in a sunny corner.

▶ A Victoria plum tree
provides summer fruits.

plum tree

pond

▲ An informal pond
benefits the ecosystem.

bulbs

▲ A variety of spring bulbs
planted in the grass.

path

▲ French oak
ties are laid
as a path.

practical projects

True cottagers grew plants mainly for practical purposes, using every inch of space available. Whether or not the plants are to be used, the cottage garden look is still very much in fashion. A multitude of plants of all kinds flourish at close quarters and all you need are plant supports and somewhere to walk.

Minimal skill required

Maintaining a cottage garden will require quite a bit of skill and hard work, but the skills involved in putting it together are not beyond the reach of anyone who can manage a few simple tools. Cottage gardens need frequent titivating, so good access is required, and every available bit of space is used for plants— including the vertical.

A freestanding support for climbing plants is useful if you don't have suitable walls or fences, or have already covered them with plants. It makes a decorative, semipermanent feature to give the garden some structural interest during the winter months when the soil is mostly bare.

The most stable support is wider at its base than at the top and a wigwam shape is ideal as it is unlikely to topple over in strong winds. Straight hazel poles, willow withies, or simple, thick bamboo poles are all equally suitable.

To make a natural looking walkway over the grass, set weather-proofed railroad ties or lengths of pressure-treated timber into the lawn or gravel surface.

◄ *When plants are grown closely together, they support each other to some extent and less staking is therefore needed.*

DESIGNER'S TIPS

• Buy a hoe. You'll need it to remove unwanted seedlings that will spring up everywhere.

• Don't lay fine gravel if you own a cat. It makes a wonderful litter tray!

• Stake tall plants with blue, pink, or red painted bamboo stakes, for protection and added color.

creating a wigwam

Choose a level site for the wigwam, and clear the ground of weeds. Decide how tall you want it to be, then add one half again to determine the length of the individual poles. This is to allow for the slope of the poles and the amount to be buried in the ground for stability.

1 To mark the position of the outer poles, drive a pole into the center of the prepared area and tie a length of string to it. Mark out a circle, approximately 1m/3ft in diameter.

2 Cut a piece of weed-suppressing membrane to the size of the wigwam at the base, make a hole in the center, and slip it over the central pole. Weigh it down with a layer of gravel, or small stones.

3 Drive the poles into the ground around the perimeter of the circle, bending them inwards. Secure them about 30cm/12in from the top with string or wire. Wind rounds of wire or flexible cane at regular intervals up the wigwam.

LAYING A TIMBER PATH

First decide on the position of each timber. Stand on the timber to prevent it moving, and cut along the edge all round with a sharp half-moon edger.

Remove the turf and line the base of the trench with a thin layer of cement. Lay the timber on top.

Tamp down the timber, making sure it is flush with the lawn. When you have finished, check the level with a level.

cottage plants and planting

The cottage garden is at its best in spring and summer, brimming with flowering spring bulbs, summer annuals, and seasonal perennials. Herbs, fruit, and vegetables among the flowers are an essential part of the look. Choose ornamental forms whenever you can. Evergreens give structure, shape, and winter interest.

Cottage garden flowers

An area of rough grass planted with bulbs adds charm to the cottage garden. For a natural look, scatter the bulbs on the ground and plant them where they fall. Choose a spot beneath a deciduous tree or shrub so that the crocuses, daffodils, and other spring bulbs can get the light they need at flowering time.

Herbaceous perennials play a key role in cottage garden planting, with annuals sown or planted out in patches in between. The annuals will self-seed in places where they feel at home and the perennials will quickly form large clumps which can be divided in spring or fall to make more plants. Plants grown close together soon get hungry. Winter gives you the opportunity to mulch the soil with well-rotted farmyard manure or your own garden compost (see pages 80–81), to feed the perennials and keep the soil in good heart.

▶ Rosa gallica *is an ancient medicinal plant.*

Small trees and shrubs

A small fruit tree makes an ornamental and useful focal point which will also provide perching places for songbirds. Half-standards (with a clear, short length of stem below the branches) are on the right scale. Attracting wildlife is part of the garden's appeal so use shrubs such as buddleja to draw the butterflies, or plant a pyracantha to feed and shelter the birds, especially in winter.

Profile plants

Aster novi-belgii 'Apple Blossom'
MICHAELMAS DAISY
'APPLE BLOSSOM'

Michaelmas daisies help to extend the life of the garden well into the fall and like all good cottage garden perennials they quickly make generous clumps. 'Apple Blossom' is a soft, old-fashioned pink and is particularly vigorous and hardy. No staking is needed, but the plant may

need to be sprayed to control powdery mildew.

ht 75cm/30in

sp 45cm/18in

Soil and situation

Very undemanding as to soil. Best in a light and sunny position but will flower even in semishade.

Foeniculum vulgare 'Rubra'
RED FENNEL

Tall, feathery-leaved fennel is a wonderful adornment and a traditional cottage garden herb. Red-, bronzed-, or purple-leaved forms lend a touch of distinction. All have flattened umbels of yellowish flowers which add to the plant's delicate architecture and attract beneficial hoverflies to the garden. 'Rubra' is a red-leaved form.

ht to 1m/3ft

sp 45cm/18in

Soil and situation

Shaded, well-drained garden soil.

Rosa gallica
FRENCH OR PROVINS ROSE

This is the apothecary's rose of ancient origin, whose purplish crimson flowers yield the best rose oil. It needs little pruning and is small and compact enough for small-scale gardens. Use it to add height in mixed planting.

ht 90cm–1.2m/3–4ft

sp 90cm/3ft

Soil and situation

Fertile, well-drained soil in sun.

▲ *Currant bushes provide vitamin-rich fruits.*

▲ *Fennel has aromatic, feathery leaves.*

SUITABLE PLANTS

Perennials

Centranthus ruber (valerian)
Dianthus (pinks), such as 'Dad's Favourite', 'Gran's Favourite', 'London Delight', 'Mrs Sinkins', 'Prudence'
Geranium (cranesbill), such as 'Johnson's Blue' and *G. renardii*
Heuchera (alum root), such as *Heuchera cylindrica* 'Greenfinch', 'Palace Purple'
Lupinus polyphyllus Russell hybrids (Russell lupin)
Nepeta (catmint), such as 'Souvenir d'André Chaudron' (syn. 'Blue Beauty')
Paeonia officinalis (cottage garden peony)
Phlox (phlox), such as *Phlox paniculata* 'Amethyst' (pale lilac), 'White Admiral' (white) and 'Windsor' (deep carmine pink)
Primula florindae (giant cowslip)
Pulmonaria (lungwort), such as *Pulmonaria officinalis* 'Mawson's Blue' or *P. o.* 'Sissinghurst White'
Scabiosa (scabious), such as *Scabiosa caucasica* 'Clive Greaves'
Verbena bonariensis

Annuals and biennials

Alcea rosea (syn. *Althaea rosea*) (hollyhock), such as 'Chater's Double' or 'Majorette'
Aquilegia (aquilegia, columbine, granny's bonnets), such as *A. flabellata* (soft blue), *A. longissima* (pale yellow flowers, very long spurs), *A. vulgaris* 'Nora Barlow' (extra frilly) and Mrs Scott Elliott Hybrids (mixed colors)
Calendula (calendula, pot marigold) such as *Calendula officinalis* 'Lemon Queen' or *C. o.* 'Orange King'
Centaurea cyanus (cornflower)
Clarkia elegans (clarkia)
Cosmos bipinnatus Sensation Series (cosmea)
Dianthus barbatus (sweet william)
Digitalis purpurea (foxglove)
Erysimum cheiri (wallflower)
Helianthus annuus (sunflower), such as 'Giant Yellow' and 'Music Box'
Lathyrus odoratus (sweet pea)
Meconopsis cambrica (Welsh poppy)
Nigella damascena (nigella, love-in-a-mist)
Papaver rhoeas Shirley Series (shirley poppy)
Papaver somniferum (opium poppy)

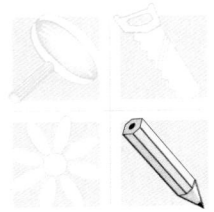

design alternatives

SKETCHES

Two layouts for more formally structured cottage gardens. Design one leads you through the garden, separating different areas with screening while design two leads you through honeysuckle archways to a central, beautiful pear tree.

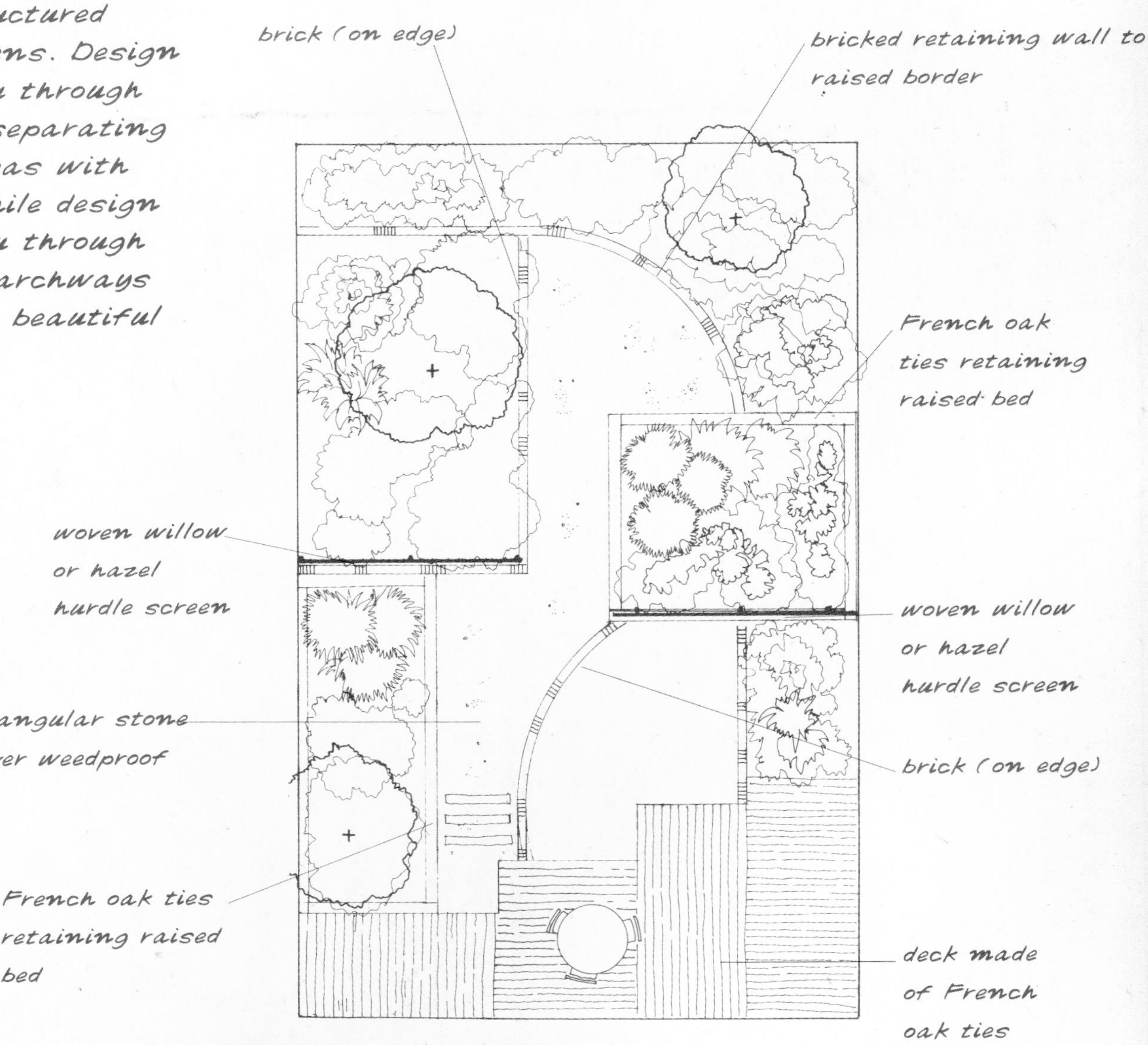

brick (on edge)

bricked retaining wall to raised border

French oak ties retaining raised bed

woven willow or hazel hurdle screen

woven willow or hazel hurdle screen

20mm/¾in angular stone chippings over weedproof membrane

brick (on edge)

French oak ties retaining raised bed

deck made of French oak ties

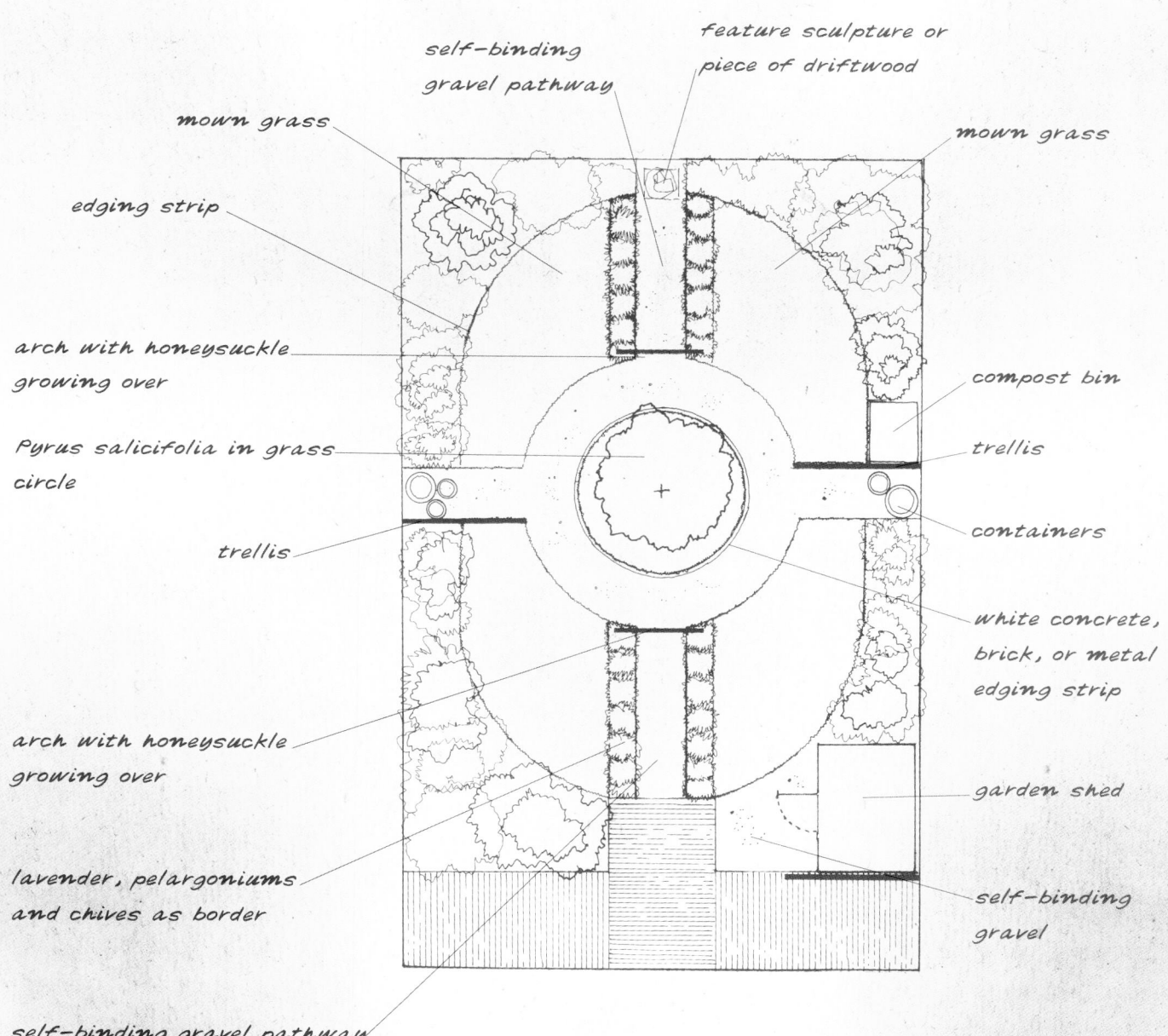

self-binding
gravel pathway

feature sculpture or
piece of driftwood

mown grass

mown grass

edging strip

arch with honeysuckle
growing over

compost bin

Pyrus salicifolia in grass
circle

trellis

trellis

containers

white concrete,
brick, or metal
edging strip

arch with honeysuckle
growing over

garden shed

lavender, pelargoniums
and chives as border

self-binding
gravel

self-binding gravel pathway

43

rose garden

Roses have been cultivated since ancient times, and gardens to honor these lovely flowers have been devised wherever they will grow. Rose gardens can be heaven on earth—a haven of scent, beauty, and repose. But they do demand good planning and careful maintenance, because roses are not always easy to grow or manage.

◀ *In this rose garden a pathway featuring a series of timber arches provides the opportunities for climbing varieties.*

Design of a rose garden

The classic rose garden or rosarium was usually a garden within a garden. Geometrically designed, it was laid out within a square or oblong, and often quartered. Its regularly shaped beds were grouped symmetrically and separated by straight grass or gravel paths; at its center a perfect circle or oval was set off by a bird bath, sundial, or piece of statuary. Wide arches covered with rambling roses might provide an entrance to the garden and frame its view, while within it other climbing roses would grow up central pillars or be trained along swags of heavy rope suspended between posts. The garden was usually defined by a formal hedge of box, yew, lavender, or rosemary. Well-placed seating allowed enjoyment of the fragrance and beauty of the garden, as well as the structure of the design.

▶ In this classic rose garden, the beds have been edged with aromatic lavender—a traditional choice that complements the roses.

This might seem excessively formal for a smaller garden wholly made over to roses, but there is still much to borrow from the classic rosarium. Treated informally, many of the ingredients can be copied to make a garden with a "time stands still" feel to it. For instance, a sheltering evergreen hedge provides a perfect backdrop; box, rugosa roses, or shrubby herbs make low to medium hedges giving structure and a textural continuity within the garden; instead of sturdy-looking pillars, hazel wigwams can be placed strategically to give inexpensive and natural-looking support to climbing roses and to add high points within the planting. Curving borders and informal planting in deep beds can help to give a relaxed feel to an otherwise formal gardening

approach. Grass, brick, stone, timber, gravel—in fact all the traditional and natural materials—make good surfaces between borders.

Planning the garden

Roses like light, air, shelter, and rich, deep soil, so for a start you need to be sure you have the right sort of plot. Plan carefully, bearing in mind the eventual size of the plants and whether or not they can be kept smaller by pruning, as well as the way each plant grows and its color and scent. It's difficult to get a rose to grow where another one has been established, so after a few years it won't be possible to move the plants around.

Today there are many roses that flower either repeatedly or continuously right up till the fall, so it's possible to choose roses that together will produce flowers over

◀ Roses provide a feast of sumptuous flowers —often deliciously scented—to be enjoyed throughout the warm summer months.

the longest possible season. Roses that have additional attractions, such as red hips or a pleasing shape, add an extra dimension, and a happy choice of companion plants provides contrast.

Companion planting

The spires of plants such as foxgloves or delphiniums, campanula, and tall graceful trumpet lilies look lovely growing among roses, while shade lovers such as violas, geraniums, or heucheras can be used as underplanting. Clematis mingles blissfully with a climbing rose; burgeoning peonies or oriental poppies make a welcome contrast. In open areas lavender, santolina, and sage, or nepeta (catmint) will add an aromatic scent to the roses' sweetness. The idea is not to be too free with companions, but to use fairly bold groups here and there, while underplanting at the roses' feet can thread its way through the whole garden to unite the scheme.

designer's rose garden

Roses evoke the quintessential character of the classic Edwardian, English garden. Their glorious colors and scents and exquisitely shaped, velvety blooms provide universal inspiration for poetry, painting, and music and they are coveted by gardeners all over the world.

▲ *This sheltered garden offers the ideal site for a range of roses. It receives enough sun and has good soil.*

GARDEN DATA

location:	▦ New Jersey
climate:	▦ mild/temperate
soil type:	▦ chalky/clay
direction:	▦ south facing
aspect:	▦ open

The brief

This slightly sloping plot is sunny and sheltered from prevailing winds. The owners have long wanted a rose garden in the romantic style and accept that their garden will be at its most attractive in summer, rather than year-round. There is plenty of support for climbers and ramblers but the garden needs a central focal point and a clearly defined ground pattern, to draw attention away from the square outline shape.

The design solution

The garden is within a modern development and we decided on a contemporary approach rather than traditional, quartered, or otherwise geometrically shaped beds. We made use of the existing boundary fences and wigwams for climbers and ramblers and grouped shrub and ground-cover roses around these schematically by color. We also introduced plants that associate well with roses and some that will provide

— 22m x 12m/72ft x 40ft —

structure during the dormant months of winter. We used log roll to edge and retain rose beds. Grass and brick look well with roses and we have used these traditional materials for surfaces and paths, making sure that the beds and borders are accessible for rose-sniffing, cutting, and pruning!

log roll

Log roll is used as edging ▲
for the planting beds.

gazebo

▲ Metal gazebo and statue
provide the central feature.

rose

▶ 'Miss Alice' is a
dramatic rambler.

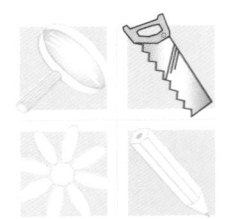

practical projects

A timber arch for climbing roses is a traditional rose garden feature, and simple arches are useful to give height and a sense of structure in many garden situations. As well as enabling you to grow climbing plants they can also frame a focal point, or allow you to separate your garden into a series of different spaces.

Framing the scene

In every size of plot attention to scale and form brings balance to the scheme. Luckily, what is comfortable for the human figure also generally delights the human eye.

An arch has to be tall and wide enough for practical purposes and ours uses posts that are 3m/10ft long so that they produce a 2m-/7ft-high opening when driven 60cm/2ft into the ground. This allows the roses to tumble down prettily while still leaving room for the tallest visitor to walk comfortably underneath. The width of the opening is 1.2m/4ft, which is nicely in balance with the height and allows plenty of room for people to walk through without getting entangled with the thorny stems. It also means that there is no problem for two friendly people to walk side by side, and space for pushing a wheelbarrow or lawn mower through the arch.

In our garden a log roll is used to make a border edge. These logs can be set at different heights, allowing you to create a raised border, and they are ideal for a curved bed.

LAYING LOG ROLL

Log roll is one of the most versatile materials for edging beds, borders and pathways, as it is flexible and can be curved in any shape you may choose. Most has already been treated. Decide how much of the edging you wish to protrude above ground level and dig a trench. Place the roll in position and, with a mallet, tap it into place, checking the level with a level. Back fill any gaps with garden soil and firm down.

building a rose arch

A timber arch makes a charming support for climbing or rambling roses and is easily made. Use chestnut, birch or thick bamboo poles. When measuring up, you need to allow at least 60cm/2ft of timber below ground for maximum stability. A height of 2.2m/7ft and a width of 1.2m/4ft will allow most adults to pass through without rose thorns catching on their clothing. For our garden we used four uprights each with three bracers and two 1.8m/6ft poles along the top, again with three bracers. The two uprights were constructed first, followed by the top section.

1 For ease of work, lay the timbers on the ground and mark on the verticals the position of the horizontal cross pieces. Chisel out cross-halving joints at the appropriate points, so that the beams will fit together.

2 Fit the posts together and screw or nail them in place. Depending on the roses' habit of growth, you may need more cross pieces than shown here.

DESIGNER'S TIPS

• Don't have too many fragrant roses in a garden—the mixed scents can be almost overpowering on a still day.

• Add companion plants to soften the woody base of the rose plants and to add variety of texture and form.

• Use bent hazel or willow wands to anchor and contain rose beds—they look gentler than stakes.

3 Assemble the horizontal top section and fix it in place with long screws.

4 Dig trenches in the ground to the appropriate depth (60cm/2ft is recommended) and insert the finished arch. Use a plumb line to make sure it is vertical. Backfill with soil.

rose plants and planting

There is a huge choice of roses, with a few for even the most difficult situations. A rose garden is a long-term creation so it pays to choose carefully. Check before buying that the rose's size and way of growing really are what you want. Visit rose gardens during the summer and consult specialist growers' catalogs.

Making preparations

Roses respond to good care even though they often thrive in polluted city air (its acidity deters mildew and black spot). They like a rich, heavy, but well-drained soil. And as they are going to stay put the ground has to be well prepared for them. At least a month before planting dig the whole garden really well and work in as much manure as you can lay your hands on as deep as possible. This will help to lighten heavy soils and give bulk to sandy soils as well as feeding the roses. It's best to plant in the fall from fresh stock, so prepare beforehand.

Planting bare-root roses

Before planting soak the roots in a bucket while you dig a deep hole wide enough to accommodate the spread-out roots. Mix crumbly soil with bonemeal, and garden compost if you have it, and add to the bottom of the hole. Sit the rose in, with the bulge called the union at the base of the stem just below the surface, fan out the roots and support the rose as you trickle in more soil, tucking it in round the roots as you go. Tread in and water well.

Care and maintenance

Roses need mulching, pruning, spraying, and deadheading. Get hold of farmyard manure if you possibly can, and give each plant a deep mulching in the fall and again in spring. Repeat-flowering roses need an extra feed in mid-summer. (You can use a proprietary rose feed for this.) Pruning is generally done in winter or early spring, and it's best to check on the requirements for each plant. Prevent mildew and black spot by spraying in early spring, and again

◀ R. *'Suffolk' makes excellent ground cover.*

◀ R. 'Wedding Day' is a dramatic rambler.

for a long period and produce bright orange-red hips.

ht 50cm/18in

sp 1.2m/4ft

Rosa 'Wedding Day'

'Wedding Day' is a light and airy rambling rose that will soon ramble over a shed or large arch or cover a pergola. It flowers very prolifically, the apricot buds opening to creamy yellow and quickly turning white. The flowers are single with a boss of bright yellow stamens.

ht and sp to 9m/30ft

Rosa 'Gertrude Jekyll'

This is a strong-growing and disease-resistant English rose (a recently developed breed of shrub roses with all the charm of old roses). Its fragrant, rosette-shaped flowers are a rich pink and it has a "true rose" scent. The shrub can be pruned annually to half its size, which produces the biggest flowers.

ht 1.2m/4ft

sp 1m/3ft 6in

throughout the flowering season depending on how prone the plant is. Look out for aphids (greenfly and blackfly). Spraying with an appropriate insecticide may be necessary but diluted washing-up liquid often does the trick just as well. During the flowering season snip off dead flowers to encourage repeat flowering but remember to leave a final flush of flowers to produce hips in the fall.

Profile plants

Rosa 'Suffolk'

This is a ground-cover rose—a low-growing, dense, and bushy shrub with large sprays of bright scarlet flowers on arching stems, which make it suitable for planters as well. The gold-stemmed flowers are produced

▶ Rosa 'Gertrude Jekyll' is rich pink.

design alternatives

SKETCHES

Here are two more designs for rose gardens. Each of them includes a bench for sitting, relaxing, and enjoying the beautiful results of your labor. Neat mown grass and fine gravel complement the delicate flowers.

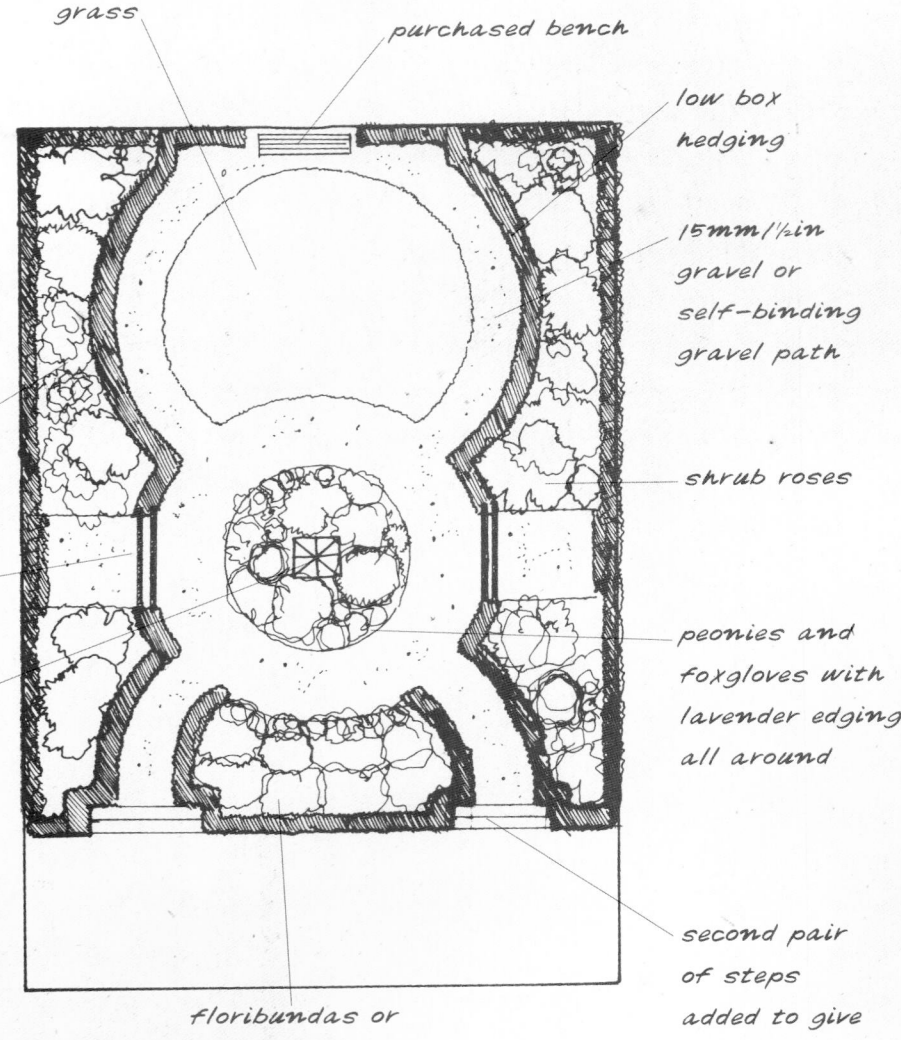

grass

purchased bench

low box hedging

15mm/½in gravel or self-binding gravel path

shrub roses

shrub roses

timber or metal double arch to support climbers

peonies and foxgloves with lavender edging all around

central wigwam or gazebo for climbing roses

second pair of steps added to give balance

floribundas or ground-cover roses

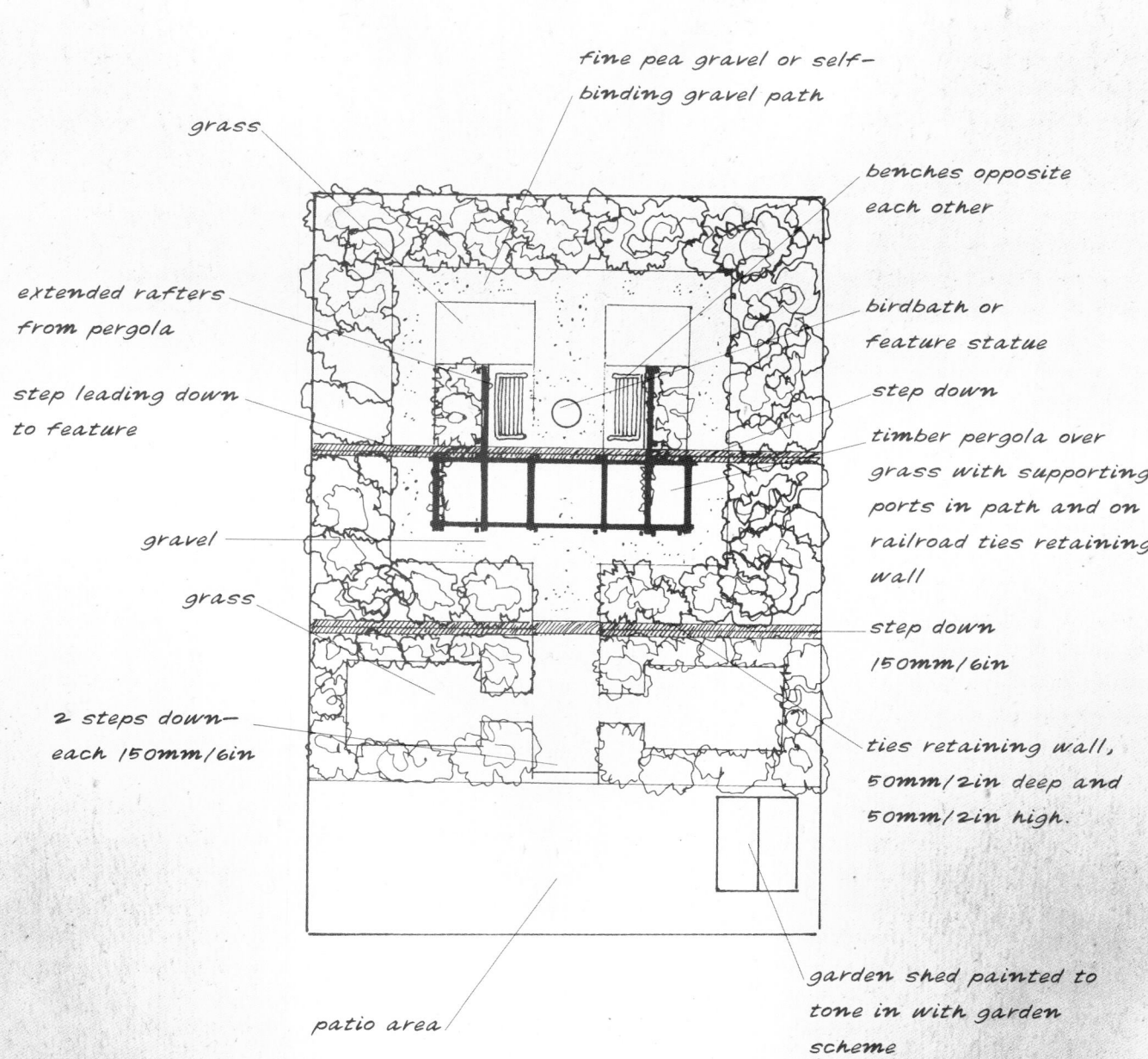

fine pea gravel or self-
binding gravel path

grass

benches opposite
each other

extended rafters
from pergola

birdbath or
feature statue

step leading down
to feature

step down

timber pergola over
grass with supporting
ports in path and on
railroad ties retaining
wall

gravel

grass

step down
150mm/6in

2 steps down—
each 150mm/6in

ties retaining wall,
50mm/2in deep and
50mm/2in high.

garden shed painted to
tone in with garden
scheme

patio area

border garden

The border, with its blend of color and mix of heights and shapes is a true garden classic, even though in fact it is really a twentieth-century creation. Just about any garden in any situation can become a border garden— generous paths and deep beds are key ingredients for successful design.

The mixed border

The traditional lush border on a grand scale was at its best in high summer but today's more relaxed planting and the continual introduction of new plants means that the whole garden can be used for borders which have something to offer all year round. While borders in the past consisted of perennials and seasonal bedding plants, today they incorporate climbers, small trees, deciduous and evergreen shrubs, spring- and fall-flowering bulbs, and annuals too.

Perennials still form the mainstay of a border, but the general mix insures there is something of interest from shape and color at almost any time of year. The spring bulbs and early summer annuals bring life and color before the high-summer perennials are at their best. Height is supplied by climbers, and shape, form, and long-term structure are derived from evergreens, trees, and larger shrubs, to make a harmonious whole allowing the color to be seen within a framework.

Most gardens have a sunny and shady aspect and you can take advantage of this to create two borders with very different characters. Hot borders have caught the contemporary imagination.

◀ *A modern mixed border uses shrubs, perennials, and grasses to create continued color, shape, and texture throughout the year.*

▶ *This border relies for much of its effect on the interplay of contrasting leaf shapes and shades of green foliage as a foil to the flowers.*

Flowers and foliage with a high intensity of color are the first ingredient, but second is the way they are mixed, in what would once have been considered "clashes," such as deep carmine, orange, and purple with blue. Most of the plants for hot borders are not just stunningly bright colors by accident, they also signal their preference for sun this way. They tend also to offer strong, spiky forms. On the shady side color can be gentle, with white and blue, cream, lilac, or pale pink, and shapes may be softer too. Dark green from evergreens and light green border plants, such as alchemilla, will tie the scheme together.

Essentials

Although the complete effect is important, part of the pleasure of a border garden is the way it leads the eye and allows the foot to follow, so that not all of it is seen at once, and there is always more to discover from a different viewpoint. Curving beds help to create this effect in even the smallest garden. If you can contrive to make the gap between the borders wide at the beginning and narrow at the end this heightens perspective.

Paths and walkways are an essential part of the scheme and you also need somewhere finally to sit and admire the whole thing after inspecting the beds in close-up, if possible at the far end, away from the house. When using curves, try to make them

◀ *Pots allow you to plug gaps in borders so you need never see any bare earth. Try a variety of materials such as terracotta and metal.*

generously sweeping, not tight and contorted. When two borders face each other in complementary curves with an open area between them they can be enjoyed from many different angles. This helps to give the garden a feeling of greater size too, as you can't take everything in at once and there is more to be revealed round the bend.

Between the beds areas of lawn are traditional, and they are the perfect foil. In a dry garden where grass would need constant attention, gravel or stone can pay a pleasing compliment to the softening effect of flowering plants. The background completes the whole. Of course the ideal traditional border is backed by a yew hedge but this takes space and absorbs nutrients the border plants would be glad to get their roots on. In a small garden, trellis with climbing plants may be better.

designer's border garden

A stunning herbaceous border has long been seen as a pinnacle of gardening achievement. But this traditional form of border was originally designed to be at its best for only a few short weeks when wealthy families visited their country houses for the summer. Today we want interest from our gardens year round.

▲ *This sloping garden offers huge potential for growing both sun- and shade-loving plants, so we schemed the borders accordingly.*

GARDEN DATA

location:	▓ *Pennsylvania*
climate:	▓ *mild/temperate*
soil type:	▓ *chalky*
direction:	▓ *east facing*
aspect:	▓ *open*

The brief

This long, east-facing garden slopes steeply downward from the house. A shed and an elderly summerhouse are to be replaced and an old apple tree, awkwardly positioned in the center of the lawn, moved. One long boundary is shady while the other is warm and sunny, so each border will have a very different planting plan, although each will cross-refer to the other by color or form of plant. The view also needs to be restricted at intervals, so that you are keen to discover what lies beyond.

The design solution

The existing layout was reshaped to form two areas of unequal size, to avoid splitting the garden into two exact halves. Within these two areas we repositioned the potting shed and made a feature of the summerhouse. The planting is vibrant and hot on one side and cool and lush on the other, moving from traditional English herbaceous plants near the main house to exotic jungly leaves near the summerhouse. The lawn is unbroken by paths as its steep slope allows good drainage to gullies.

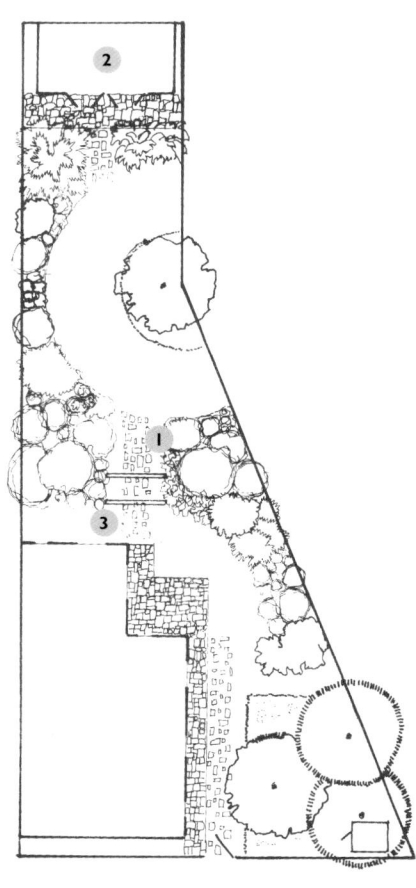

— 28m x 15m/90ft x 50ft —

path

▲ *A path set in mown grass leads through the garden.*

summerhouse

arch

▲ *The old summerhouse was replaced.*

▲ *A metal arch was installed for climbers.*

practical projects

Planning the shape and content of the borders is one of the chief projects for this garden, bearing in mind the plants' height, size, shape, and color. Once you have got your designs worked out on paper, trace them in on the ground to see how they will fit and then have fun getting the plants together.

Planting schemes

The aim is to arrange the plants you choose for the border so that there will always be something at its best to take over as other plants fade, to keep it going for the longest possible period. Generous curves can be made on the ground using a length of rope and a peg as a radius. A general principle is to have taller plants at the back and shorter at the front, but not in a regimented way.

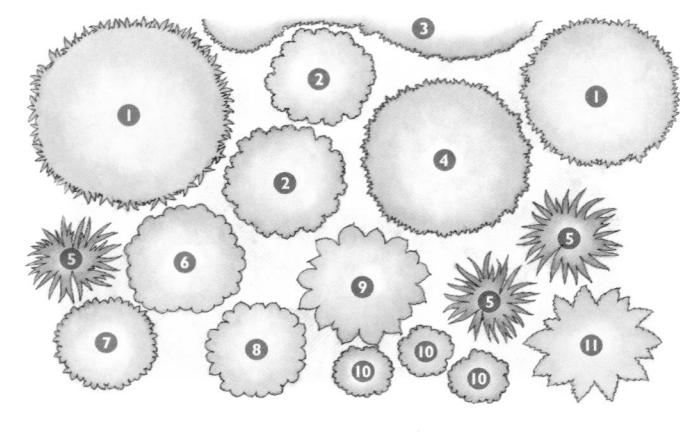

1. Aucuba japonica 'Salicifolia'
2. Thalictrum rochebruneanum
3. Hedera helix 'Glacier'
4. Viburnum tinus
5. Phormium tenax
6. Saxifraga hirsuta
7. Epimedium
8. Trillium grandiflorum
9. Hosta crispula
10. Viola odorata
11. Athyrium filix-femina

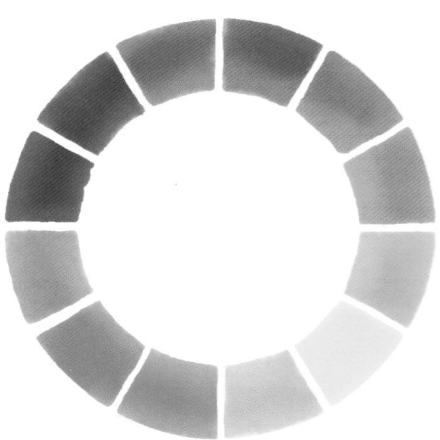

▲ *Color is a key aspect of design. Opposite colors tend to blend well, while neighboring colors work less well together.*

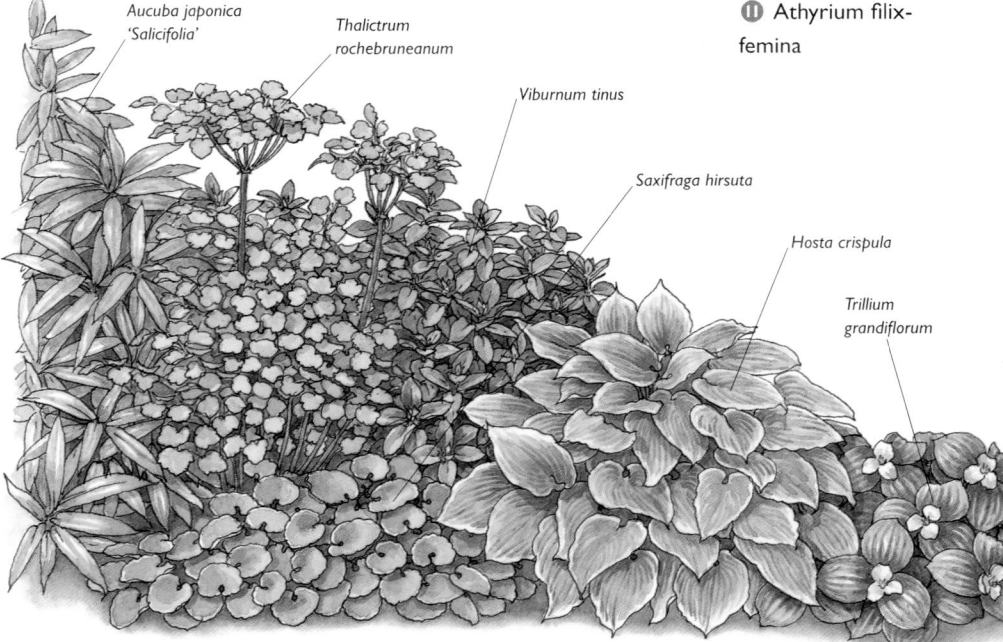

Aucuba japonica 'Salicifolia'

Thalictrum rochebruneanum

Viburnum tinus

Saxifraga hirsuta

Hosta crispula

Trillium grandiflorum

staking plants

Many tall border perennials benefit from staking, particularly those with heavy heads of flowers that can easily flop over, such as peonies or delphiniums. The traditional method is with pea sticks or rods of hazel, and these have the advantage of being unobtrusive once the plants have grown to cover them.

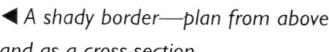
◀ *A shady border—plan from above and as a cross-section.*

1 In early to mid-spring, cut lengths of branching, twiggy hazel (pea sticks) up to 1.2m/4ft long using sharp pruners.

2 Drive the sticks into the soil around the plants, arching them inward, and burying them up to one third of their length.

3 Unless the sticks are very twiggy, it may be necessary to tie the plant stems loosely to them as they grow, with wire, horticultural twine or raffia. Once the plant has reached flowering size, tie in any loose stems.

AN ALTERNATIVE METHOD OF STAKING

Proprietary link stakes are available in garden centers and by mail order and are usually made of metal coated with green plastic. These stakes have the advantage over pea sticks in that they can be used year on year and are more readily available. The fresh growth will soon hide them from view.

At the start of the growing season, insert the uprights in the ground around the plant, pushing them deep into the soil so that the horizontal members support the emerging growth. As the plant grows, gradually raise the stakes until there is enough support against wind damage.

Ring stakes have a circular horizontal disc with a coarse mesh through which the plant stems grow. This type is suitable for plants with tall, thin stems.

border plants and planting

With border planting it's the overall effect that matters, even though of course seeing individual plants at close quarters is part of the pleasure of growing them. Small is beautiful—a limited number of plants well used is much more effective than too many. Foliage makes a foil for flowers and can act as a link between groups.

▲ Hosta 'Whirlwind' provides strong shapes for a shady border.

Planning and planting

As a general rule repeat planting creates rhythm and harmony and planting in groups (massed planting) is much more effective than planting singly. At the same time, repeating at regular intervals is very dreary— varied repetition is what's called for. Bear in mind when planning the planting what the individual plant's eventual spread will be and don't be tempted to crowd too much in. You will need a few gaps for your feet when tending the plants, and bare patches can be filled with annuals or with plants in pots.

If you are starting from scratch you will need to prepare the border well before you plant, working in plenty of manure or other organic matter in the fall. Although you can improve and control the growing conditions your garden offers to some extent, it's better to concentrate on plants that prefer the conditions you can offer in terms of soil, light, shelter, and exposure than to aim at something difficult to achieve. (See pages 224–227). Most gardens offer at least two aspects, so that there is a range of conditions to exploit, as long as plants with similar needs are grown together.

▶ Viburnum 'Opulus roseum', suits a sunny border.

Brimming borders

Make the border as deep as you can—1.5–2.5m/5–8ft, or more if you have the space—so that you can grow plants in bold clumps, with plenty of room at the front for smaller plants and space for shrubs, trees and climbing plants behind. As well as grading heights from front to back in this way, plan also for varying heights along the border, with taller groups at intervals. Choosing plants that are hardy will avoid disappointments, and if you select plants that need as little support as possible, or

◄ Calendula *'Pacific Beauty'*.

spring to prevent non-flowering,
tangled growth.
ht to 5m/17ft
sp 1.5m/5ft
Soil and situation
Fertile soil, with its head in the sun
and its feet in the shade.

plant them so that they can support
each other, you will have less work to
do. Don't be in too much of a hurry
to tidy up when the fall comes. Some
plants look wonderful covered with
winter frost or topped with a dollop
of snow, and many seed heads are
attractive, as well as providing food
for birds.

Profile plants

Magnolia stellata
STAR MAGNOLIA

A starry-flowered magnolia of
modest size and beautifully spreading
habit, this is a gift for the border,
although it will also stand alone in
the lawn. It bears a multitude of
fragrant, white, long-petaled flowers
before the leaves in early to mid-
spring. Spring-flowering bulbs such
as scilla and crocus or cyclamen
corms can flourish at its feet. It needs
shelter from cold wind but is more
robust than it looks.
ht to to 3m/10ft
sp to 4m/13ft
Soil and situation
Fertile soil; light but sheltered position.

Heuchera cylindrica 'Greenfinch'
ALUM ROOT

The scalloped, mottled leaves of this
heuchera form shiny mounds, above
which stand tall, wiry stems carrying
spikes of tiny lime-green flowers in
stiff, airy panicles. An adaptable plant
that's good for hot or cool borders, it
flowers in early summer. Similar
greenish-flowered heucheras include
H. c. 'Chartreuse' and *H.* 'Greenfinch'
ht 90cm/3ft
sp 60cm/2ft
Soil and situation
Fertile soil that is well drained but
not too dry, in sun or partial shade.

Clematis 'Etoile Violette'
CLEMATIS

This is a viticella clematis with
masses of small, nodding violet-
colored flowers from early summer
right through to fall. Incredibly
pretty scrambling through a climbing
rose or over a yellow-leaved plant
such as *Euphorbia polychroma* or a
golden-leaved philadelphus. Another
viticella hybrid is 'Abundance' with
rose-pink flowers. Cut back each

BORDER MAINTENANCE

Routine work includes:
• mulching round plants with compost or
stripped bark in fall/spring to conserve
moisture and suppress weeds
• staking in early spring
• watering in dry periods
• hoeing to keep down weeds during
summer
• feeding during the flowering season
• controlling pests such as slugs and snails
(hostas, dahlias, and delphiniums are
particularly at risk)
• removing faded flowers to extend
flowering (except where seed heads are
wanted, as on Japanese anemone, sedum,
and the opium poppies, *Papaver somniferum*)
• dividing over-large plants in the fall

PLANTS FOR THE BORDER

A selection of summer border perennials
• carnations or pinks (*Dianthus* species),
delphiniums, echinops (globe thistle),
eryngiums (sea holly), geum, hollyhocks,
irises, lupins, peonies, phlox
• Border plants for fall
summer hyacinth (*Galtonia*), chrysanthemums,
Clematis vitalba, dahlias, michaelmas daisies
(*Aster* species), montbretia, sedum, see also
Plants for cottage gardens, pages 40–41

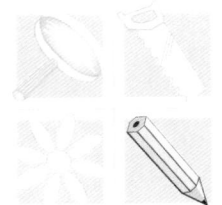

design alternatives

SKETCHES

These alternatives, hot and shady borders, have been designed according to color. You could create different color planting, e.g. "hot," "cool blue," and "white" as shown in the first variation.

terracotta tiles or crazy paving

garden divided into border areas bounding lawn, by two clipped-box hedges

grass

"cool blue" and spot of yellow e.g: Delphinium, 'Pacific hybrids', lavender and Verbascum 'Gainsborough'

"hot" garden: cannas phormiums, Dahlia 'Bishop of Llandaff', Hemerocallis 'Chicago Apache', Crocosmia 'Lucifer'

terracotta tiles or crazy paving

yellows, e.g. Achillea 'Moonshine', Solidago 'Goldenmosa', Rudbecki. 'Goldstrum'

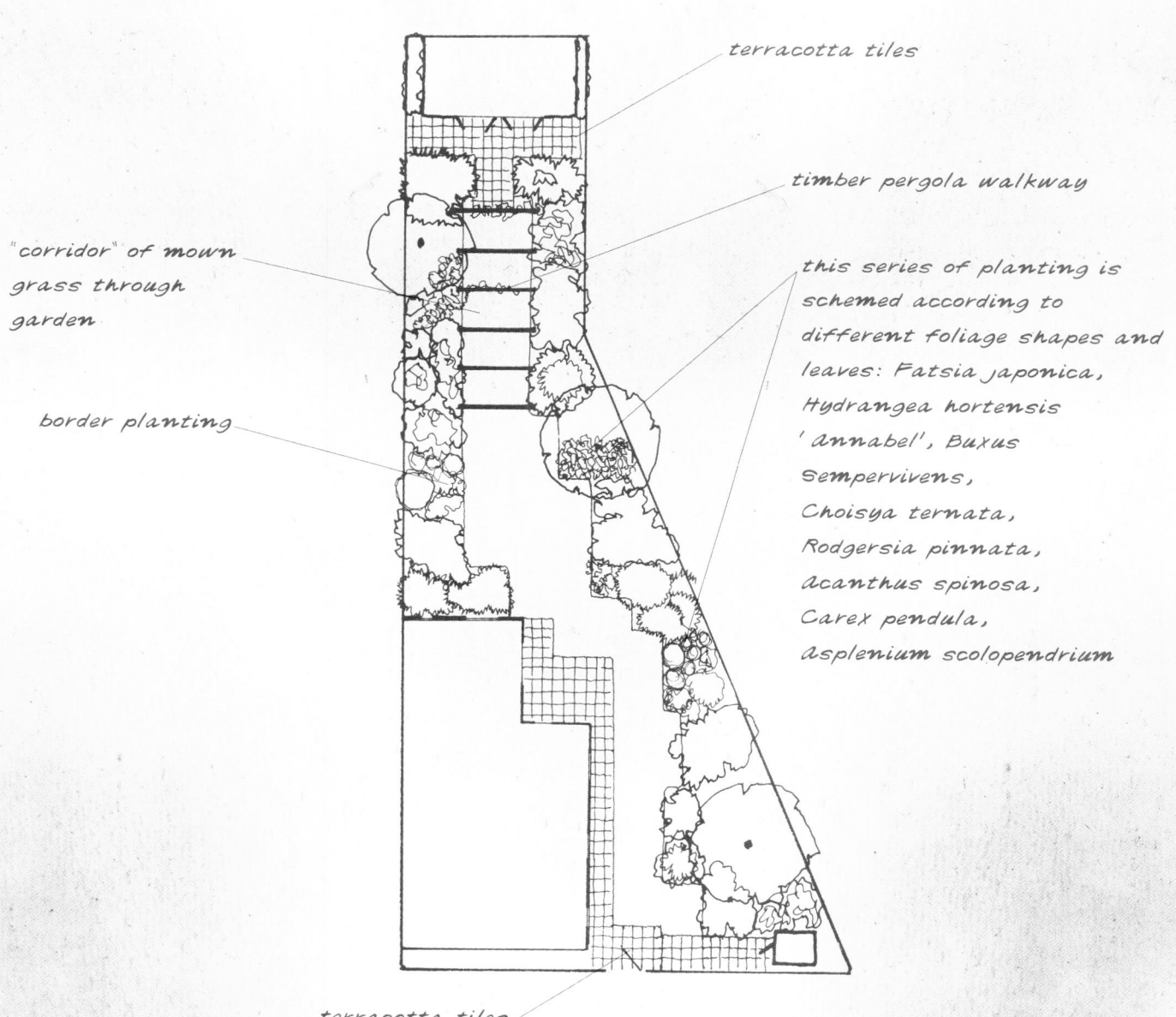

terracotta tiles

timber pergola walkway

"corridor" of mown grass through garden

this series of planting is schemed according to different foliage shapes and leaves: Fatsia japonica, Hydrangea hortensis 'annabel', Buxus Sempervivens, Choisya ternata, Rodgersia pinnata, Acanthus spinosa, Carex pendula, Asplenium scolopendrium

border planting

terracotta tiles

courtyard garden

A courtyard garden can be made from a space which is partially or totally enclosed. It's usually near the house, perhaps linked to it by a patio or terrace, and bounded by walls, fences, or hedges. While some are suntraps, a courtyard at basement level is often cool and shady—a place for intermingled shades of green.

◄ *Black bamboo in galvanized metal containers contributes much to this minimalist courtyard. Stylish dining furniture completes the look.*

An outdoor room

A small enclosed garden at the back of a terraced town house is the ideal candidate for the courtyard treatment. Well-defined by boundaries, it offers a private area generally with no view to worry about losing. Mellow country cottages often have a paved, cobbled, or brick-set area immediately outside the house, with or without a garden beyond, and these areas too make perfect courtyard gardens, although here it may be important not to become too enclosed, as this would risk losing views of the rest of the garden or of the countryside beyond.

Being (generally) next to the house a courtyard becomes another room—a perfect place for dining and entertaining, sun-bathing, dozing, or even to sit and work in. Apart from its "room" quality, the essence of the

▶ In a suntrap courtyard a spiky-leaved plant grown in a classic terracotta container will give a tropical touch.

courtyard is also its hard-landscaping. If you have the stone or brick floor already, be advised to keep it. If not, choose materials that will suit those of your house. Small-sized units are best in a small area.

Again, your courtyard may have natural boundaries already. If not you will need to start by supplying boundaries for enclosure. Be aware that the higher they go the greater your privacy but also the greater the shade. Walls in the same material as the house are unbeatable, with wires or trellis attached firmly to give support to climbing plants. A dense evergreen hedge will offer great privacy but will take several years to grow and will rob the limited amount of soil of its nutrients. Both hedges and walls create dry areas at

the base which are inhospitable to plants. Lightweight fencing can be a very satisfactory alternative, acting as a screen and support for plants, while still letting in light. Screening trellis is right in formal settings while hazel or willow hurdles look good in a more rural country garden.

Structuring the garden

Restraint and some formality are required for courtyard gardens. Decide on your theme and don't try to cram too many ideas into a small space. A lot of the planting will probably be in containers, but it's

◀ Courtyard gardens can be home to many plants, both growing in containers and trained on trellis against the wall.

worth contemplating building raised planting areas filled with earth (with drainage) as these can supply structure and will also need less watering than containers. Again, the materials used should be in sympathy with those of the house and with the enclosure. You may well be looking at the garden from above a lot of the time, for example from a first-floor living room or bedroom, so make sure that the scheme will look as well from this angle as it does when you are actually sitting in it. Because of the shelter it gains from its boundaries a courtyard can be warm and still at night, and is a natural place for fitting subtle lighting for the evening. Good-quality garden furniture can be a key feature.

designer's courtyard garden

A courtyard garden is at its most elegant when it follows clean contemporary lines, with sleek modern furniture. But if you prefer a traditional look you can fill it with pots and containers, and cover the walls with climbers. Paving, tiles, and gravel make the surfaces, and your containerized plants can be changed to suit your mood.

▲ *Contrary to first impressions this dark, overgrown courtyard offers surprising possibilities for a major transformation.*

GARDEN DATA

location:	▦ Maryland
climate:	▦ mild/temperate
soil type:	▦ chalky clay
direction:	▦ north facing
aspect:	▦ urban enclosed

The brief

This tiny space is dark and shady because of long-neglected boundary plants that have grown out of control. The owner is not a keen gardener but would like some variety of color and interest through the year and would like to use the courtyard as an extra summer room for relaxing and entertaining friends.

Courtyards on the north or east side of the house will be cool and shady whereas ones that face south can be real suntraps. When planning a courtyard garden the first thing to do is to decide how it will be used—somewhere to sit and soak up the sun, a quiet place, or a social area.

The design solution

The area was cleared wall to wall to maximize space and light and the dilapidated fencing was replaced with color-stained screening trellis to allow light to filter through but retain privacy. Small spaces work best if they are not too busy, so we

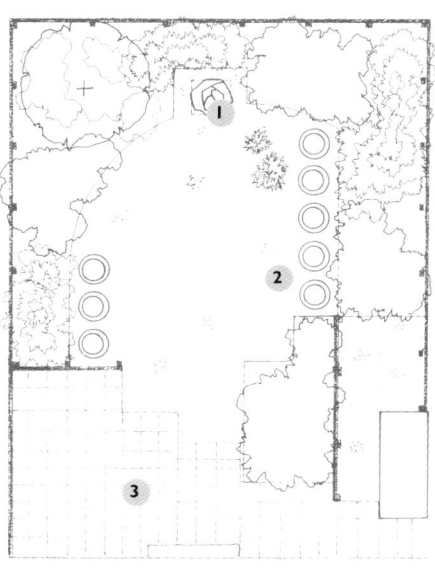

—7m x 9m / 22ft x 30ft —

chose unfussy paving to replace the dark, brick patio and combined it with creamy gravel to reflect as much light as possible. Planting is bold and simple, with splashes of color provided by containerized annuals that can be replaced each year. We installed automatic irrigation and one uplight to make a dramatic focal point of the owner's beautiful piece of contemporary sculpture.

sculpture

▲ A large sculpture provides a
dramatic focal point.

pots

▲ Matching containers
always look stylish.

paving

◀ A paved patio provides an unfussy seating area.

practical projects

▲ *This wood trellis permits a glimpse through to another part of the garden and allows the garden to have different components to it.*

◀ *The delicate white and purple flowers of* Clematis sieboldii *complement this trellis. It is an especially good climber.*

A courtyard garden is defined by its enclosures. You may be lucky enough to have a ready-made area adjoining the house, but if not, a sturdy, well-supported trellis makes a quick and straight-forward enclosure and shelter from winds.

Making an enclosure

A courtyard garden is a garden on a small scale, where everything is visible at close quarters. It also has a degree of formality that comes from being closely attached to the house, and is an area where you will be sitting and looking around a lot of the time. For all these reasons, good workmanship is important.

Since a large part of the effect will come from plants growing up the enclosure, anything you build needs to be strong enough to take the weight of plants climbing or twining over it, and also sufficiently well finished to make sure that it will wear well.

If you use ready-made trellis panels, choose the strongest available and fix them between strong posts. For easy fixing as well as long life, special metal post holders can be used. Trellis looks good painted to go

with the house or with other features. Dark garden green forms a restful background to plants and French gray is a calming color. If you prefer the look of bare wood, protect with wood seal. Paints, seals, and varnishes are all available in nontoxic, water-based formulas.

DESIGNER'S TIPS

• Choose hard-landscaping materials that complement or match the materials of your house.

• Don't try to create a tropical hotspot if the courtyard is exposed to wind or cold.

• Don't choose a shady and dry area for your courtyard. Unless you use an automatic irrigation system the plants will die and you'll be left with a brown dustbowl. If it's cool it needs to be damp and that may not suit your purpose.

• Decide on a single, main theme for your courtyard: don't have too many ideas crammed into its small space.

• The higher the boundaries, the more shady your courtyard will be.

putting up trellis

Trellis panels are easily erected, but if
they are to be a lasting feature in the
garden, it is worth taking the trouble to
put them up correctly. Good fence
posts will carry a guarantee of 15 years
or longer. The panels are fixed to
timber uprights firmly anchored in the
ground. These can either be cemented
in or held in place by means of the
special fencing posts illustrated here.
Most fencing materials sold today have
already been pressure treated to make
them weatherproof, but check before
you buy.

1 Check the position of the uprights carefully,
making sure they are the correct distance
from each other and that they are square on to
each other.

2 Drive the fencing posts into the ground,
using a lump hammer and a wooden block.

3 Knock the uprights into the metal shoes and
bolt them in firmly. Use a level to make sure
that the post is upright.

4 Screw the panels to the uprights, using rustproof metal plates.

5 Fix finials to the tops of the posts. Not only
are these decorative in their own right, but
they will deflect rain that would otherwise collect
at the top of the post and cause rotting.

courtyard plants and planting

Small enough to take in at a glance, courtyard gardens offer special opportunities for planting. Planting within the courtyard will usually be in containers or raised beds, while the boundaries can be used to great effect, with hedging plants if you want a "live" boundary or climbing plants to cover walls or trellis.

A courtyard theme

For the best effect stick to a strong scheme, even if you want the effect to be exotic, dramatic, or riotous. Too much going on in a small place will otherwise risk looking muddled. Use containers that are similar in style, whether it's brightly painted buckets,

◄ Yucca filamentosa *in flower.*

old stone troughs, or Versailles planters. Have a strong theme for plants and don't use too many "highlight" plants—one glorious flowering climber given prominence can be more successful than several in uneasy competition.

Container plants for a sunny courtyard

A sunny courtyard, if also well sheltered, can be host to the most exotic plants. The following can all be grown as striking specimens in large containers in a tropical-style courtyard. All need rich, easy-draining compost.

Agapanthus 'Blue Giant': drumheads of blue flowers on tall stems, broad, strappy leaves
ht 1.2m/4ft
sp 60cm/2ft
Ensete ventricosum (syn. *Musa ensete*): banana-like plant from Ethiopia with enormous leaves in bright olive-

green and huge bronze and white flowers
ht to 6m/20ft
sp to 4.5m/15ft
Hakonechloa macra 'Aureola': golden-leaved, mound-forming grass—smaller than most grasses—looks stunning in a container
ht 35cm/14in
sp 40cm/16in
Musa basjoo: a banana plant from Japan with long rippled leaf blades and exotic brown and yellow flowers followed by inedible fruit
ht to 4.5m/15ft
sp to 3.6m/12ft
Phormium tenax (New Zealand flax): clump-forming plant with tall, architectural, strappy leaves and even taller stems of dark red flowers
ht 3m/10ft (leaves), 3.6m/12ft (flowers)
sp 1.8m/6ft
Yucca filamentosa (Adam's needle): rosettes of sharply pointed leathery leaves and upright heads of small cream flowers
ht and sp 90cm/3ft

◀ *Parrot tulips have striking frilly flowers.*

small. Try some of these varieties:
Hedera colchica, 'Dentata' and *H.c*
'Dentata Variegata': large
green/variegated, tooth-edged leaves,
vigorous growth
Hedera helix 'Gold Heart': small
lobed leaves with yellow centers;
modest growth
Hedera helix 'Maple Leaf': less
vigorous ivy with deeply serrated,
maple-like leaves

Climbers for warm courtyards

These plants will need support from
wires or trellis if grown up a wall.
All grow to 5m/16ft or more.
Clematis armandii: scented, cream-
flowered, early clematis
Clematis montana var. *rubens:* pink-
flowered version of the vigorous
early summer-flowering clematis

Lonicera periclymenum 'Serotina': late-
flowering, very fragrant honeysuckle
Passiflora caerulea (passion flower):
exotic, starry, crown-of-thorns
flowers in creamy white with purple-
blue markings
Rosa 'banksiae': pale yellow or white
clusters of slightly scented flowers in
early spring
Solanum crispum (Chilean potato
vine) 'Glasnevin': vigorous purple-
flowered jasmine-like climbing plant,
but with no scent
Vitis coignetiae grapevine whose leaves
color a rich purple red in the fall
(black grapes are not edible)

Ivies for shady walls

Green ivies are the perfect wall-
climbers for shady courtyards, and
need no support. Ivies with yellow
variegation prefer some sun. Many
leaf forms are available, large and

◀ Solanum crispum *is a vigorous climber.*

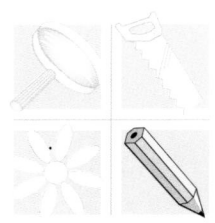

design alternatives

SKETCHES

These two design
alternatives both
feature sculptures
as their focal point,
adopting on the left a
contemporary, lush feel,
while on the right a
more traditional
approach.

path lights

Dicksonia antarctica
(New Zealand Tree Fern)

low surround
of ferns or
Aegopodium
podagnia
variegata

box hedging

large flat
pierced stone
with water
trickling over

paddle
stones all
round path
(laid over
weedproof
membrane)

10mm/½in
gravel

tiled patio 300 x 300mm/12 x 12in
quarry tile

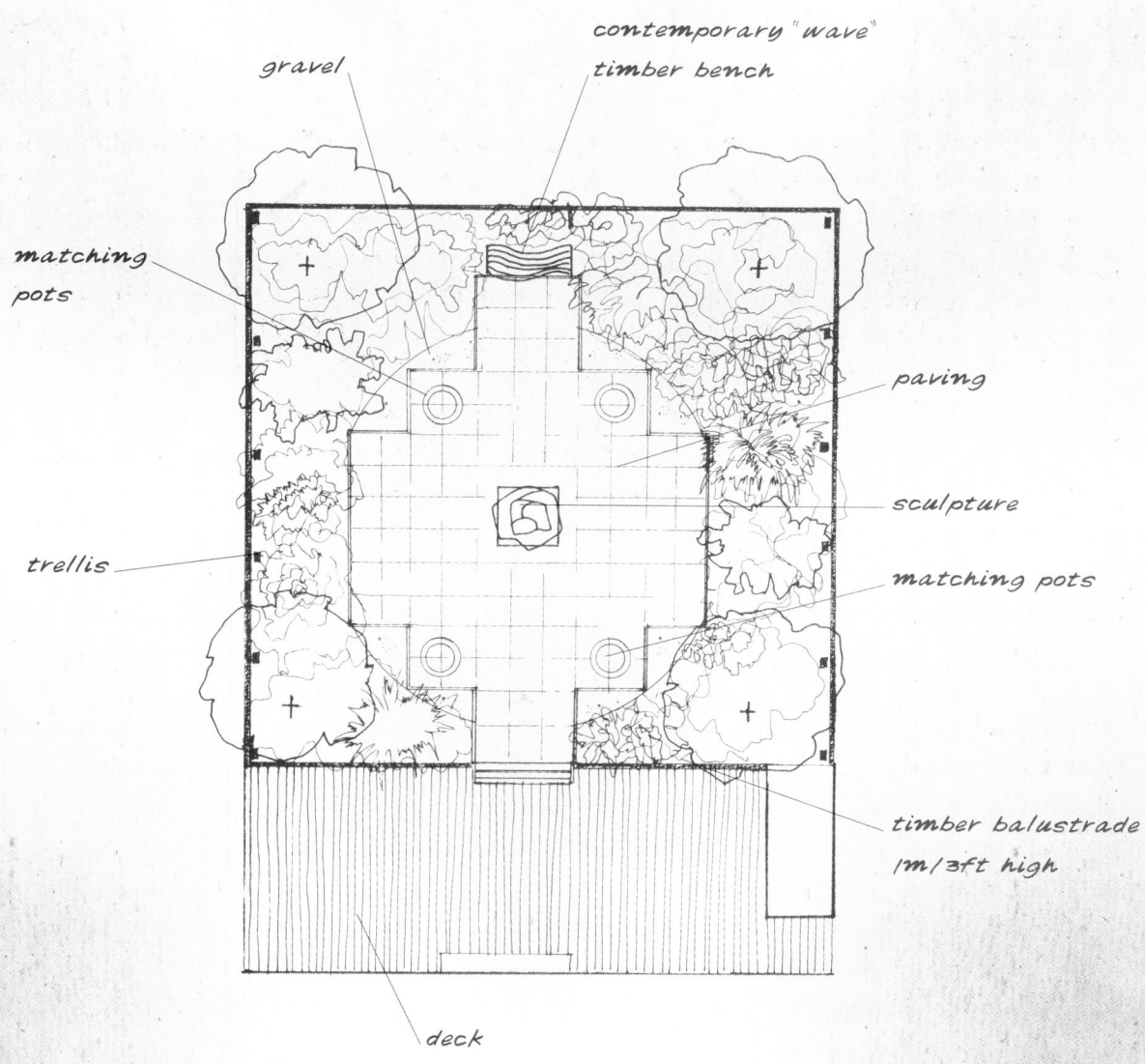

gravel

contemporary "wave"
timber bench

matching
pots

paving

sculpture

matching pots

trellis

timber balustrade
1m/3ft high

deck

useful gardens

Growing vegetables and herbs makes gardening useful as well as enjoyable. But if you have a small garden you probably don't want the whole plot to look too utilitarian. It doesn't need to—kitchen gardens and herb gardens can be designed so that they are a pleasure to look at as well as productive, and they don't have to exclude flowers.

kitchen garden

There's no denying that growing vegetables, herbs, and maybe some fruit for the kitchen takes time and trouble. But this is more than compensated for by the pleasure it gives. This is an orderly way of gardening that many people find not only intensely rewarding, but also very relaxing.

Planning and preparing

To get the best out of the soil you need to grow vegetables in rotation, and you also need plenty of access to tend and harvest the plants. For these reasons separate, rectangular plots divided by narrow paths work well. However, if you prefer a more informal design with curves you can still move your vegetables around from area to area. In this case, make sure that your design allows you easy access to the plants.

For the kitchen garden there are three main types of vegetable crop to be planned for: root vegetables (beets, carrots, turnips, radishes), brassicas (cabbages and kale) and legumes (peas and beans). The onion family can be given a permanent plot or can be moved along with the legumes. Leeks, going in at a different time from most other vegetables, can be put in as and where there is space. They are planted out in summer, and are finished with by the following spring, leaving the ground free for something else. Lettuces can be planted with the roots or legumes and can also go in as "catch crops," to be removed and eaten as their neighbors grow and need the space.

Preparing the plot

Vegetables are greedy feeders, so the soil needs to be well prepared before

◄ *This formally laid-out kitchen garden has raised beds which help to provide good drainage and warm the soil.*

◄ *If you haven't the time or energy for a kitchen garden, grow occasional vegetables and herbs among your flower borders.*

you plant. Ideally you should dig it over well in the fall before you begin and lay a thick layer of manure or garden compost on top (or dig it in); then fork over again in the spring. Finally, rake the beds smooth and level to prepare them for seeds and seedlings.

Reasons for rotating

One reason for moving types of crop from area to area is that it discourages the build-up of pests and diseases. There is something nasty specific to almost anything you may wish to grow, and such diseases and predators are much less likely to get established

if the crop varies from year to year.

Different types of vegetables also have different requirements, as well as having different effects on the soil. Peas and beans enrich the soil with nitrogen, which is needed by brassicas and leafy vegetables, while root crops help to make the soil comfortable for the legumes. Root crops do best where manure was applied for the previous growing season. Too rich a soil makes them fork under the ground and produce leaf instead of root.

In a big garden, as well as providing beds for three main crop types, you might plan to have a fourth plot for potatoes, which do best on freshly manured soil and which would go around in rotation preceding the root vegetables. Home-grown potatoes are delicious and justify the room—and the work—they take, but not everyone has space to grow and store them in quantity. In our garden we grow a few choice potatoes with the roots and use a fourth area as a permanent site for soft fruits—equally rewarding and worthwhile. You can then pick them at the peak of perfection.

◄ *A well-stocked kitchen garden with ornamental herbs and vegetables provides a feast for the eye as well as for the table.*

designer's kitchen garden

Many of us do not have the time and energy needed to grow enough vegetables and fruit to supply the kitchen without ever buying produce from a farmers market or supermarket. So think laterally and mix flowers, fruits, herbs, and vegetables in small quantities, to avoid a glut and satisfy the taste buds.

▲ *A sloping or terraced site is ideal for a kitchen garden. We took advantage of the banks to plant annual flowers and vegetables.*

GARDEN DATA

location:	▦ New York State
climate:	▦ mild
soil type:	▦ chalk
direction:	▦ south facing
aspect:	▦ slopes towards house

The brief

The plot is south facing and open —ideal for early warming of the soil in spring and for growing crops to benefit from even exposure to sunlight. The garden is terraced upward away from the house and these terraces will form the basis for the vegetable beds.

The design solution

Following the linear layout of the garden we used a mini rotivator to level each terrace, to avoid the seeds being washed away by the first rainstorm. The ground was cleared of stones, weeds, and debris and the soil raked to a fine tilth. The brick retaining walls were crumbling so we replaced them with low, but sturdy walls of new, tanalized or reclaimed railroad ties, supported at regular intervals by sawn timber posts. (Reclaimed ties tend to leach messy tar preservative which can contaminate plants.) These also provide a step up from the path and a place to sit while hand weeding or shelling peas! Paths were laid with bark mulch to intersect the beds and provide a soft but firm surface for wheeling a barrow back and forth. Trellis panels were fixed over sloped banks to help climbers.

▲ *A pot of bright pelargoniums.*

flowers

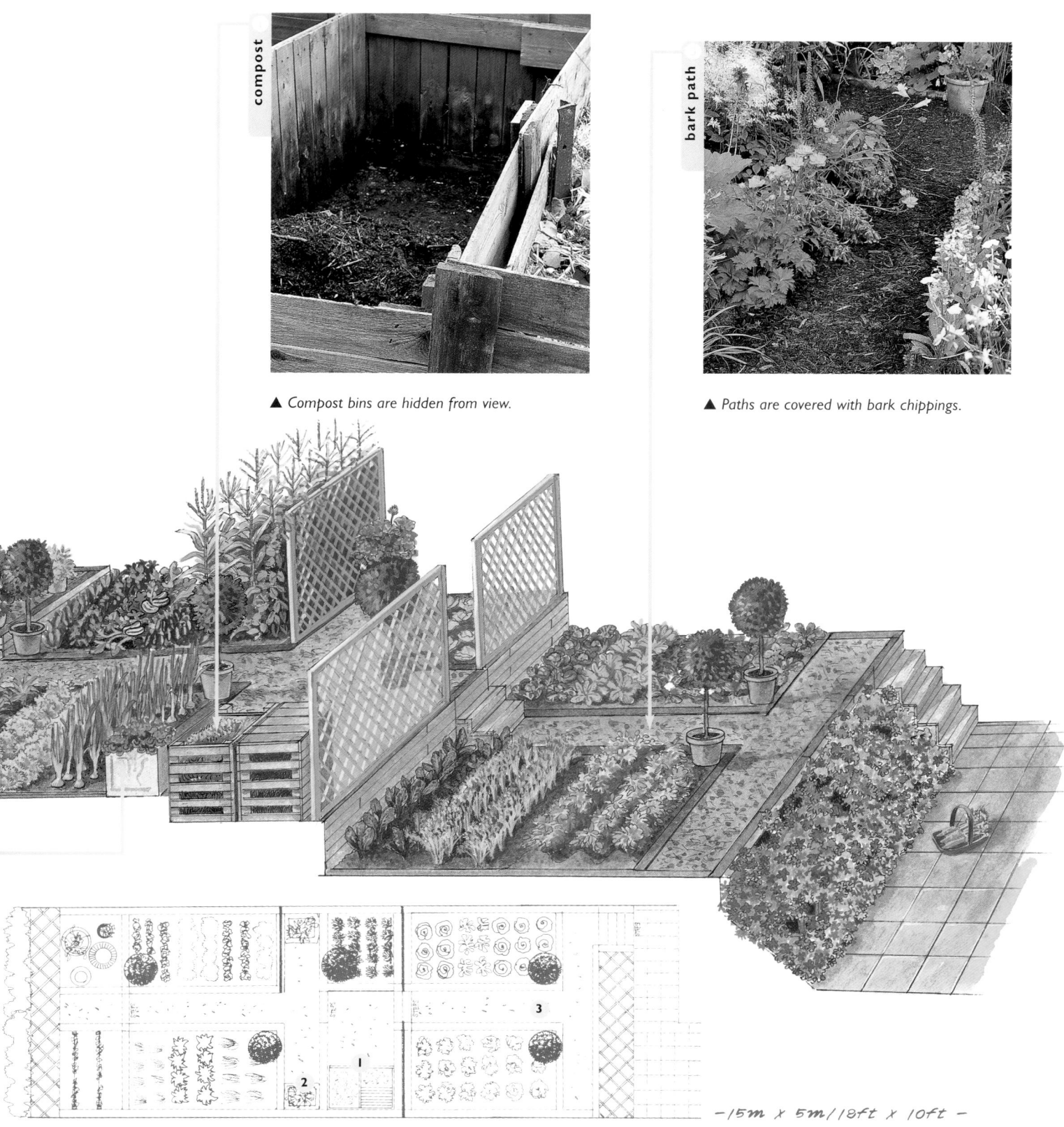

▲ *Compost bins are hidden from view.*

▲ *Paths are covered with bark chippings.*

compost

bark path

−15m x 5m/18ft x 10ft −

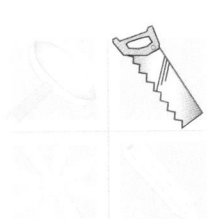

practical projects

Compost making is important in any garden, but especially so for vegetables. We used pressure-treated timber to make our own simple compost container, then set diamond trellis over a weedproof membrane as a support for our decorative climbing beans. Other crops can be grown by planting through the membrane.

Feeding your food

Making your own compost is wonderfully satisfying and is also very easy. There are several schools of thought about the finer details of compost making, but everyone agrees that to rot away into beautiful, sweet-smelling plant food, compost in the making requires air and a degree of moisture. If you make your own compost bin (or buy a proprietary bin) and fill it with thick layers of kitchen vegetable waste, grass clippings, annual weeds (not perennials such as dandelions as their roots can grow anywhere), plant clippings, and even the contents of the vacuum cleaner bag, you cannot go far wrong.

HOEING

A practiced hoeing technique is important: keep away from vegetable stems and penetrate not more than 2.5cm/1in below soil surface.

▲ *If you don't have time to build your own compost bin, or your garden is very small, there are excellent, commercially available varieties.*

Layers of soil between vegetable matter speed up the process of beneficial decay, and the faster the bin is filled the more efficiently its contents rot down. Stems and sticky bits and pieces help to admit air, but twigs or branches are too big and won't rot down. Coarser stems are best crushed to give them a good start. You can also put in loosely screwed up paper and card, fall leaves, and waste bits of potting compost from repotting.

building an organic compost bin

The movable compost bin illustrated here is quick to make, and, since it allows excellent air circulation, it will rapidly produce good compost.

1 Any sort of timber is suitable, provided it is pressure treated. Cut the timber into lengths, ideally of around 1.2m/4ft. (A smaller bin will not make such good compost, as insufficient heat will be generated.) Cut notches toward each end of the timbers so they will fit together.

2 Slot the timbers together. There is no need to screw them in place: in fact, this makes it easier to dismantle the sides once the heap is ready. The bin can then be reassembled elsewhere in the garden.

3 Carry on until the bin is of the desired height. Ideally, make two bins side by side. Once the material in the first bin has rotted down, use it while making a fresh pile in the second bin.

TRELLIS AGAINST A MEMBRANE

Weed-suppressing membrane is the vegetable gardener's answer to prayer and minimizes the amount of back-breaking weeding necessary to keep the vegetables growing strongly. It is designed for use on flat ground, but can also be used against a bank provided you overlay it with trellis panels to hold it in position. Prepare the ground first, then stretch the membrane over it. Cut trellis panels to fit and lay them over the membrane. Nail the trellis in position using long, rustproof nails. Cut holes in the membrane as usual and plant the vegetables through the membrane.

kitchen plants and planting

The most useful kitchen gardens concentrate on produce that can be cropped throughout the season. Flowers for cutting can be grown to jolly the plot along, though many vegetables are ornamental in their own right. Herbs will also give an authentic look and help make full use of your plot.

Mixing in flowers

On the whole it's best to grow flowers separately as they have different growing requirements and get in the way when you are weeding between the vegetables and picking the crop. Many flowers attract beneficial insects such as bees and hoverflies, making them useful as well as pretty, and many have similar requirements to herbs so can be mixed with or grown near them. For the main plan we have grown herbs mostly in containers, but chives or parsley make a neat edging to a bed, where they are easily reached for cutting, and perennial herbs such as rosemary or thyme can be given a permanent home. Little flowers such as *Bellis perennis* (bachelor's button daisies) make a neat edging to herbs or vegetables, and nasturtiums, parsley or chives also look good.

Essentials

Mastering the use of the hoe is essential for those with a kitchen garden as the vegetables you grow must not be placed in competition with weeds for the soil's nutrients. Neatness and orderliness are also an essential part of successful kitchen gardening. Annual weeds can be hoed out without disturbing the crop if attacked while still young. This is best done when the ground is dry so that the weeds won't take root again.

Profile plants

Borago officinalis
BORAGE

With its nodding heads of flower buds and clear blue, five-petaled flowers, borage is a lovely ornament to the kitchen garden. Tiny white

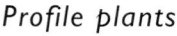 *Borage has attractive blue flowers.*

▶ *Cobbles set in concrete surrounding a small water feature are a strong design focus of this formally laid-out herb garden.*

coloring, such as gold-leaf forms of sage or lemon balm, thrive if given shade from the summer sun at its strongest. Many aromatics actually prefer soil that is not too fertile.

The garden design

Traditionally, herb gardens have been planned rather in the same way as rose gardens (see pages 44–53) with small plots arranged within a formal, geometric structure, each bed enclosed by a low hedge of clipped box. The geometry and formality are complemented by the use of gravel, brick, or stone paving for paths and the whole is intricately ornamental. Herbs growing in beds without an enclosure can spill out onto the hard surface for a more informal look, and they also take very well to being

planted in containers, which can be used to give more height. Either of these treatments can work well for a patio garden.

While a symmetrical plan based on mirrored beds within a square or rectangle can look over-designed in a smaller garden, the formality of straight-edged planting areas, evergreen edging, and hard surfaces

can be adapted in many ways to produce a garden with a true herbarium appeal but without the over-demanding symmetry. This sort of solution is particularly suitable for an irregularly shaped plot. The materials used for the hard-landscaping of the garden should be in sympathy with the house.

It's worth remembering that a highly formalized herb garden with clipped hedging needs to be kept constantly manicured to look at its best. An informal style can benefit from a slightly negligé look. However you decide to organize your own herb garden, remember that you will need to be able to reach the plants for harvesting, so the depth of bed should not be too great.

◀ *Many herbs lend themselves to a relaxed, informal style of gardening; they look at their best when they are allowed to grow naturally.*

designer's herb garden

Apart from the many culinary herbs, there are hundreds of different herbal plants used in medicine, aromatherapy, cosmetics and perfume, and for dyeing cloth. Some traditional herbs, which self-seed easily, are considered to be little more than weeds by some gardeners, but many more are highly ornamental.

▲ *This dark garden looks unsuitable for herbs, but with some work and careful use of light, it can easily be brightened up.*

GARDEN DATA

location:	Kentucky
climate:	mild/temperate
soil type:	chalk
direction:	west
aspect:	sunny, open to the south

The brief

This small, narrow garden faces west, but is denied a lot of natural light because of its high boundary walls, which are overgrown with ivy and other old, woody climbers. A brick-paved passageway opens to a small sitting area in front of the shed and utility area.

The design solution

We removed all the existing climbing plants. The walls, brick shed, and paving were all jet-hosed to remove dirt and debris, then scrubbed with an antifungicide. All walls were checked for cracks and loose mortar and repointed where necessary.

We painted the walls on either side of the passageway a soft yellow. Trellis panels were color stained sea-blue and battened to the wall along the south boundary. The shed door was painted to match. We replaced the existing rotten wooden arch with a removable, bamboo curtain hung from a simple metal arch, and

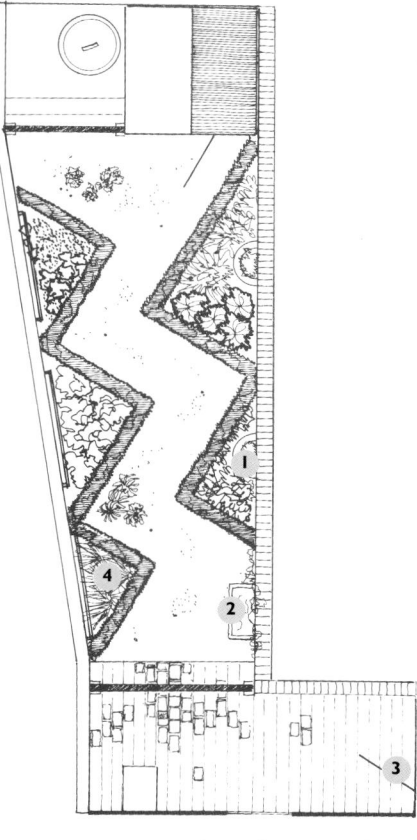

— *16m X 6.5m/52ft X 21ft* —

positioned another one across the steps to the utility area. Gravel replaced the grass patch and the butler's sink became the basin for the ceramic, "lion" water feature.

fountain

◄ *Masque water feature creates a focal point for the brick walls.*

gate

▲ *A decorative wooden gate creates an old-fashioned look.*

container

▲ *Wall-mounted containers are a perfect accompaniment for a brick wall.*

herb bed

◄ *Strong triangular-shaped beds widen this narrow garden.*

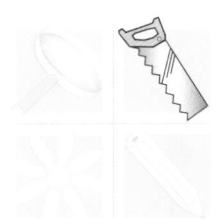

practical projects

Trellis battened to a wall makes a useful framework for many plants. Whatever you intend to grow, make sure that the trellis is fixed just clear of the wall to allow air to flow. In a herb garden it can be used to support nasturtiums (whose leaves, flowers, and fruits are edible), hops, blackberries, and ornamental fruit.

Support and shelter

One of the skills involved in creating a herb garden is to appreciate, and provide, the conditions herbs require. Most herbs (like most vegetables) need warmth and good light, and don't enjoy wind. Providing shelter will be necessary if you have an open position. Bamboo screens can fulfill this function while also being a good-looking way of hiding any unsightly or purely functional parts of the garden. Although temporary, they have a lovely natural look that blends with the simple shapes and planting of the herb garden, and they are cheap and easy to replace.

If you are lucky enough to have a walled garden it will provide maximum shelter. Make optimum use of the wall by growing suitable companion plants up it. Flowering plants such as roses and climbing vegetables such as pole beans, as well as ornamental vines and fruits, can all be grown on trellis and have a natural affinity with herbs.

SCREENS AND CURTAINS

In our client's focus garden (see pages 88–89) we used bamboo curtains to screen off the garbage cans and to separate out different

parts of the garden. These curtains can be put to many different uses—for example in our focus roof garden they are used to

disguise the safety railings (see pages 186–187). Here is a selection of some of the different designs available.

trellis against a wall

In order to grow twining climbers against walls, it is necessary to provide them with some kind of support fixed to the wall. One of the simplest methods uses ready-made trellis panels. If you are using wooden panels, make sure they have been treated with a preservative before proceeding.

1 Cut small wooden battens on which to mount the trellis and drill holes through the length of them. This avoids damage to old walls.

2 Use a masonry bit to drill holes in the wall at the appropriate intervals.

DESIGNER'S TIPS

• Trim clump-forming herbs after flowering, to avoid straggly, woody-stemmed plants.

• If you don't want your herbs to self-seed, trim before they flower. But remember you will have to replace annual herbs with new plants next year.

• Harvest herbs before they flower, in dry, but not hot, conditions.

• Herbs with variegated leaves may be less hardy than those of single-color foliage.

• Chamomile lawns can get untidy and weedy very quickly; be warned.

• Don't experiment with herbal remedies or use them in cooking without reading instructions. Some herbs are very poisonous.

• Beware of rue. It can give you nasty blisters when handled.

• If you have heavy, clay soil, grow your herbs in raised beds.

3 Tap in Rawlplugs to hold the screws. Place the battens in position so that the holes in the battens line up with the holes in the wall.

4 Using long screws, screw the trellis to the wall through the battens. Using battens (rather than fixing the trellis directly to the wall) allows for good air circulation behind the plant.

herb plants and planting

There are dozens of culinary herbs that would grace any garden. And apart from these, herbs in a wider sense include some beautiful and ornamental plants that were once grown for their usefulness, especially in medicine, but which are now known best as garden flowers and shrubs.

FLOWERING HERBS FOR USE AND ORNAMENT

Angelica—*Angelica archangelica:* tall, stately plant; the stems can be candied and the leaves cooked with fish

Borage *—*Borago officinalis:* has a cool, cucumber flavor; both young leaves and the brilliant blue flowers are edible

Chamomile—*Chamaemelum nobile:* apple-scented leaves for pot pourri, white flowers for soothing tisanes

Comfrey—*Symphitum officinale:* a tall, leafy plant with purple-blue flowers, used in folk medicine as a general curative, but unsupervised home use is not now recommended. The whole plant makes excellent garden fertilizer

Feverfew—*Tanacetum parthenium:* flowers are white with yellow centers; leaves eaten in sandwiches may be effective against migraine, flowers deter moths

Lemon balm—*Melissa officinalis:* tiny white flowers attract bees; leaves and flowers can be made into a soothing tisane

Nasturtium—*Tropaeolum:* velvety, spurred flowers yield green knobby fruits that can be pickled like capers; flowers and leaves are edible, with a peppery flavor

Flowers for herb gardens

If you include flowers such as lilies, foxgloves and roses in your herb garden you will be continuing an old apothecary-garden tradition as well as enlivening the garden with spires and mounds of alluring flowers. Selecting widely, you will be able to achieve great variety using only those plants once grown for their use. While it is not advisable to use any of the more powerful plants from the old herbals for self-treatment, growing them to look at is another matter.

As well as the flavoring herbs with which we're still familiar, herbs less widely known, some for kitchen use and some with ancient domestic uses such as keeping away fleas (pennyroyal—a mint) or for making sweetmeats (elecampane), can still be bought from specialist growers. Look out for yellow-headed tansy, blue-leaved rue, red-flowered bergamot and mint-like, blue-flowered hyssop. Add these to the well-known classics such as chamomile, pot marigold, mint, thyme, and lavender.

▶ *Rosemary traditionally accompanies lamb and many Mediterranean dishes.*

Profile plants

Rosmarinus officinalis
ROSEMARY

Rosemary makes a lovely shrub with evergreen piney needles and small light blue flowers which may appear from November until early summer.

ht and sp to 1.5m/5ft but can be cut back
Soil and situation
Well-drained soil that is not too rich and a sheltered position in full sun.

Tropaeolum
NASTURTIUMS

Nasturtiums are well-loved flowers that bring bright color to the herb garden. Bushy and climbing varieties are both easily grown from seed.

ht 30cm/12in (bush) 1–3m/3–10ft (climbing)
sp 45cm/18in (bush) 1.2m/4ft (climbing)
Soil and situation
Well-drained soil that is not too rich in a sunny position.

Salvia officinalis
SAGE

Sage makes lovely purple-blue flowers as well as having attractive, felty gray-green leaves. Golden-leaved and purple-leaved varieties are also available ('Aurea' and 'Purpurascens').

ht 75cm/30in
sp 90cm/3ft
Soil and situation
Fairly fertile soil that is light and well-drained, in a sunny position.

▲ *Nasturtiums have edible flowers.*

▲ *Use home-grown sage for Christmas stuffing.*

SOME COMMON HERBS FOR THE KITCHEN

Annual and short-lived herbs

Basil—*Ocimum basilicum*
spicily aromatic, used in pesto and salads; has an affinity with tomatoes
Dill—*Anethum graveolens*
cool, aromatic flavor blends with fish and potato salad
Garlic—*Allium sativum*
bulbs have strong piquancy for a Mediterranean flavor
Parsley **—*Petroselinum crispum*
indispensable garnishing herb
Rocket **—*Eruca sativa*
brings a pungent, peppery flavor to a mixed-leaf salad

Perennial and shrubby herbs

Bay—*Laurus nobilis*
leathery evergreen leaves for bouquet garni (bay can be grown as topiary)
Chives **—*Allium schoenoprasum*
onion-flavored green leaves for garnish; accompanies cream cheese well
Fennel *—*Foeniculum vulgare*
feathery leaves have a slightly aniseed taste
French tarragon *—*Artemisia dranunculus*
a subtle aniseed flavor for chicken and sauces
Marjoram *—*Origanum vulgare*
a good herb for soups, stews, and bouquet garni; also for pizza
Mint ** *Mentha spicata*
well-known cooling and refreshing herb for

mint sauce, new potatoes, and peas (also known as spearmint), pineapple mint (*M. suaveolens* 'Variegata'), and eau-de-cologne mint (*M.x. piperata* f. *citrata, syn.* M. *citrata*) are some more unusual varieties
Rosemary *—*Rosmarinus officinalis*
aromatic needles go well with lamb; also for pot pourri and cosmetic uses
Sage *—*Salvia officinalis*
for pork dishes and sage and onion stuffing
Salad burnet *—*Poterium sansquisorba*
cucumber-flavored leaves for salads and summer drinks
Thyme *—*Thymus vulgaris*
aromatic herb for bouquet garni and to add to soups and stews

  * *needs sunshine and good drainage*
** *needs moisture and semishade*

▲ *Thyme and the annual basil make an aromatic and decorative combination.*

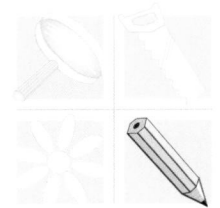

design alternatives

SKETCHES

The first alternative employs rustic secondhand bricks, traditional herbs, and an old-fashioned butler's sink to create a medieval herb garden effect. The second plan is more modern with raised beds, clipped bay trees, and sharper, straighter lines.

pots of small herbs—thyme, pineapple mint, tarragon, basil

butler's sink with pebbles at bottom, to hold oxygenating water plants such as pontederia cordata lanceolata or seolz watermint

secondhand or old stock bricks (must be frostproof) to make irregular-shaped path through garden to shed

10 mm/½in pea gravel over weed-proof membrane, herbs planted directly into this

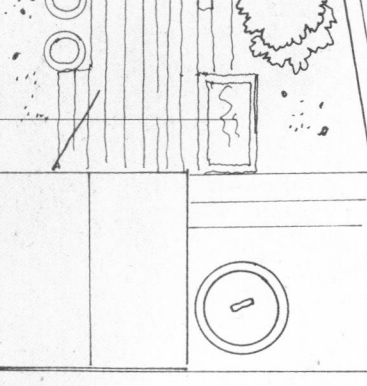

94

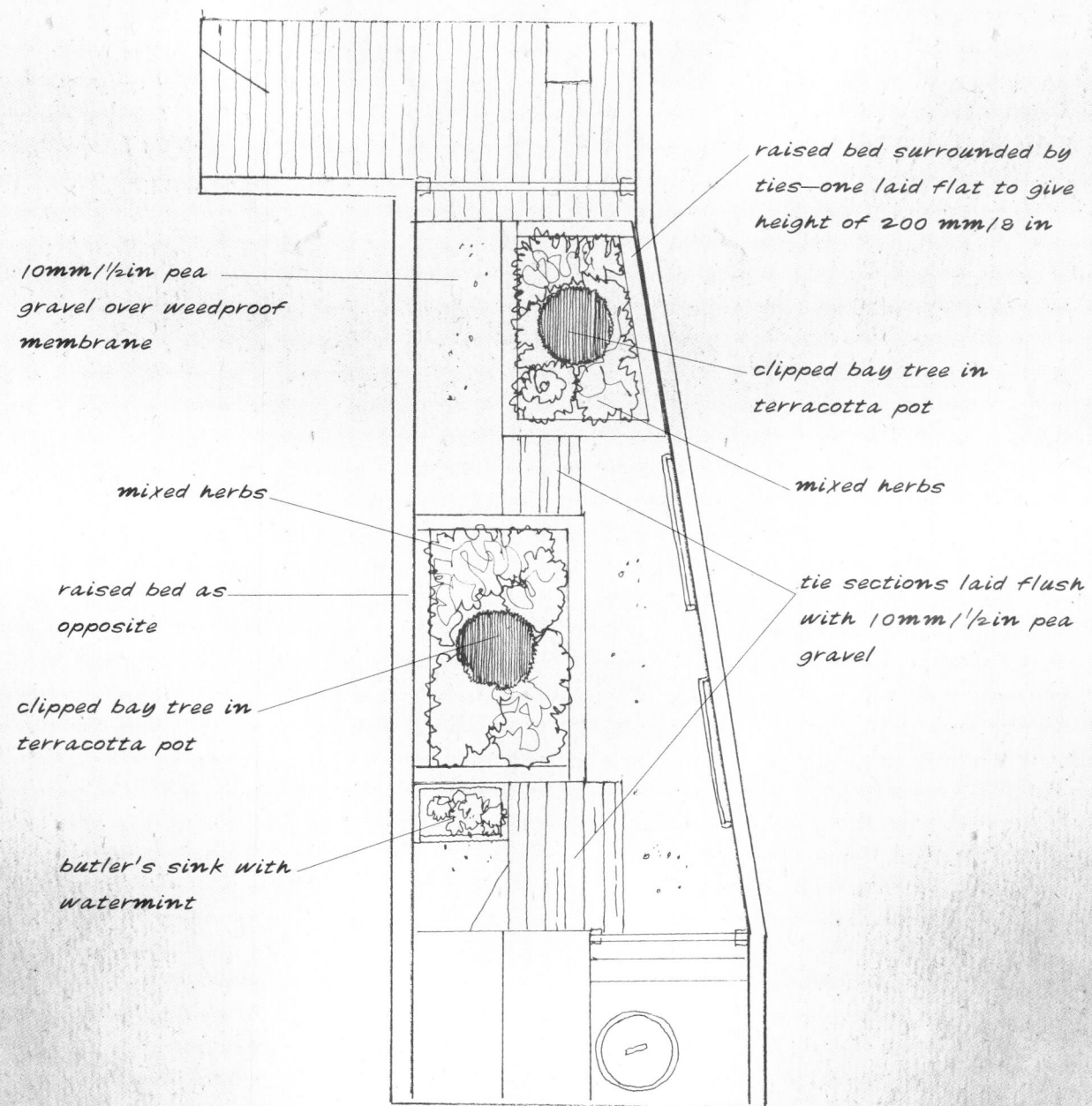

raised bed surrounded by
ties—one laid flat to give
height of 200 mm/8 in

10mm/½in pea
gravel over weedproof
membrane

clipped bay tree in
terracotta pot

mixed herbs

mixed herbs

raised bed as
opposite

tie sections laid flush
with 10mm/½in pea
gravel

clipped bay tree in
terracotta pot

butler's sink with
watermint

peaceful gardens

The gardens in this section for contemplation and meditation are gardens to sit in, gardens to look at, and gardens in which to find peace. All gardens provide this to some extent but this is the explicit aim of these particular schemes. Of course the peaceful garden may be the result of a lot of preliminary hard work—but the calming results will be worth the effort.

meadow garden

Leave your garden to grow by itself and you'll get a tangle of ineradicable weeds, linked—or partly hidden—by scrambling bindweed and a blackberry thicket. It follows that growing a meadow hazily dotted with wild flowers like an Impressionist painting must be an art and the meadow as a garden must be deceptively contrived.

◀ *Grasses, swaying gently in the slightest summer breeze, are an essential ingredient of every successful meadow garden.*

Wild delights

What a dream of a garden the apparently artless meadow is—and many a plot has room for a little flowering meadow area of its own even when the rest is more conventionally cultivated. A tiny area of meadow in a lawn can be just as effective as a flower bed and can assuage that longing to be at one with nature. An important incidental feature of a wild meadow garden is that it attracts insects to the garden, bringing a peaceful summer hum. With luck, these will include beneficial insects that prey on garden pests, such as hoverflies, ladybirds, lacewings, and bees for pollination.

Many of the plants suitable for a meadow garden are wild native plants, but many more have been borrowed from gardens. Growing in grass and fending for themselves they will be smaller and more subtle. Growing a meadow garden is doing our bit for nature, as native flowers in the wild are a disappearing phenomenon, thanks to the use of herbicides, the ripping up of hedges, the grooming of the countryside and ever-spreading building, as well as the loss of wild areas in towns. But foxgloves, cornflowers, forget-me-nots, scabious, and verbascums were once as common in the wild as poppies on a construction site and ox-eye daisies on a highway bank, and these are typical meadow garden plants for us to grow from seed. Other plants for meadow planting, such as larkspur, tulips, love-in-a mist, and lupins, are wild flowers of another part of the world, and add a slightly foreign charm to the meadow.

Maintenance

The main work in presiding over a meadow garden is in the preparation and planting (see pages 104–105). After that the care needed is much

less than that for a lawn or flower bed. Meadows are self-supporting once they are established and the plants must be allowed to seed themselves. This means that the flowers and grasses must have gone to seed before you do any cutting.

Some cutting is necessary to keep down aggressively competitive weeds and grasses. So, depending on the look you want, cut in the fall for a summer-flowering meadow or at the beginning of summer for spring meadows. The summer meadow can then be kept cut until late in the following spring to keep it at a reasonable height and to continue to discourage unwanted competitors, but it may be left if you prefer. A spring meadow can be mown or

scythed during the summer unless it is also planted with summer flowers, in which case after an early summer cut it won't need to be cut again until fall.

Many people prefer to make the first cut a close one. In any case, the mowings must be raked up, not left on the soil to feed it, as the essence of a successful meadow garden is a soil of fairly low fertility. Every so often competing plants may gain the upper hand. Weeding your meadow will help to keep them under control, but sometimes the only answer is to start again.

▶ Once established, a meadow garden will be self-supporting, but will look slightly different each year as different plants flourish.

▲ In meadow planting carefully selected grasses and wild flowering plants mingle and flourish as nature would have chosen.

designer's meadow garden

A wildflower meadow humming with insect activity in high summer is a rare and delightful sight. Even in a small garden you can create a minimeadow, either by leaving an area of lawn to grow and produce its own colony of plants or by the deliberate introduction of a mix of wild flowers and grasses suited to the soil type.

▲ *Transforming an area of this large garden into a meadow will attract wildlife whose survival depends on nectar-rich plants.*

GARDEN DATA

location:	▦ Rhode Island
climate:	▦ cold/windy
soil type:	▦ light clay
direction:	▦ west facing
aspect:	▦ sloping towards trees

Design brief

The open space designated for this small patch of meadow planting is part of a large garden which is planted very informally. The soil is thin and chalky—ideal conditions for a dry-meadow planting. The owners want to add a splash of summer color which will be visible from the house and are prepared to learn how to use a scythe in order to "mow" the meadow in late summer. Otherwise, apart from removal of unwanted weeds, it will be left untouched.

Design solution

To avoid unwanted competition from vigorous grasses we stripped the existing turf. We undertook no further soil preparation other than removing surface stones.

There are many possibilities for flower and grass mixtures and even for a minicornfield. Here we chose a selection of plants which can cope with dry conditions and the slightly alkaline soil. Apart from myosotis

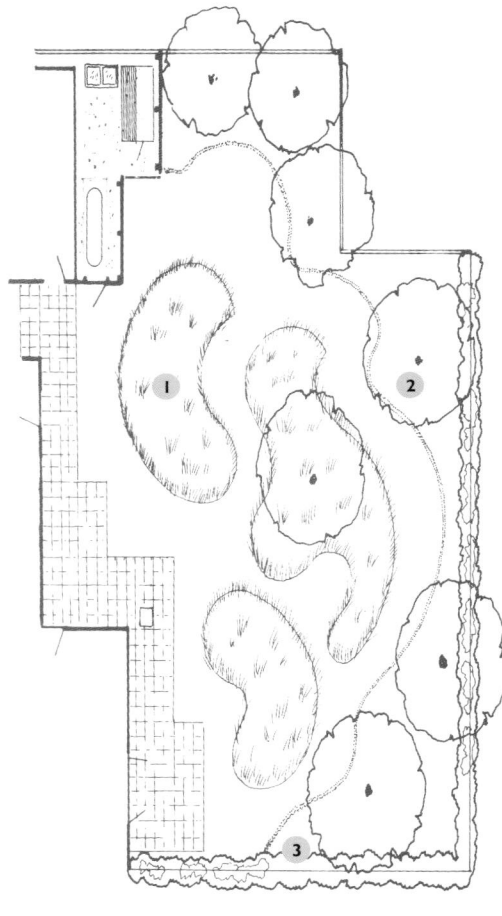

— 25m x 13m/80ft x 42ft —

(forget-me-not) the plants are summer-flowering and after two or three years will establish and start to spread more or less vigorously.

flowering cherry

◀ *A flowering cherry is a focal point in the center of our designer's garden.*

ox-eye daisy

▶ *A traditional country hedge is a wonderful boundary for a meadow garden.*

traditional hedge

◀*Ox-eye daisies were once common in meadows and will grow well in a garden.*

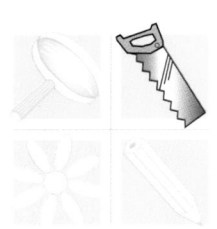

practical projects

To achieve a meadow haze you will need to become adept at raising plants from seed. But most meadow plants are either long-lived perennials or else self-seeding annuals, so once you have done the groundwork your garden should work for you. Seeds are available as named meadow or wild flower varieties and in mixes.

Easy sowing

Most suitable meadow plants can be grown easily from seed, and this is generally the best way to grow plants needed in such large quantities. Some seeds have to be sown directly into the ground as the young plants don't like to be disturbed, while others, such as the meadow cranesbill in our garden, can be started in seed trays and planted out into position as young plants. Seedlings always need light and warmth as well as moisture once they are growing, which means that seeds are generally sown outside only when the earth has warmed up, and the ground needs to be well watered unless it's been raining. Like the grass in our designer's meadow, seeds specifically sold as meadow mixtures are normally sown direct into the ground.

Individual plants

For accent plants, a very good alternative is to buy plug plants, which have been germinated and started off in ideal conditions. These are potted on into larger pots before being planted out in their chosen positions. (See page 227 for more information on buying and transferring plants.)

Grown in this way individual plants benefit from not having their roots disturbed when being moved on. Primrose, harebell, red campion, cowslip, ox-eye daisy, and cornflower are some of the meadow plants frequently available, and of course you can grow your own seedlings in the same way which will give you an even wider choice.

BROADCAST SOWING

For any meadow mixture, prepare the ground as you would for a lawn, except that no fertilizer should be added.

Rake over the surface to make it smooth and level. Scatter the seed by hand. Water in with a fine sprinkler.

sowing meadow seed

If you want more control over the final result than can be achieved by broadcast sowing, as described on page 102, sow individual types of seed according to their specific requirements. Remember that germination rates vary depending on the species, and some will self-seed freely, so that the meadow will never look the same two years in succession.

1 Prepare the ground as normal, but add no supplementary fertilizer. For larger seeds, make shallow trenches with a trowel.

2 For smaller seeds, mark rills in the soil with a hoe. Some seed can be surface sown.

3 Sow the seed thinly. For large seed, allow a space of about 1cm/½in between seeds. Fine seed can be mixed with sand. Gently draw the soil over the seeds. Seedlings can be thinned once they have germinated.

4 By summer, the meadow will be a sea of color. The majority of meadow plants will self-seed, and over the course of the years the species best suited to the site will predominate.

meadow plants and planting

The key to a successful meadow garden is to encourage nature to do its best, not try to interfere with it. Having prepared the ground thoroughly, start your meadow by sowing seed in spring. Nature does the rest. Some plants will thrive in a wide range of meadow conditions, but patience is critical to success.

Before you sow

Perennial weeds can be a problem in a meadow garden and eliminating as many as possible before you begin is the aim. Start with a bare plot. Some meadow growers advocate plowing. In a smaller area you might consider rotovating—laying down black plastic for a year to suppress weeds—or even spraying the whole area with a harmless weedkiller (a glyphosate type). Planting with potatoes for a year (a well-known clearing crop) is also a recommended way of preparing the ground. Those devoted to the task will remove perennial weeds by hand before they begin. Most meadows thrive on soil that is not too fertile so it may be best to remove the top layer of earth in an established garden, especially if the soil is of the fertile, loamy type or has been well cultivated over the years.

To select plants that will be at home in the type of soil and situation you have to offer, spend some time assessing this first, and then browse over the catalogs. The three main types of soil are the more fertile, medium to heavy soils (sometimes called "loamy" or "pasture"), and the poorer chalk, and sandy soils. You also need to assess whether the soil is dry/well-drained (usually in a sunny, open position) or whether it tends to be moist (and often more shaded). Ready-mixed seed such as 'cornfield

◀ Briza media *is a perennial grass.*

▲ Allium sphaerocephalon, *commonly called drumstick allium.*

▲ *Meadow clary will attract bees and insects to your wild garden.*

MEADOW PLANTING

Meadow in a lawn

You can sow meadow seeds directly onto grass in spring or fall. Cut the grass as low as possible and rake the lawn well to open it up. Broadcast a general "meadow mixture" seed and rake in lightly. (The soil should be moist.) Firm the area with a roller.

Keep the grass fairly closely cut during the first year so that it does not get ahead of the flowers. From year two, cut the grass in early May, then after summer flowering in late August, and again in late October

Moist meadow plants

astilbe	celandine
lady's smock	meadowsweet
mimulus	meadow buttercup
trollius	purple loosestrife

Plants for chalk and limestone

comfrey	cowslip
flax	harebell
hawkbit	knapweed
pinks, Cheddar	toadflax

Shady meadow plants

These plants are also suitable for growing under trees.

betony	bugle
forget-me-not	foxglove
herb robert	purple loosestrife

Bulbs, corms, and tubers for naturalizing

Scatter the bulbs and plant where they land, using a bulb planter. Plant each bulb with twice the amount of soil above it as its own depth. Bulbs are hungrier than true meadow plants and can benefit from an annual dressing of a high-potash fertilizer.

Plants marked (W) are also suitable for woodland conditions and shade.

bluebell (W)
crocus
celandine
daffodil (*Narcissus pseudonarcissus*)
grape hyacinth
lily-of-the-valley (W)
snowdrop (W)
wood anemone (W)
wood tulip (*Tulipa sylvestris*) (W)
wild garlic (*Allium ursinum*) (W)

Plants for thin, dry soils

Also for windswept areas and coastal conditions. Plants marked (S) are for sandy soil.

California poppy (S)

clover	convolvulus
corncockle (S)	corn marigold (S)
evening primrose (S)	flax
harebell	lupin
mullein	pinks, Cheddar
St John's wort	toadflax
vetch	yarrow

mix', 'hay meadow mix' (early-flowering), 'flowering lawn mix' (for shorter grass), and 'meadow flowers' (the most wide-ranging) are available. You will also find mixtures on offer for the various soil types, including acid or alkaline soils. Be prepared to spend some time selecting plants that will be at home in your plot. Otherwise of course, you can chance your luck and learn as you go.

Meadow grass

It's important to have suitable grass so that it doesn't dominate the wild flowers but instead acts as a foil for them. The grass itself will produce plumes of beige and buff flower heads which are part of the charm of a meadow garden.

Grass seeds are also available for starting meadows, while some flower mixtures contain a suitable grass seed as well, so check when you buy. If in doubt ask your seed supplier for advice before buying.

Profile plants

Geranium pratense (meadow cranesbill) is one of the few meadow plants that require rich soil. *Leucanthemum vulgare* (ox-eye daisy) thrives in a multitude of situations. *Briza media* (quaking grass) is a delightful grass for a meadow.

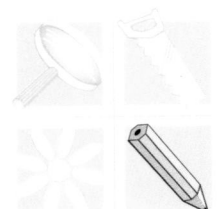

design alternatives

SKETCHES

You can apply these
meadow planting ideas
to just a small patch of
lawn, say 3m x 3m/
10ft x 10ft—just choose
"wet or dry" plantings
depending on your soil
conditions.

θ   meadow cranesbill

△   ox-eye daisy

◐   Tulipa parrotica

◎   Allium sphaerocephalon

○   Nepeta faassenii

+   Briza media

•   Salvia pratensis

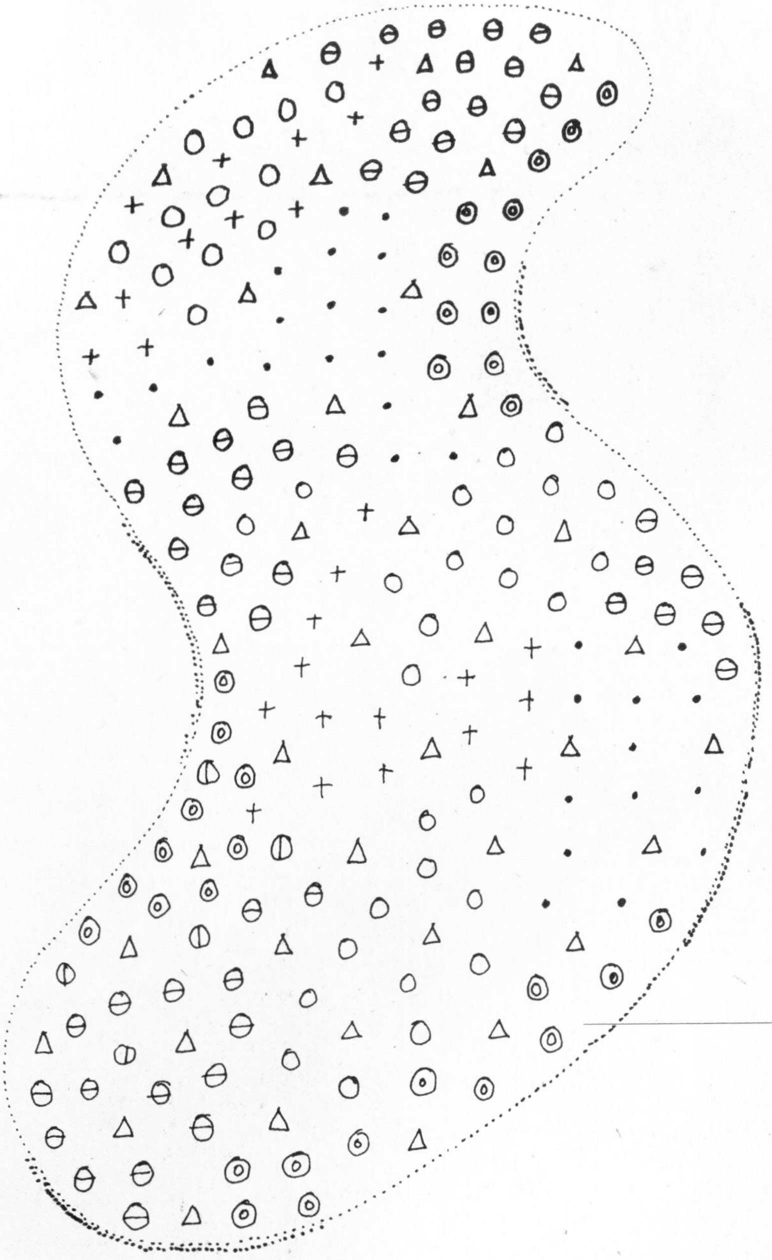

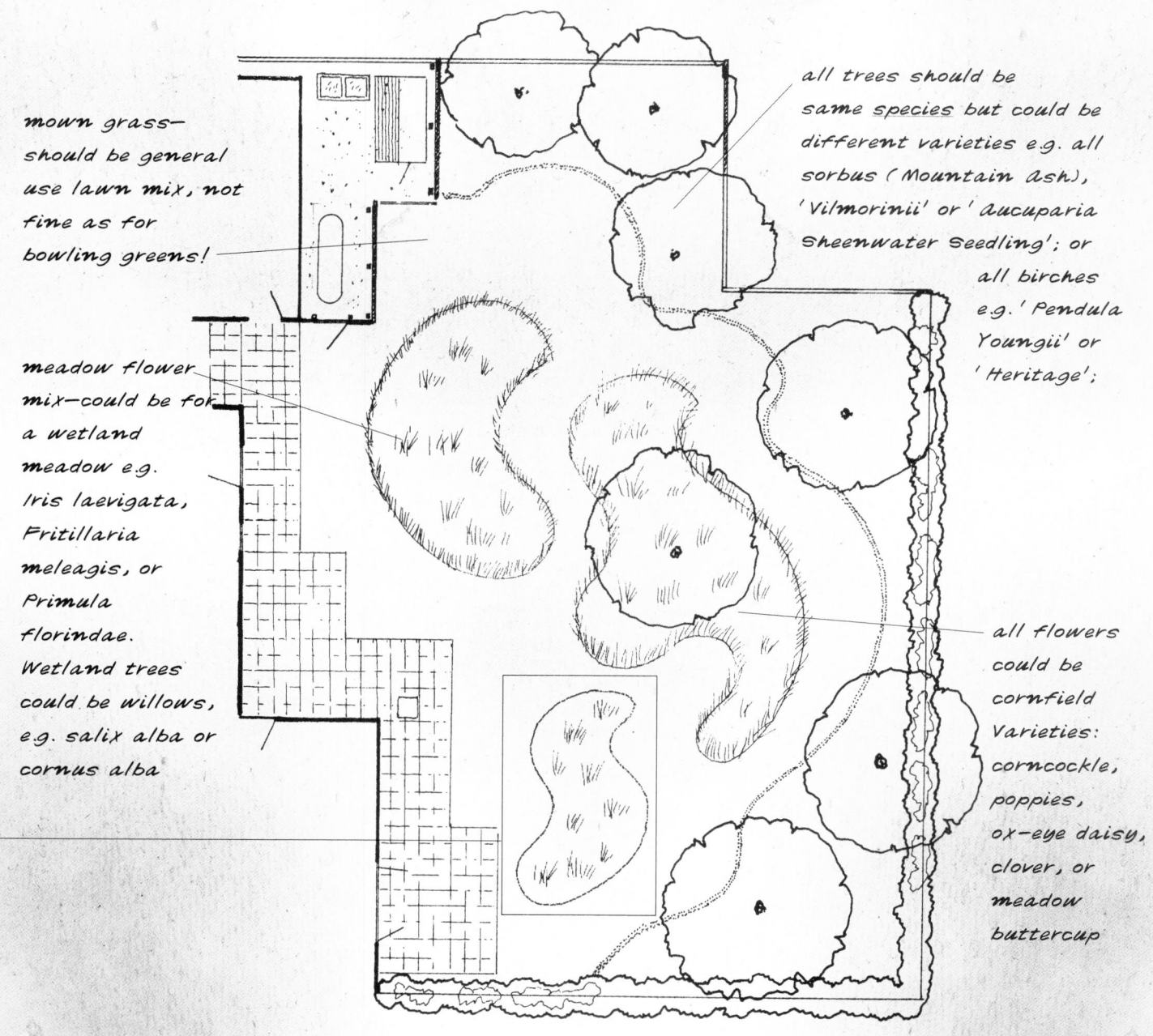

mown grass—
should be general
use lawn mix, not
fine as for
bowling greens!

all trees should be
same species but could be
different varieties e.g. all
sorbus (Mountain Ash),
'Vilmorinii' or 'Aucuparia
Sheenwater Seedling'; or
all birches
e.g. 'Pendula
Youngii' or
'Heritage';

meadow flower
mix—could be for
a wetland
meadow e.g.
Iris laevigata,
Fritillaria
meleagis, or
Primula
florindae.
Wetland trees
could be willows,
e.g. salix alba or
cornus alba

all flowers
could be
cornfield
Varieties:
corncockle,
poppies,
ox-eye daisy,
clover, or
meadow
buttercup

107

shade garden

If your garden is naturally shady, why not go along with it and turn it into a green and pleasant place? And if you'd like to be out of the sun in a more exposed garden there are plenty of ways of creating a shady spot for an afternoon snooze and for indulging in green thoughts in the shade.

◄ *Hostas, astilbes, lamiums, and lady's mantle are among many plants that positively thrive in the shade and will look wonderful in any garden.*

A shady situation

Sometimes shade in the garden is dictated by the aspect or by neighbors' planting. If you live downhill your garden may well be shady, and if neighbors on the uphill side grow anything in the least bit tall this will exaggerate it. Or it may simply be that the folks on all sides have a taste for trees and this robs your garden of light. If so don't fight them, join them and make your neighborhood into a leafy oasis. Tall buildings, including your own house, can put your garden in shade for much of the time and in this case there is nothing you can do about these shady areas but learn to enjoy and work with them.

Shade is often associated with moisture and there are lots of plants that can be grown in moist, shady situations. If you are unlucky enough to have dry shade, or shade that is wet and water-logged in winter and dry and cracked in summer, your choice will be more limited. Like any peaceful garden, a shaded garden needs to provide you with somewhere to sit. It would even be possible to create a shady bower overhung with green climbing and twining plants in a sunny garden. It is best to locate your shade garden in a spot where it gets a ray of light in the morning or evening if this is possible as these are the times you are least likely to want to flee the sun.

A woodland theme

If your garden is big enough, or if the location is suitable (for example the house is in a wooded area or adjacent gardens already have trees and tall shrubs), a wonderful way to create shade is to grow a woodland garden.

Naturally the trees will take some years to grow, so you need to intend to stay put. There are some lovely plants to grow under deciduous trees, which let through a lot of light in winter and spring before the leaves come out and then cast a magical green dimness. To blend with a woodland theme you'll need a winding path, and open "glades" of grass. Bark chippings and log stepping stones are sympathetic materials for paths. You might also borrow from the meadow garden

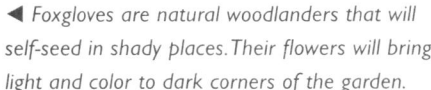
◀ *Foxgloves are natural woodlanders that will self-seed in shady places. Their flowers will bring light and color to dark corners of the garden.*

(pages 98–107) and have some areas of rough grass with woodland- or shade-loving wild flowers.

Bulbs naturalize beautifully under deciduous trees. Scattered and planted naturally, the spring-flowering bulbs look even prettier in newly growing grass and criss-crossed with the shade from branches of trees overhead.

A shade garden with only deciduous trees can look empty in winter. Using evergreens will continue the green theme into the bare season and also help to give a more decisive form to the garden. Many evergreen shrubs grow naturally in forests and supply either brilliant flowers in contrast to their leaves or unexpected scents for winter days or summer evenings.

It will be best to link the woodland area to the house by lower-growing and more formal planting. You don't want to step straight out into a wood, but rather to see it somewhat in the distance. An area of formally planted shrubs and flower companions, perhaps defined by low evergreen hedges, will arrange things beautifully.

◀ *A potted fern brings a touch of sophistication to this shady corner. Ferns suit container planting and can be moved in winter if tender.*

designer's shade garden

A shady site can be turned into a lush and leafy green oasis, or a woodland garden. It need not be without color at most times of the year and can always be planted with a variety of leaf textures and shapes. Dry shade under the canopy of large trees is more difficult, but even here ivy or gaulteria will cope adequately.

▲ *In this garden we decided to screen the summerhouse with trees to create an element of surprise and provide privacy.*

GARDEN DATA

location:	▪▪ Pennsylvania
climate:	▪▪ temperate
soil type:	▪▪ neutral—alkaline
direction:	▪▪ north facing
aspect:	▪▪ overlooks railway bank

Design brief

The north-facing garden forms a long rectangle, shaded on three sides by neighboring trees and on the fourth side by the house. Some year-round interest is required together with planting to balance the tall surrounding trees. There is a small summerhouse at the far end.

Design solution

We decided to turn the shadiness of the site into a positive feature by creating an informal woodland area round the summerhouse. We planted graceful birches, which will still allow some light through to the woodland floor. We massed different ground-cover plants beneath the trees to flower at different times of the year. A camellia puts on a stunning spring show against the dark green backdrop of the surrounding yew hedge. The planting was surrounded by a deep bark mulch—leaf mold would be even better—and we marked a gently meandering path

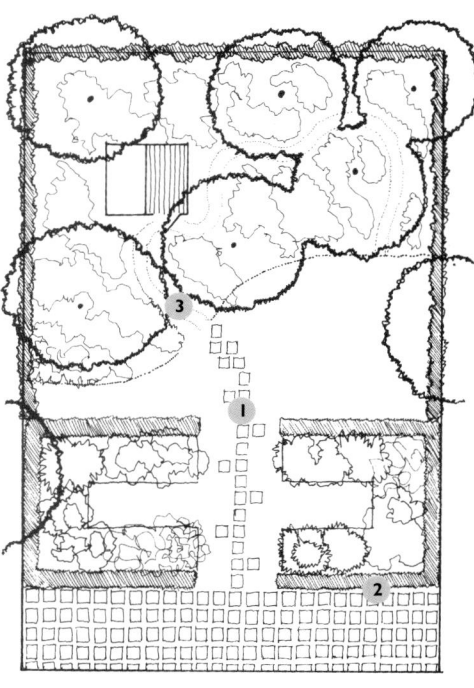

– 19m x 11m/60ft x 35ft –

with a coarser grade of bark chippings in a lighter color. Nearer the house we contrasted the informality of the woodland with a geometric matrix of slabs set in closely mown grass. Formal box hedges enclose perennials and flowering shrubs and frame the path through the garden to the wood.

box hedge ②

▲ *Flower beds are edged with clipped box.*

bark chips ③

▲ *Bark chippings are used as a path to the summerhouse, and to provide ground cover.*

paving slabs ①

▲ *Paving slabs are set in the mown lawn.*

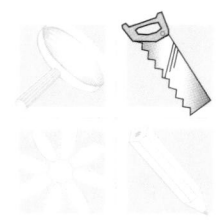

practical projects

Hedging is a useful feature in many types of garden and a dense evergreen hedge will always add a formal touch and provide structure. A low hedge can be used to divide one part of the garden from another and a high hedge is a perfect way of concealing the "hard work" area of the garden from view.

An evergreen hedge

Box '*Buxus sempervirens*' is *the* plant for a traditional low evergreen hedge. It is ideal for a shady garden as the leaves can lose their strong green color if the light is too strong. We

◄ *There are many types of tools available for trimming box hedge, including shears, pruners, and clippers. Ask your garden center for advice.*

used it to make a neat dwarf hedge to enclose areas of looser planting.

If your budget can run to it, buying young plants is the best way to start, as establishing a hedge is a long-term project without the additional wait for cuttings to take root. However, it is possible to grow a temporary "hedge" using other plants (such as the annual summer cypress, *Kochia scoparia*) while you produce your own box plants, and growing plants from cuttings is very satisfying. So if you know someone whose box hedge needs trimming, step in and volunteer to help.

The best time to take cuttings is late summer, when the new growth is just beginning to ripen and become more woody. When taking cuttings the aim is not to let the plant material dry out. Therefore it's best to do it on a dull, damp day, and

to keep the cuttings in a plastic bag as you cut them. Cut off lengths up to 30cm/12in long, if possible taking them from side shoots. When you have enough, trim the cuttings to the same length, just below a leaf joint, and dip the cut ends into hormone rooting powder. Plant in pots or cutting mix or in a reserved area in the garden. You will need to add horticultural sand to the soil and cover the cuttings with cloches if you strike them in the garden.

planting a box hedge

An evergreen hedge needs to be very carefully planted and maintained because its success depends on its formal quality. Planting lines should be marked with strings attached to pegs and the plants are normally spaced about 30cm/12in apart for a taller hedge of about 60cm/2ft high, and only 15cm/6in apart for a dwarf hedge. The hedge needs to be trimmed two to three times a year to keep it immaculate.

1 Mark the line of the hedge with a string stretched taut and attached to pegs driven into the ground. Dig a trench along the string.

2 Set the plants in the trench at the appropriate distance from each other and firm them in. Water well, then water daily until the plants are established and growing strongly.

CLIPPING A BOX HEDGE

Box responds well to clipping, which produces a sheer surface of tight, dense growth. Unless you have a very good eye, it can be a good idea to run a horizontal line at the height you wish to trim the hedge.

Box can be trimmed with shears, pruners, or the special clippers shown here. Hold the blades as near flush to the surface as possible. Be sure to trim wayward shoots right back. Trim in spring and mid- to late summer.

shady plants and planting

The garden we designed has shade of its own and needed a selection of plants that would thrive in and enhance it. In other gardens you may wish to grow plants in a light position in order to create shade. Deciduous plants will insure that shade is reduced to a pattern of shadows in winter when you want more light.

Green arbors

Climbing plants grown over an arbor or pergola can create areas of shade in a sunny garden. These structures need to be strongly made—or, if you buy them in kit form, well assembled and installed—as they eventually bear a strong weight and it's disheartening to have to dismantle and rebuild them just as the plants are reaching their peak of glory. Ideally a pergola should lead somewhere or extend all the way along the length of a wall. Plants to grow up trees or large shrubs should be planted some distance from the roots and guided toward their host with canes or strings.

Plants for creating shade

Honeysuckle (*Lonicera periclymenum*) and wisteria (*Wisteria sinensis*) are two lovely scented climbers, along with a few climbing roses. Russian vine (*Fallopia aubertii*, syn. *Polygonum aubertii*) is a terrifically fast climber for creating a green shade, though it will need to be kept severely within bounds—not for nothing is it known as mile-a-minute vine. A true vine, *Vitis coignetiae* provides cooling green leaves that overlap to form a lovely density, followed by a warm red glow in the fall. The hop plant (*Humulus lupulus*) is another leafy climber with flat, overlapping leaves, in green or a sharp greeny yellow *(H. l.* 'Aureus'). All these are deciduous, but shade is not such an objective in the winter, when the twining stems create their own beauty and the extra light will be welcome.

Wall plants in shade

As climbers to provide all-year green in shady places the ivies (*Hedera helix*) are invaluable. Or for a sheltered, shady wall there is *Trachelospermum asiaticum*, with waxy, scented flowers. The climbing hydrangea, *Hydrangea petiolaris* is a vigorous and tolerant wall plant which though deciduous looks good when bare.

◄ *Astilbes are excellent shade plants.*

HOSTAS FOR SHADE

Hostas are the perfect plant for moist and shady places, with their generous mounds of overlapping, heart-shaped leaves and stems of small tubular flowers. They love the humus-rich soft earth under deciduous trees, where they get dappled shade. There is now a multitude of hostas, grown mainly for their leaves—often crinkled or rippled and having contrasting margins—in shades of green, golden green, or blue-green. Perhaps the best way to make a selection is to choose what appeals from your local plant center. Some special cultivars are listed here. It's essential to protect hostas from slugs and snails, which are particularly partial to this snack.

Hosta selection

H. 'Blue Wedgwood'

Hosta fortunei var. *aureomarginata* (syn. *H.* 'Aureomarginata')

H. 'Frances Williams'

H. 'Halcyon'

H. 'Honeybells'

H. 'Sum and Substance'

Hosta sieboldiana var. *elegans*

H. *tokudama*

H. *undulata* var. *albomarginata*

H. *venusta*

H. 'Wide Brim'

▲ *The black birch has beautiful peeling bark.*

Profile plants

Betula nigra 'Heritage'
BLACK BIRCH

This is a tall but graceful birch for a woodland area, its whitish young bark peeling to reveal orange-brown new bark. In early spring it bears long, brown catkins and the brown leaves turn yellow in the fall.

ht 18m/60ft

sp to 12m/40ft

Soil and situation

Fertile, moist soil; shade.

GROUND–COVER PLANTS FOR SHADE

Lamium maculatum (dead nettle), *Tiarella cordifolia* (foam flower), epimedium (barrenwort), and *Vinca major* (periwinkle)

Ajuga reptans
BUGLE

A low-growing, spreading woodland plant with whorls of small, deep blue, or bronze flowers in spikes above the small green leaves.

ht 15cm/6in

sp 60cm/2ft

Soil and situation

Moist soil and partial shade.

Astilbe 'Fanal'
ASTILBE

There are many different astilbes for growing in shady conditions, mainly in cream or shades of pink. 'Fanal' is an unusual variety in deep red with very dark foliage.

ht 60cm/2ft

sp 45cm/18in

Soil and situation

Dry soil and semishade.

▼ *Ajuga reptans has spikes of deep blue flowers.*

design alternatives

SKETCHES

As a general design principle, when designing a formal, symmetrical garden, always work out the exact dimensions of the hard-landscaping first. This avoids the problem of having to cut the slabs to fit a fixed layout of plantings.

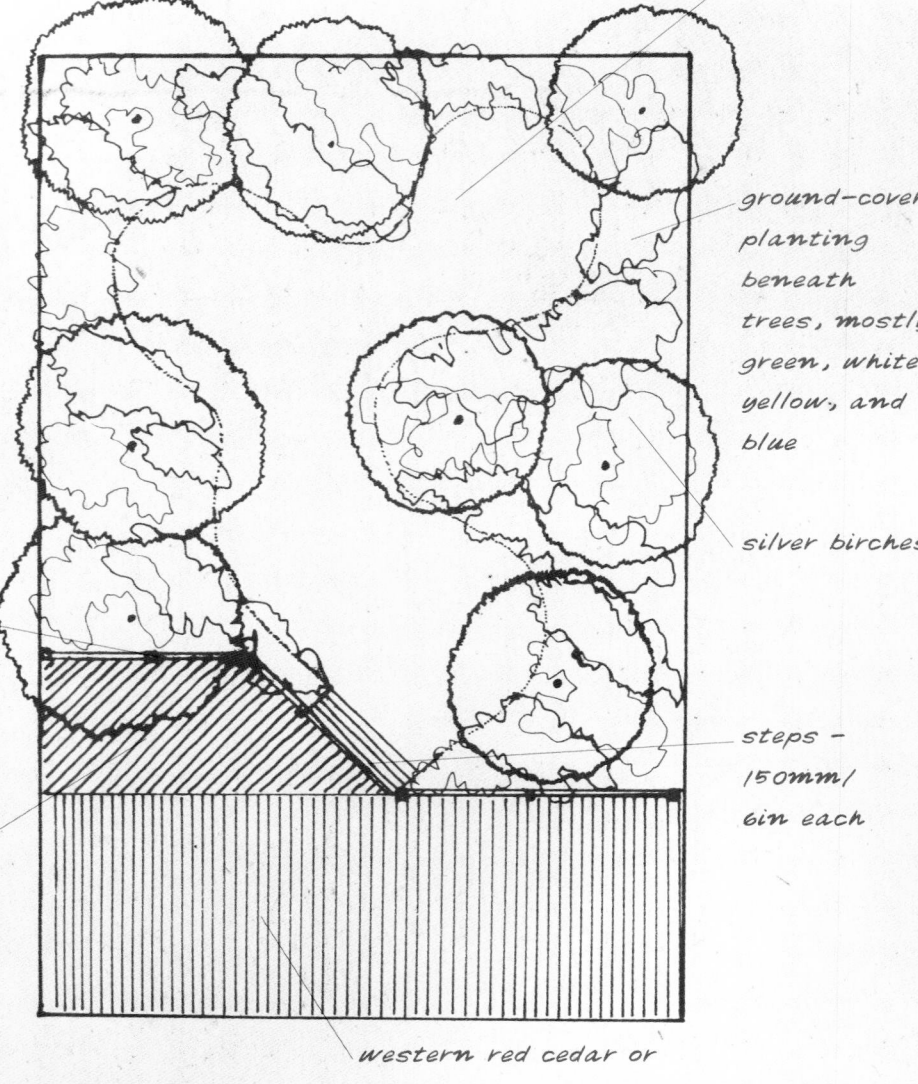

grass

ground-cover planting beneath trees, mostly green, white, yellow, and blue

silver birches

steps – 150mm/ 6in each

balustrade around deck

deck raised approx 300mm/ 1ft above ground level

western red cedar or similar deck raised approx 15cm/6in above lower level

summerhouse 2.4m x 3m/8ft x 10ft,
painted white, or soft yellow

1.5m/5ft hedge of
Thuja plicata
aurea on 3 sides

two matching beds of
white hydrangeas or
Choisya ternata at
either end of garden

sculpture or
statue as main
focal point

creamy white 20mm/
³/4in angular stone
chippings

clipped box hedges
75cm/30in high

clipped buxus (box)
hedge 75cm/30in
high—immediately
next to thuja hedge

Victorian rope edge tiles
in terracotta or dark
slate blue

cream or white slabs
45cm x 45cm/
17in x 17in

nb: This garden is ideal for non-gardeners—
only maintenance is clipping the hedges.

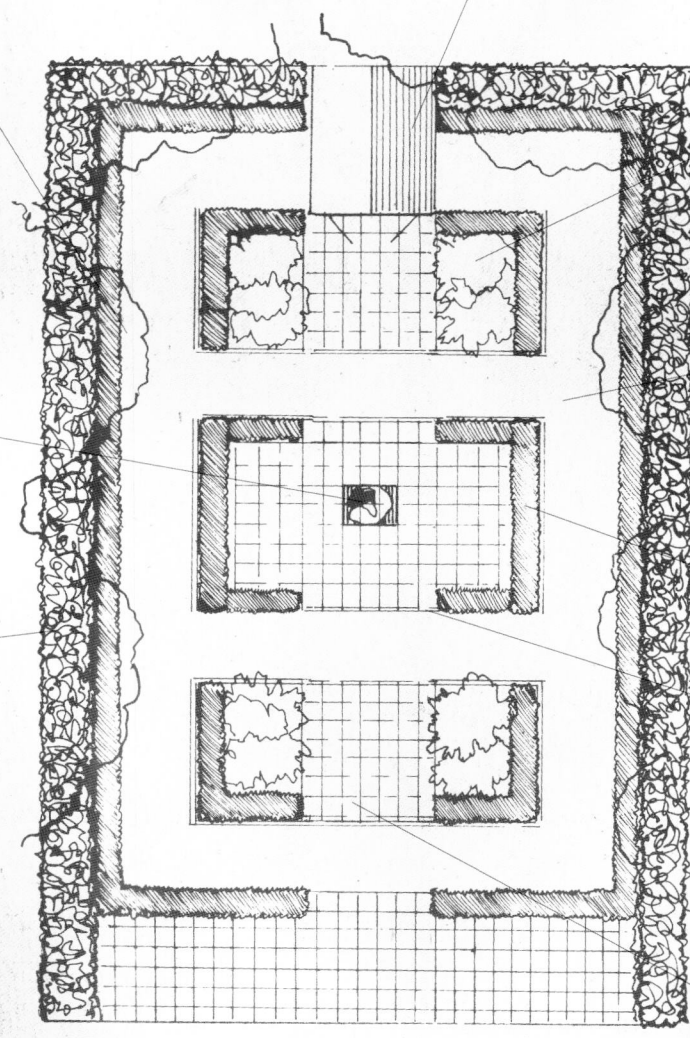

117

scented garden

Spring and summer are the best times for perfume in the garden, but winter offers its own heady delights—all the more so for being singled out through lack of competition. A scented garden has an added sensuous dimension, but some perfumes can be overpowering on a warm still day, so don't overdo it.

The role of scent

Scent is extremely evocative and appeals to a primitive and powerful part of the brain. The compelling power of scent to affect the emotions is intensified by the beauty of many scented plants. At the botanical level scent draws pollinators to a plant. Pale-colored plants often give out their fragrance most strongly at night, when their paleness shows up best, and this is a two-pronged attraction for night pollinators, the moths. Colorful flowers attract day-time pollinators, the bees and butterflies, by their bright color, and therefore in general the more brightly colored flowers tend to offer less scent. Nature is generous, however, and gives us many colorful flowers (such as wallflowers, some roses, and hyacinths) that are also strongly perfumed. Aromatic—as

◄ *Roses are among the most richly scented of all plants and no traditional garden would be complete without their distinctive presence.*

◄ Combining a range of scented plants will produce a heady fragrance that hangs in the air and induces a romantic mood.

opposed to fragrant—plants have essential oils in their leaves to protect them from heat exposure. The scents of the oils are intensified by heat and give out their best when grown in southern, tropical-type climates. Less sensuous than invigorating, their scent indicates an antiseptic or medicinal value: thought to help protect the surrounding plants and flowers from disease.

Ingredients of the garden

Apart from the main distinction between fragrant and aromatic, it's very difficult to classify scents without referring to other scents— usually those of other flowers. So that roses are described as smelling of violets, lily of the valley, orange blossom, or even lemon, while pinks smell of cloves, and choisya of orange blossom, although buddleja is agreed

to smell of honey. Aromatherapists refer to the "notes" of fragrance, descending from the light and evanescent top notes (for example, associated with lemony scents), to the heavy and lingering base notes, with middle (floral) notes in between. The base notes, found in plants such as the strongly scented lilies, jasmine, night-scented stocks, tobacco plants, and many roses, can be quite overpowering. It's a good idea to mix your plants so that a happy blend is inhaled on the air, with top, middle and base notes all participating. And it makes sense to measure out the more overpowering scents by having areas of quietly scented companions. Scented plants offer so many

▶ These beds of aromatic plants are surrounded by hedges of tightly clipped box, which has a curious scent of its own.

pleasures that you will want to linger and breathe in the different parts of the garden. They also seem to go best with a soft approach: curving lawns, which can act as a path unless the garden is large; loose planting, with plants allowed to merge into each other to blend the gentle colors of most scented plants. To coordinate the relaxed and natural theme, willow hurdles form a sympathetic material for plant supports and boundaries. And this is another garden theme that needs seating. A scented seat at the end of the garden will give you somewhere to rest when you're swooning from the mingled scents and pleasures of your plot.

designer's scented garden

A scented garden is essentially a romantic and feminine garden and is at its best on a warm summer's evening. The best site, even if it is just one corner of a larger plot, is a sheltered, warm position. Most fragrant plants release their perfumes in warm air and you will enjoy their scent more if it is not being blown clean away.

▲ The narrowness of this garden will be disguised by the clever use of screens, which also provide shelter from the wind.

GARDEN DATA

location:	▓▓ Northern California
climate:	▓▓ variable—mild
soil type:	▓▓ slightly acid
direction:	▓▓ south facing
aspect:	▓▓ open

The design solution

This garden is long and narrow and the restricted feeling of a corridor is made worse by the long, straight path which splits the garden into two even narrower slivers.

We designed a more sensuous, but simple ground pattern, employing wide, curving borders with a slim ribbon of grass running between them and screens to shelter each garden room. These both help contain the perfumes of the plants and act as supports for some of the climbing plants. There is a bench from which color, form, and scent can be enjoyed and the garden is lit on summer evenings, to encourage you to linger on with your glass of Chardonnay. We used romantic whites, creams, soft yellows, and blues in this scheme.

The grass path provides a lush, green carpet through the garden that does not distract from the scented air and the hum of bees.

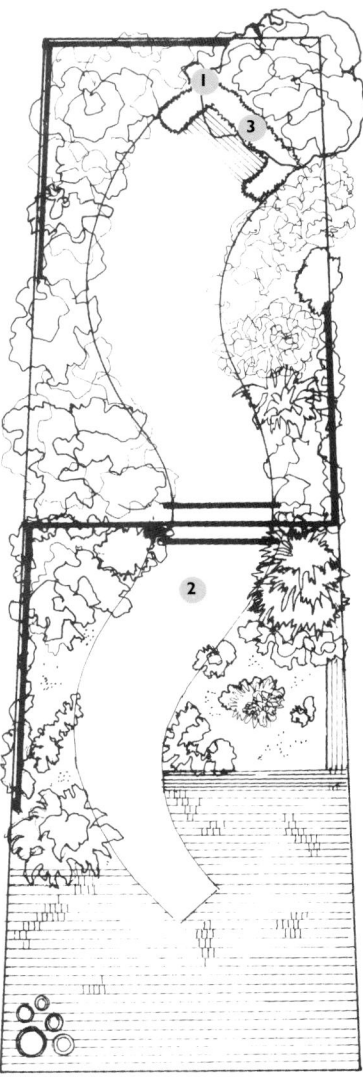

— 15m x 6.5m / 48ft x 21ft —

▶ Willow fences provide shelter.

screens

lawn

▲ The lawn curves intriguingly, giving a sense of discovery.

seat

▲ A seat surrounded by scented plants offers an ideal place to unwind

121

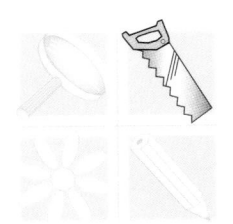

practical projects

▲ *There are many types of scented seats; this one has been carefully clipped into shape and surrounded by climbing roses.*

▲ *How better to relax and enjoy the sunshine than on a scented recliner? Simply grow a bed of thyme in the shape required—then lie back!*

To be complete, a scented garden will need a scented seat. This should be located where you will get a view over a large part of the garden, while some of it is still tantalizingly hidden, to give the illusion that there is yet more to be enjoyed.

A scented seat

The smell of box adds a cool, green note to a scented garden, and clipped box makes a lovely, rather architectural surround for a garden seat. As an alternative, you can create an informal scented seat in a covered arbor, made from a kit—or from your own design if you are sufficiently resourceful. Planted with climbing roses, jasmine, or honeysuckle this will give perfumed shade.

If you have the patience you can make a seat from an earth bank, solidly compacted and planted with thyme or camomile. But such seats, though most romantic, are in truth fragile. Far better is to build a seat into the retaining wall of a raised flower bed and use ordinary cushions for comfort. The scent of the herbs or flowers you use in the bed will still be released as you sit among the plants.

You can also import a stone or wooden seat, make a back for it with box or other clipped shrubs in beds

▲ *For artful simplicity, a rustic wooden seat is placed inside an arbor draped with beautiful scented leaves and flowers.*

or containers and grow beautifully scented plants in boxes at either end. Any ordinary garden bench can be made to look like a more permanent feature and incorporated into the garden by having an alcove made around it in this way.

building a scented seat

Filling a planter with low-growing scented and aromatic plants is a quick and easy way to concentrate perfume in the garden. If you position the planter near a garden seat or bench you can be sure of having fragrance to enjoy whenever you take a break from your labors. Painting the planter to match the seat makes it blend with the scheme.

1 Using a plant-friendly product, paint or stain the planter to match your seat.

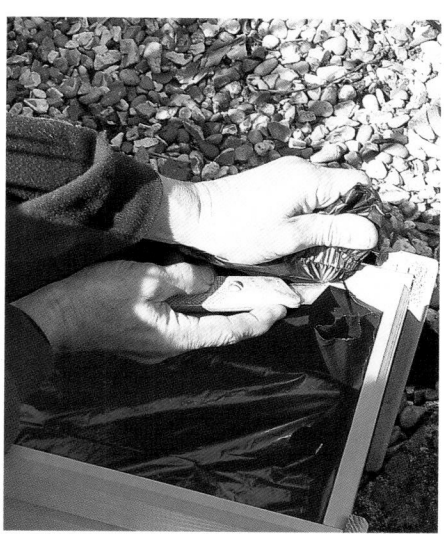

2 To make the planter watertight, line with heavy-duty polyethylene. Cut the polyethylene to fit around the top and staple it in position. Punch holes at the bottom for drainage.

BOUNDARIES FOR SCENTED GARDENS

Ideal boundaries are old, warm and mellow brick or stone walls, against which scented climbers can be trained.

Most of us don't enjoy this luxury so use 1.8m/6ft trellis battened to your fence supports.

Grow an aromatic hedge to border your scented garden. *Rosmarinus,* 'Miss Jessup's Upright', or the slow growing *Buxus sempervirens* will make hedges up to 1.2m/4ft high.

3 Plant with your selected plants. Here we used thyme and lavender. A top-dressing of grit looks attractive and improves drainage.

4 Brushing your hand gently over the plants, particularly in hot weather, will release their distinctive aroma.

scented plants and planting

Plants in the scented garden are carefully arranged to make sure that there is something to offer at almost any time of year and at every level of the garden. They cover both fragrant and aromatic plants, including those which flower at nose level and those whose perfume rises up from the ground.

Profile plants

Philadelphus 'Belle Etoile'
MOCK ORANGE

A heavenly scent of orange blossom drifts from the creamy white, four-petaled flowers in early summer. In this species the flowers have a dash of maroon at the center, and the shrub is small enough for any garden. Should be pruned after flowering.

ht and sp 2m/6.5ft

Soil and situation

Well-drained soil; sun or partial shade.

Erysimum × *allionii*
(syn. *Cheiranthus* × *allionii*)
SIBERIAN WALLFLOWER

This is a wallflower with stunning bright orange coloring and a powerful scent to match. A short-lived perennial, it is always grown as a spring and early summer bedding plant.

ht 40cm/16in

sp 30cm/12in

Soil and situation

Fertile, well-drained soil, preferably neutral or alkaline, and a position in full sun.

Viola odorata
ENGLISH VIOLET
OR SWEET VIOLET

A spreading and very fragrant violet, flowering all spring with deep violet-purple flowers, sometimes white or pink. Violets are lovely low-growing plants for naturalizing in moist, cool places. Various named hybrids are grown (known as florists' violets), including the double violet 'Duchesse de Parme' and the pink-flowered 'Coeur d'Alsace'.

ht 15cm/6in

sp to 40cm/16in

Soil and situation

Fertile, well-drained soil in a semi-shaded position, or in sun as long as the ground is cool.

▶ Erysimum *x* allionii, *Siberian wallflower.*

◀ Philadelphus *'Belle Etoile' or mock orange.*

Shrubs and trees for scent

Choisya ternata
(Mexican orange blossom)
(see pages 198–199)

Daphne mezereum—small, heavily
scented, purple-pink flowers in
winter/spring; must have alkaline soil
ht to 90cm/3ft

Caution: the berries are poisonous

Fothergilla major and *F. gardenii*
(see page 247)

Magnolia grandiflora—magnificent tree
for sheltered areas; summer flowers
with a spicy fragrance
ht 9m/30ft
See also *Magnolia stellata*
(Star Magnolia)
(see pages 60–61)

Rhododendron luteum
(Ghent azaleas)—rhododendrons and
azaleas are not noted for fragrance,
but these hybrids have a strong, warm
honeysuckle scent and brilliant
yellow flowers in late spring; need
acid soil
ht to 3m/10ft

Sambucus (Garden elder)
(see pages 248–249)

Syringa cultivars (lilacs)—flowers in
purples through to white, with wafts
of the most heady scent toward the
end of spring
ht 1.8–4.5m/6–15ft
(see also pages 144–145)

Viburnum cultivars—all the winter-
and spring-flowering viburnums have
delicious scent
(see page 249)

A SELECTION OF SCENTED PLANTS

Scent in full summer

Heliotropium arborescens (syn. H. *peruvianum*)
heliotrope or cherry pie plant
Lathyrus odoratus sweet pea (see page 231)
Lavandula species lavender (see page 242)
Lilium regale and other lilies (see page 237)
Matthiola bicornis night-scented stock
Matthiola incana Brompton stock
Nicotiana tobacco plants (see page 232)
Pelargonium crispum and *P.* x *fragrans*
pelargoniums with scented leaves
Petunia hybrids petunias
Phlox paniculata garden phlox (see page 243)

▲ *Midsummer flowering* Lilium regale.

Scent in spring and early summer

Convallaria majalis lily-of-the-valley
Dianthus species pinks and carnations
Erysimum species (syn. *Cheiranthus*) wallflowers
Hesperis matronalis dame's violet or sweet
rocket
Hyacinthus cultivars hyacinth
Narcisssus jonquilla (jonquil) and many other
narcissi
Paeonia 'Sarah Bernhardt'—peony in apple
blossom pink
Primula vulgaris and *P. auricula* primrose and
auricula

Roses for perfume

Almost all roses are perfumed but this is a
selection of favorites
Rosa 'Boule de Neige'—a repeat-flowering
bourbon rose with large flowers like white
camellias
ht 1.5m/5ft
Rosa 'Cardinal de Richelieu'—a gallica rose,
with dusky purple red flowers
ht 1.5m/5ft
Rosa centifolia 'Robert le Diable'—a cabbage
rose, in mauve, pink, violet, and crimson
ht 1.2m/4ft
Rosa damascena—the damask rose has
varieties in white, pink, red
ht to 1.5m/5ft

Rosa gallica officinalis—deep crimson/striped
(see pages 40–41)
Rosa 'Margaret Merril'—small floribunda or
cluster-flowered rose with delicate flowers in
blush white
ht 75cm/30 in
Rosa moschata (musk rose)—creamy white
old-fashioned climber
ht to 4m/13ft
Rosa 'Mme Pierre Oger'—a bourbon rose,
globular flowers in silvery pink all summer
ht 1.5m/5ft
Rosa 'Penelope'—a hybrid musk with flowers
in pale salmon pink all summer
ht to 1.2m/4ft
Rosa rugosa 'Blanc Double de Coubert'—
rugosa rose with white flowers all summer; big
red hips
ht 1.8m/6ft
Rosa 'Zéphirine Drouhin'—climber for wall or
trellis with masses of deep rose-pink flowers
all summer (suits a shady wall)
ht 3.6m/12ft
Rosa 'William Lobb'—a repeat-flowering old
moss rose with deep crimson flowers fading
to pale violet
ht 1.8m/6ft

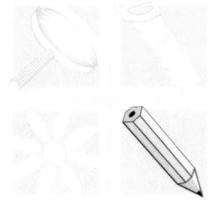

design alternatives

SKETCHES
These plans feature
different garden
"rooms" which lead one
through an adventure
of scents, textures,
and colors.
The combination of
herb, rose and
perennial "rooms"
insures there is scent
throughout the
gardening year.

a perennials garden
with mown lawn as
center

a herb garden with
mown lawn

a rose garden with mown
lawn

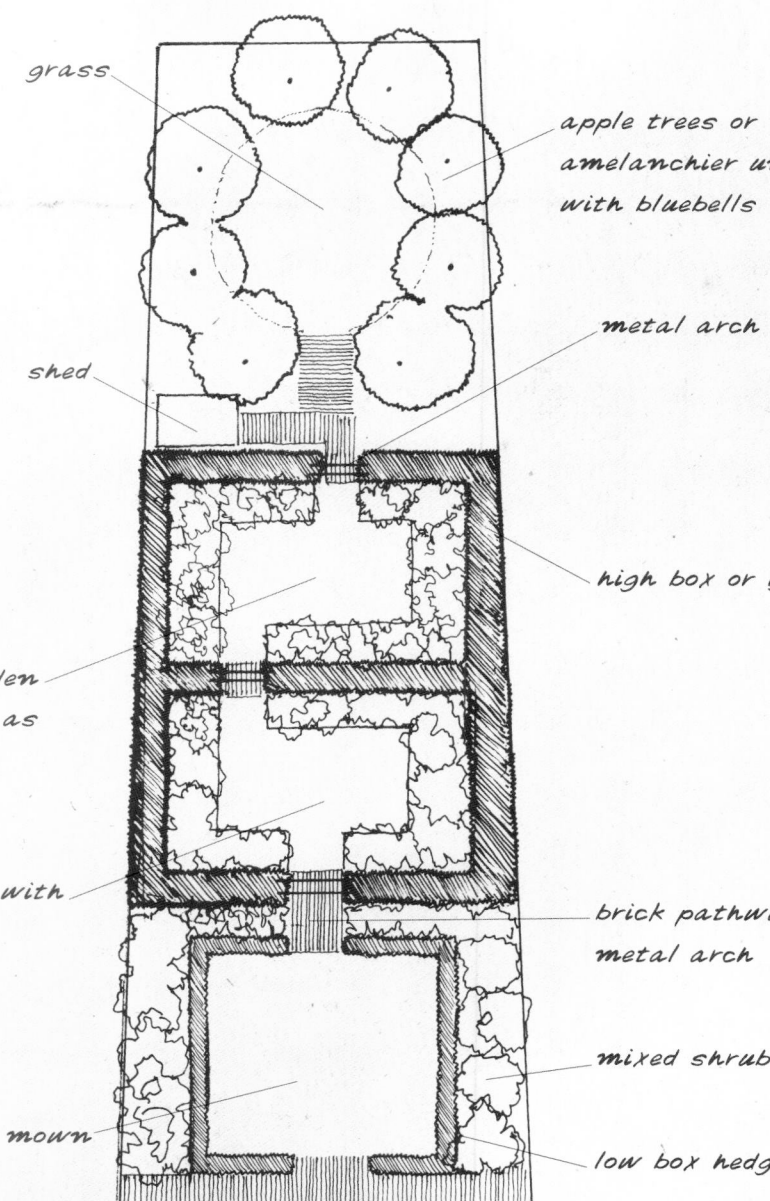

grass

apple trees or
amelanchier underplanted
with bluebells

shed

metal arch

high box or yew hedge

brick pathway under
metal arch

mixed shrub roses

low box hedge

brick patio

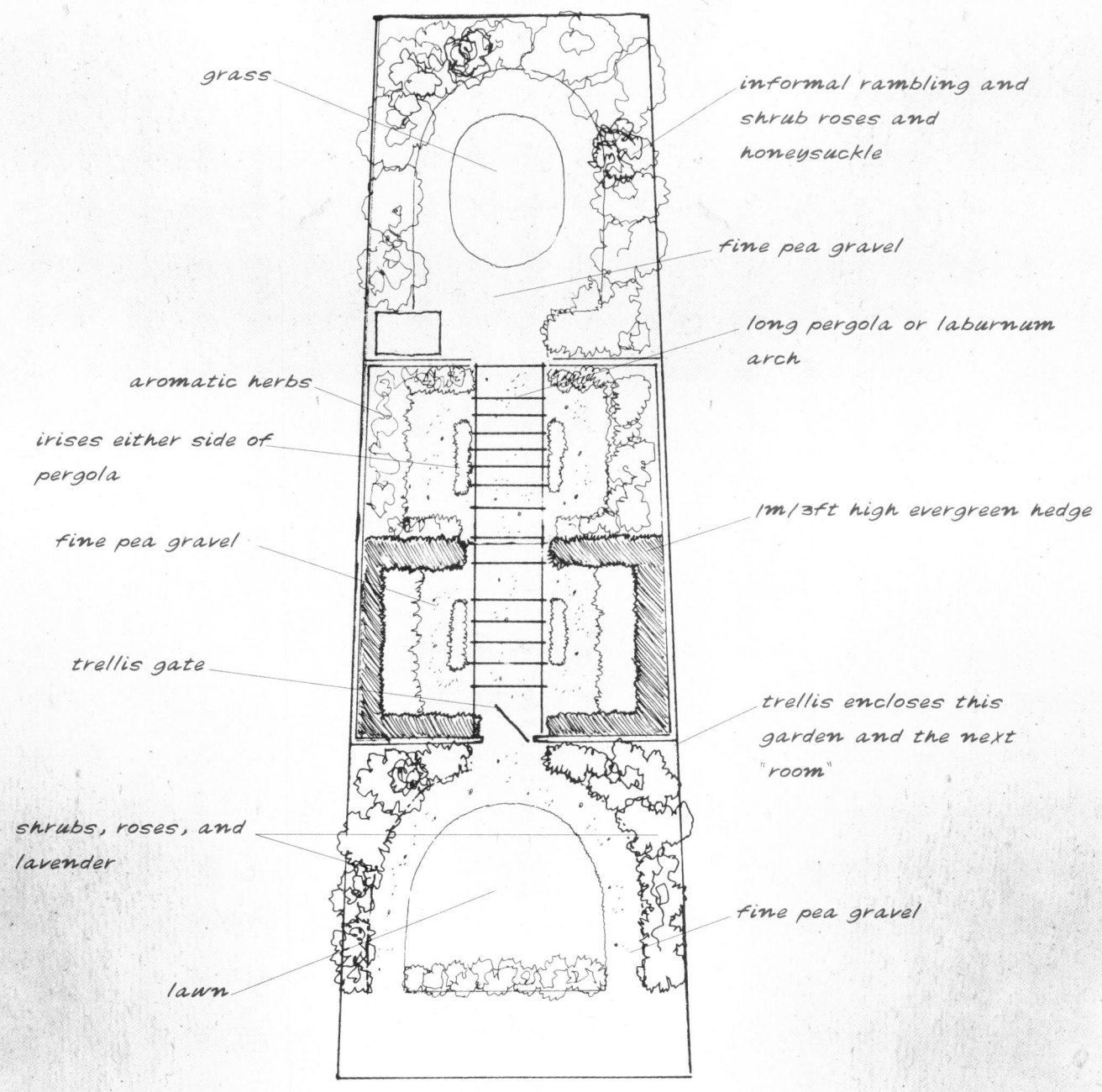

grass

informal rambling and shrub roses and honeysuckle

fine pea gravel

long pergola or laburnum arch

aromatic herbs

irises either side of pergola

1m/3ft high evergreen hedge

fine pea gravel

trellis gate

trellis encloses this garden and the next "room"

shrubs, roses, and lavender

fine pea gravel

lawn

Zen garden

A Japanese Zen garden is understood not in terms of its ingredients but only by looking at its overall meaning—nothing is fortuitous or haphazard. All the elements employed in the garden have a symbolic significance related to a quest for spiritual enlightenment. Restraint and simplicity are the keys.

What are the elements?

Whether or not we understand Zen symbolism, we can borrow ideas from Japanese gardens to make our own peaceful and beautiful retreats that, with care, do not look too much out of place in a Western setting.

When you relax at the end of the garden, perhaps you will think about your spiritual journey through the world. If not, it will still be a nice calm and peaceful place to sit.

While some elements come from Buddhist monastery gardens, the Zen garden of today is largely based on a Japanese invention of early medieval times, and its development responded to the practices of the tea ceremony, which was given mystical and ritual dimensions by the Zen priests and their disciples who took part in it. The participants at a tea ceremony reflected on nature and sought inner stillness by contemplating flowers, pottery, and beautifully illustrated calligraphic scrolls in the confines of a tea house. The Zen garden was the medium through which they passed on their way to the sanctum of contemplation.

A spiritual journey

The garden sought to imitate nature in the wild, and provided a path representing a mountain journey— a metaphor for the spiritual journey in search of the eternal. So the

◀ *Traditionally the clean, simple design of a Zen garden creates a retreat, and the possibility for quiet, tranquil contemplation.*

▶ *Boulders and gravel in Zen gardens symbolize mountains and water, associated in Buddhist thought with visions of paradise.*

essence of the Zen garden is that we move through it and lose our baser selves on the way. The ingredients, charged with symbolism, were an entrance (the journey's beginning), a path (the way to knowledge or enlightenment), a seat on which to break the journey and pause in meditation, a gate or threshold, beyond which to move on, leaving behind the social world of the city and entering the world of nature. Finally, there was somewhere to wash the hands, representing a mountain stream and symbolic of purification, and at the journey's end, a tea house as a place of final contemplation.

Symbolism in the garden

Paradise in Buddhist thought was symbolized by mountains surrounded by water, and in a Zen garden water and rocks represent these elements. Much play is made of the contrast between rocks or pebbles and water. When using boulders it's important to lay the stone in accordance with its natural grain. (If you are serious about it, you won't even lay the stone on its side while maneuvering it into position.) Placing the stone in this way makes sense aesthetically, and is spiritually significant. Evergreen plants are used to symbolize

immortality. Twisted or gnarled plants represent longevity, and bonsai is a concentrated form. Japanese maples, with their twisted stems, can be used to express longevity too, while the flowering cherry, with its fleetingly beautiful blossom, represents the evanescence of the material things of this world.

Water itself need not be present. The raked gravel of Buddhist gardens, which has now caught on in the West, is used to represent flowing water. Raking it quietly each morning or evening can be a soothing meditation. Rocks or boulders set within the gravel represent the water-surrounded mountains of paradise. They should be placed at the far end of the garden, as paradise is always distant. Straight lines are to be avoided—the spirit of contemplation follows best a winding path—but they can be broken, and begun again, and this will slow down the rush of energy that is not conducive to contemplation. Overall balance in design is achieved by a measured lack of symmetry.

Colors should be subtle and limited. The natural colors of stone, timber, and bamboo, and the green of bamboo plants and evergreen shrubs form a calm, quiet backdrop.

◀ *This contemporary interpretation of Zen principles features neatly raked gravel and a delicate purple iris planted in bamboo.*

designer's Zen garden

Buddhist monks designed the earliest Zen gardens around 900 years ago. In these gardens austere, abstract arrangements of rocks, water, and plants represent nature in miniature. Western gardeners have returned again and again to this deceptively simple combination of materials to try to recreate this timeless style.

▲ *Recent travels in the Far East inspired the owner of this rectangular plot to design a minimalist Japanese garden.*

GARDEN DATA

location:	▦ *Massachusetts*
climate:	▦ *temperate*
soil type:	▦ *sandy*
direction:	▦ *west facing*
aspect:	▦ *urban*

The brief

Steve traveled extensively in the Far East before recently acquiring his first house. His rectangular garden is ideally shaped and he would like to use this to advantage to create a minimalist garden with a distinct Japanese influence.

The design solution

For complete privacy and shelter we enclosed the garden on three sides, using screening trellis panels wired to thick bamboo poles. This focuses attention entirely on the garden, ignoring the surrounding landscape and buildings. The basic design flows through three distinct areas in the garden. Inside the boundary a hedge was planted, which will be clipped to form hill shapes as it grows. Large rocks, smaller boulders, pebbles, and paddle stones were carefully chosen to complement each other in size, markings, and color, positioned to create a balanced, asymmetric design. The main surface material is fine stone chippings, raked to suggest the flow of water. Stepping stones lead to a still, calm pool, positioned to reflect the ever-changing sky.

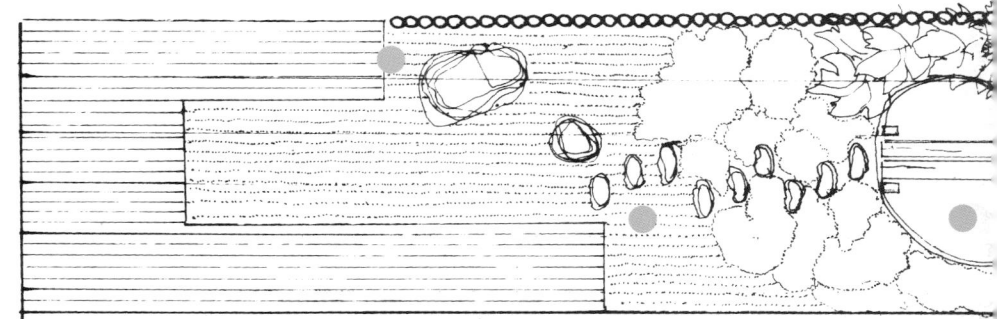

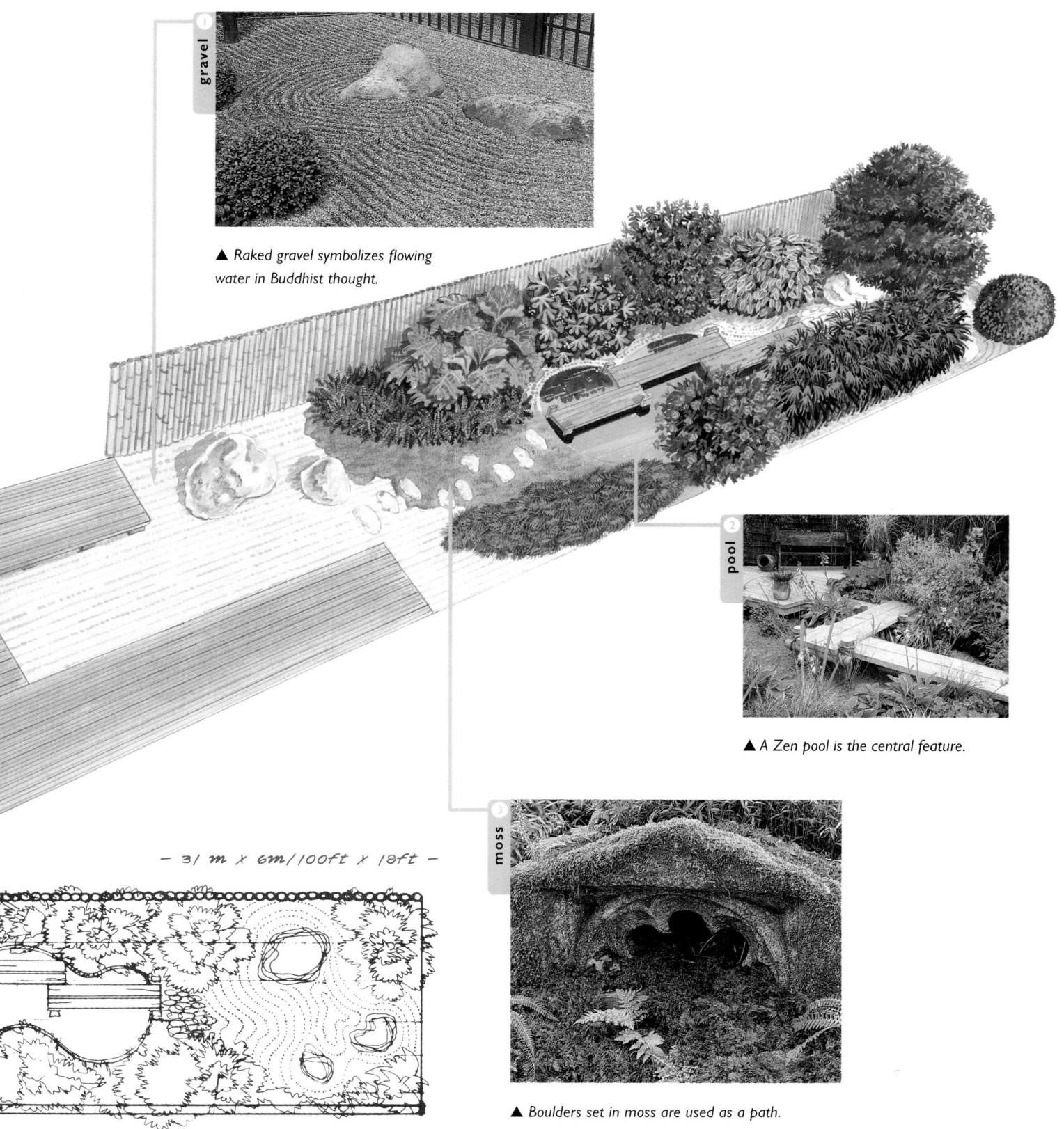

gravel

▲ Raked gravel symbolizes flowing water in Buddhist thought.

pool

▲ A Zen pool is the central feature.

moss

– 31 m x 6m/100ft x 18ft –

▲ Boulders set in moss are used as a path.

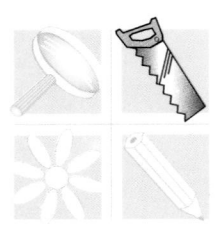

practical projects

In a Zen garden stone and wood combine with the element of water, and paths and bridges are of symbolic as well as practical importance. All materials must be chosen with care—everything should be natural in an elemental way—and a simple wooden bridge over the water is in complete harmony in this garden.

Zen bridges

We advise you seek professional garden or building advice before building your bridge. There are many designs to inspire, the essential difference is how the timber is laid, lengthways or crossways. Use hardwood or treated softwood in a firm base.

DESIGNER TIPS

• Stone, water, and plants are the three main elements of a Zen garden.

• If possible, choose local stone for all the stones and boulders used in your garden.

• Position large stones and boulders singly, or in groups of three, five, or seven.

• Zen gardens are never symmetrical. Balance is achieved through controlling the asymmetric design.

• Big stones may weigh a ton, or more. Make sure access to your garden is sufficient and be prepared to pay installation costs, which may be much greater than the cost of the stone itself.

• Choose Japanese stone or concrete lanterns and similar ornaments with care— they can look too obviously mock-Japanese.

TRADITIONAL SAND PATTERNS

Raked gravel, or sand, is a feature of many a Japanese garden, particularly temple gardens. The sand, and the lines you draw through it, is meant to imitate water. Since the essence of Zen is to achieve spiritual enlightenment through meditation, the very act of raking the sand promotes contemplation and you will find it an extremely restful occupation. Remember that the patterns you make will be temporary and need to be renewed daily. But that allows you to experiment with different designs.

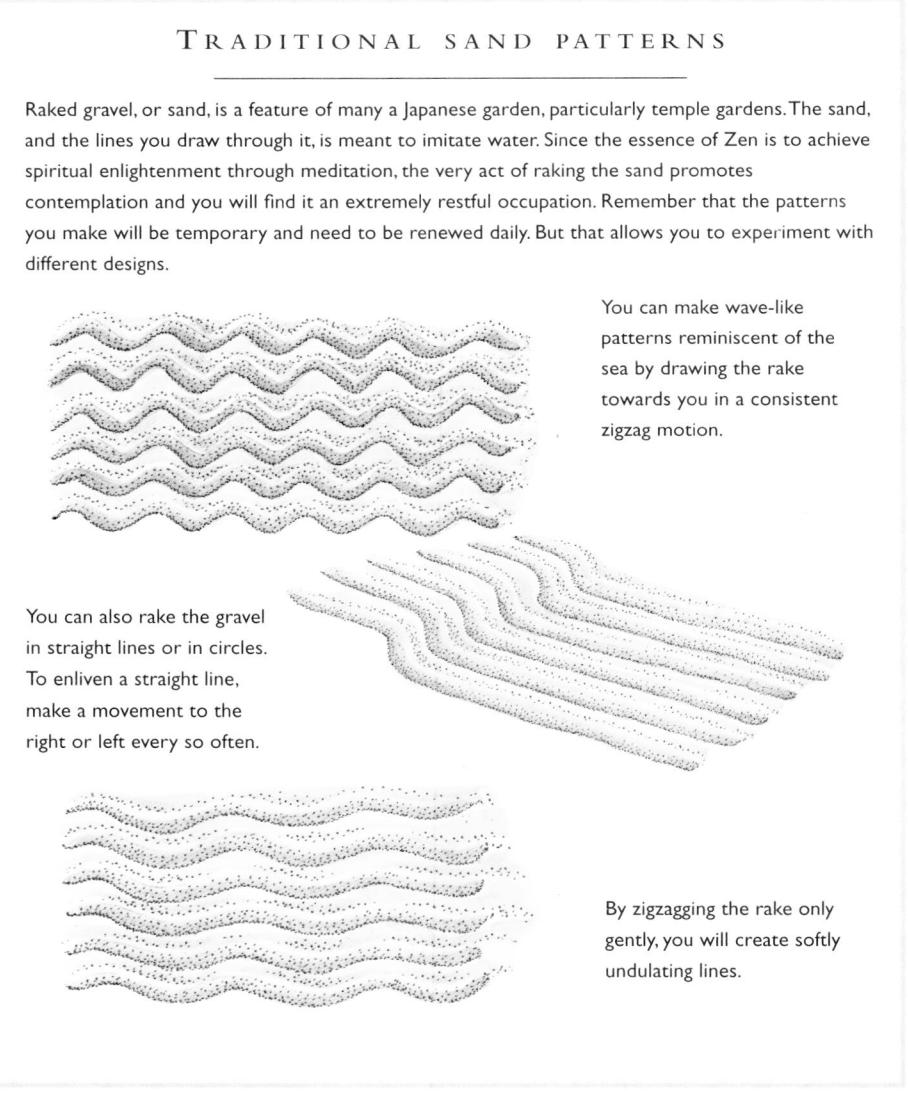

You can make wave-like patterns reminiscent of the sea by drawing the rake towards you in a consistent zigzag motion.

You can also rake the gravel in straight lines or in circles. To enliven a straight line, make a movement to the right or left every so often.

By zigzagging the rake only gently, you will create softly undulating lines.

▼ This elegant wooden structure is reminiscent of Monet's Japanese Bridge of Giverny, in Northern France. It is a wonderful example of the beauty of simple design.

▲ Simplicity is the keynote of any Japanese garden. Rocks, plants, and gravel all play a key part and are each placed with great precision.

Concrete foundation pads provide a reliable support for an otherwise traditional timber bridge.

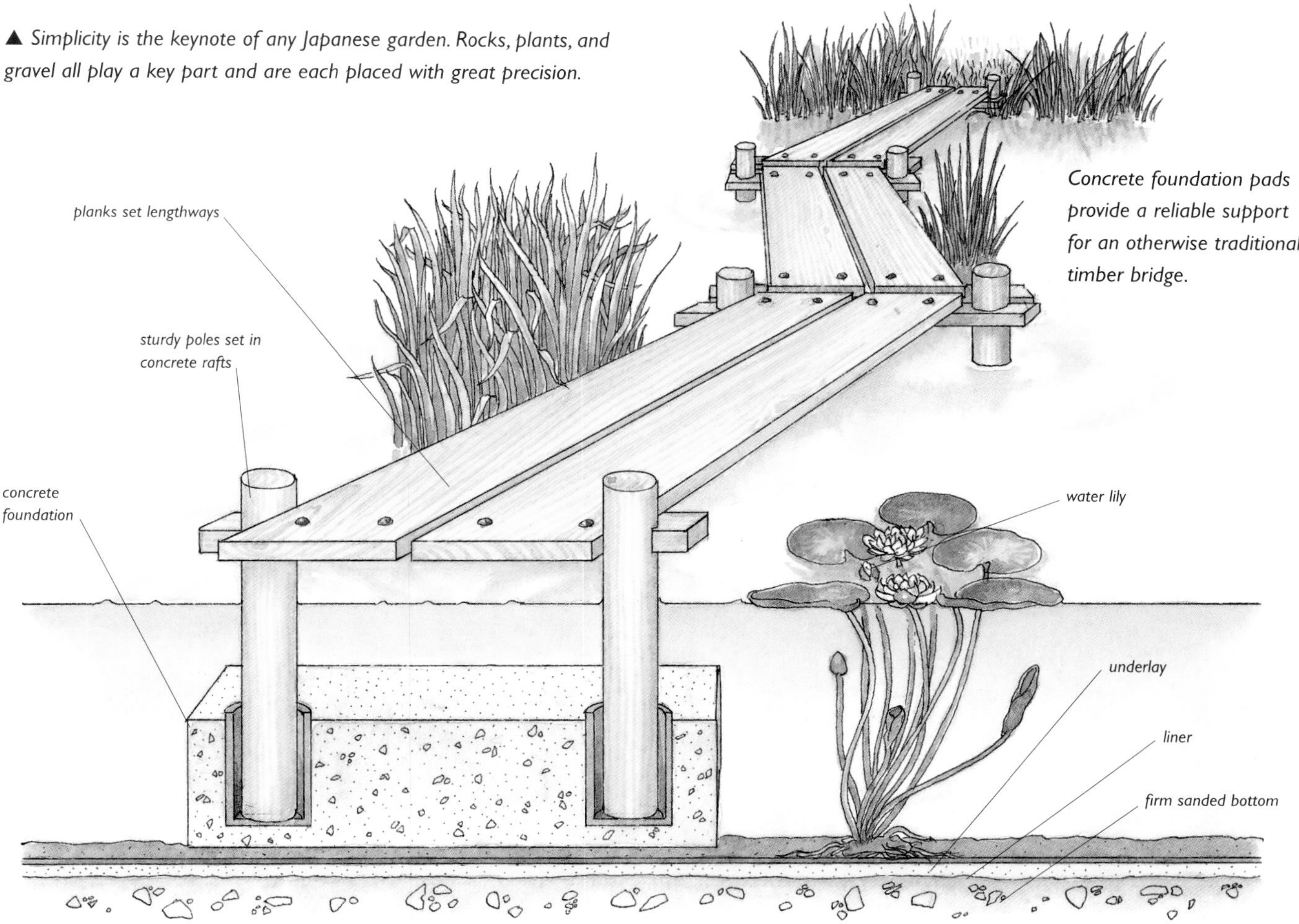

planks set lengthways

sturdy poles set in concrete rafts

concrete foundation

water lily

underlay

liner

firm sanded bottom

▲ This Zen bridge follows a traditional Japanese zigzag course.

Zen plants and planting

Restraint is the theme in planting a Zen garden. Green is the main color from plants, to contrast with the natural materials used in the garden. A limited amount of blossom—ideally in red—is permitted. The best plants are bamboos; evergreen, glossy-leaved shrubs; and Japanese maple, or a flowering cherry tree.

Bamboos and their care

Closely related to grasses and sedges, bamboos are evergreen, and as well as providing architectural shapes and delightful foliage, they also bring gentle movement and rustling sound to the garden. They grow up to 4m/13ft, in some species even more, and can make island clumps whose spread may sometimes overstep the limits (but see below), as well as lovely hedging and screening plants. Their hollow, woody culms take about three years to mature into canes. The canes are high in silica, which makes them very strong, and they can be cut for use, either as plant supports or for more ambitious projects such as screening. Bamboos are not all fully hardy and are best grown in a sheltered place.

Cultivation

Bamboos appreciate moisture, so when you plant them add plenty of fibrous organic material such as coir or—if you can get hold of it—chopped straw to absorb and retain water. Don't use garden compost, however, as it will be too rich. An occasional feeding with calcium silicate will help them to grow strong culms but otherwise they need no supplementary feeding.

The best time for planting out bamboos is in spring, and it should be just before it rains. The leaves should not be allowed to become dry as they will quickly wither and die,

◀ *Japanese maples suit a Zen garden.*

so look after them until the plants are established by spraying them with water. You can restrict the spread of bamboo by digging around the clump at the desired limits and inserting a rigid, nonperishable plastic collar about 30cm/12in deep or to the depth of the roots.

Profile plants

Acer palmatum var. *heptalobum* 'Rubrum'
JAPANESE MAPLE

More of a shrub than a tree, this form of the Japanese maple has bronze leaves which are red as they first open and which turn a fiery red in the fall. Its spreading and contorted branches give a very authentic Zen appearance.

ht and sp to 6m/20ft

Soil and situation

Fertile, moist but well-drained soil,

preferably neutral or acid, and a sheltered position.

Camellia japonica
CAMELLIA

There are literally thousands of Japanese camellias, a most magnificent group of evergreen shrubs with dark green, polished leaves and luscious peony-like winter flowers (also other forms, including single, semidouble and double). The flowers must have shelter from morning sun in areas prone to frost as hastily melted frost makes the petals brown. *A. j.* 'Alexander Hunter' is semidouble, deep red, with yellow stamens; 'Paul's Apollo' (aka 'Apollo') has red, semidouble flowers and suits a temperate climate. 'Dr. H. G. Mealing' is blood red and semidouble; 'Kouron-jura' is dark red and fully double; 'Letitia Schrader' has dark red, large peony flowers.

ht to 8.5m/26ft

sp 7.3m/24ft

◀ *Bamboos are essential in any Zen garden.*

◀ *A red form of* Camellia japonica.

Soil and situation

Must have moist, fertile, well-drained, acid soil and should be mulched with shredded bark. In the northern zones a sheltered north- or west-facing position is ideal.

HARDY BAMBOOS FOR SMALL GARDENS

Chusquea culeou (Chilean bamboo)—delicate, whitish green leaves
ht 4.5m/15ft
Fargesia murieliae (umbrella bamboo)—grayish green culms and apple-green leaves
ht 3.6m/12ft
Phyllostachys nigra var. *henonis* green and very leafy, not completely hardy
ht 9m/30ft
Phyllostachys viridiglaucescens—green and very leafy, not completely hardy
ht to 7.5m/25ft
Pleioblastus auricomus—yellow and green variegated leaves; purple-green culms
ht 1.5m/5ft
Pleioblastus simonii 'Variegatus' (syn. *Arundinaria simonii* 'Variegata')—white-striped leaves
ht to 3m/10ft
Pleioblastus variegatus—cream-striped leaves and pale green culms
ht 75cm/30 in
Pseudosana japonica (arrow bamboo)—olive-green culms mature to light beige
ht to 4.5m/15ft
Sasa veitchii—white-edged green leaves and purple culms
ht to 1.8m/6ft
Semiarundinaria fastuosa (Narihira bamboo) thick green culms mature to dark red
ht 6m/20ft
Yushania anceps (anceps bamboo)—shiny, dark green culms, arching when mature
ht 2–3m/6.5–10ft

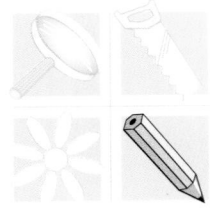

design alternatives

SKETCHES

These alternative layouts
follow the same **minimalist**
principles, using natural
materials and restrained
planting. Both suit slightly
shaded, rather than fully
open positions, so that
mosses and ferns can
flourish. Use just one
section of these gardens to
make an outdoor Japanese
courtyard or "room."

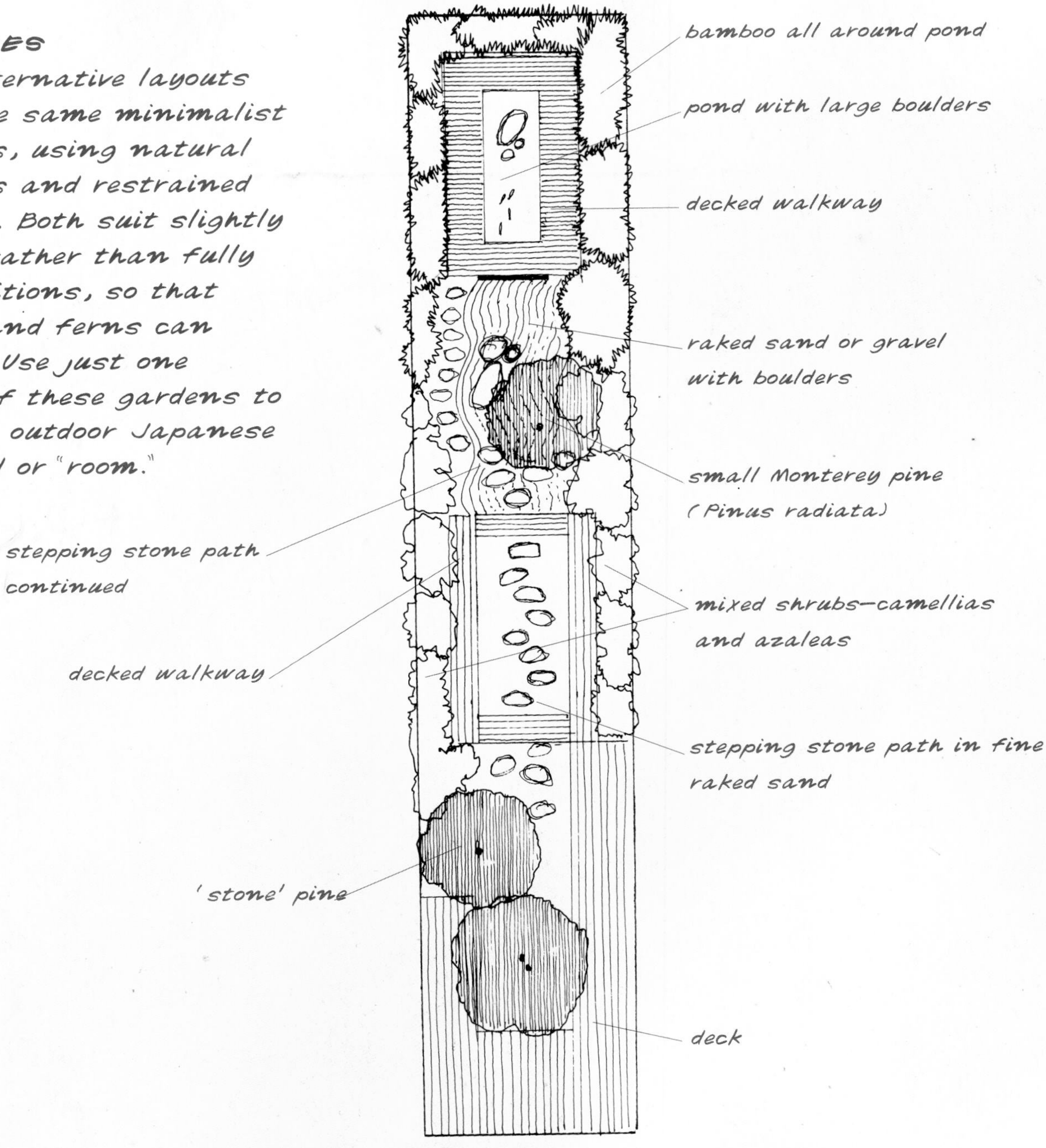

bamboo all around pond

pond with large boulders

decked walkway

raked sand or gravel
with boulders

small Monterey pine
(Pinus radiata)

stepping stone path
continued

decked walkway

mixed shrubs—camellias
and azaleas

stepping stone path in fine
raked sand

'stone' pine

deck

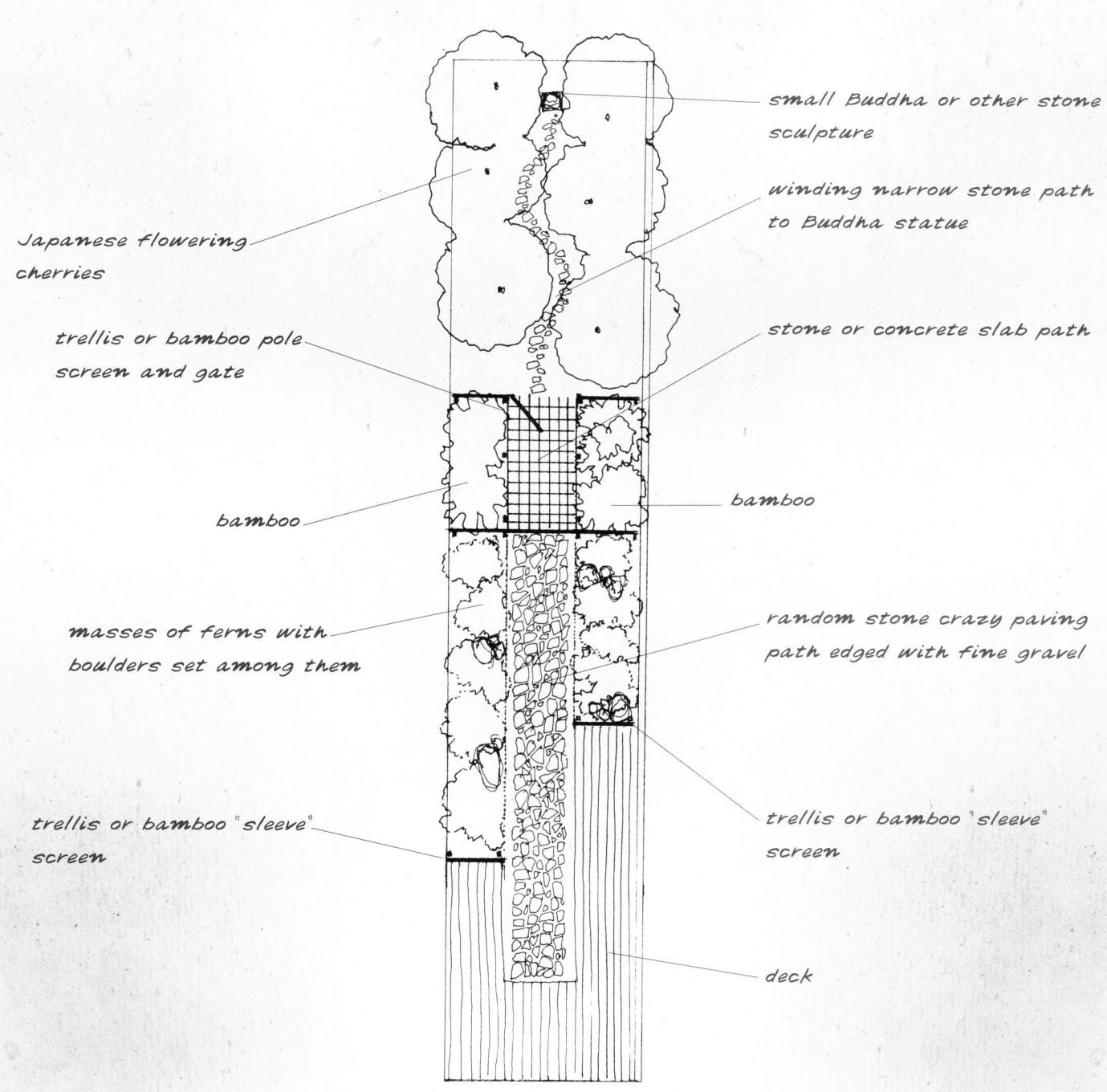

small Buddha or other stone sculpture

winding narrow stone path to Buddha statue

Japanese flowering cherries

stone or concrete slab path

trellis or bamboo pole screen and gate

bamboo

bamboo

masses of ferns with boulders set among them

random stone crazy paving path edged with fine gravel

trellis or bamboo "sleeve" screen

trellis or bamboo "sleeve" screen

deck

night garden

Somewhere to eat; ways to walk in safety; the drama of the garden brought out by lighting; nighttime scents—these are the ingredients of a garden to be enjoyed by night. Even if your garden is not intended specifically to be used at night it's a factor to take into account when you're thinking about its design.

◄ *These uplights cast interesting shadows on the rocks, in a minimalist urban garden with strong hard-landscaping.*

Designing for night

Dining outside is always a pleasure, and an area near the house for this is an asset in any garden. In the later summer, dusk begins to come early and it's often at this time of year that hot days leave a lingering warmth behind them. Lighting will be needed, and even by candlelight or by the light of little table lamps, the immediate light has a strange effect on the surrounding darkness, which can make it seem almost threatening. So lighting in the garden comes into play. And it can be used to dramatize the garden and create theatrical features, such as the pale slender stem of a silver birch, a piece of statuary or sculpture, or moving water. (Do remember, however, that your neighbors won't want the light shining on to them, and neither will you want it shining in your eyes.)

▶ *Special submerged lamps are used to illuminate the fountains, while further lighting is used to make a dramatic backdrop.*

Lighting and installation

Lighting for gardens must naturally be safely installed and is not normally a job for the home improver, particularly if you decide you need a mains-voltage system, with a standard 120-volt line for brilliant, intense lighting. For softer lighting a low-voltage (12V) is all you require and to adapt the power supply you need a transformer, which can be plugged into an indoor socket. Low-voltage cable must be safely hidden away so that you can't trip over it or cut into

it in the garden, whereas mains voltage cable must be thoroughly insulated and safely and deeply buried—not to be attempted by an amateur, however capable. Cable-free solar lighting, of course, needs no installation at all, but solar lights can't be expected to provide more than low-level lighting.

Key points

For best results remember less means more. A small amount of well-sited lighting is by far the most dramatic. Lighting should be at different levels, using uplights and downlights set at different heights, and of course the nuts and bolts should not be visible. The basic fittings are flexible spots or broadly rectangular floodlights. Spiked in the ground or fixed at low level these can be used as "uppers" for uplighting, to focus on trees, sculpture, arbors, or large shrubs;

◀ *Carefully positioned lighting will bring a hidden corner of the daytime garden to life after the sun has gone down.*

fixed high up they function as "downers" for downlighting to light paths, patios or trees (in which case called "moonlighting"). Spotlights can also wash light across a wall ("grazing") or give backlight to silhouette plants with architectural shape such as phormiums or with alluring movement such as grasses and bamboo. Shaded lights, such as mushroom types, are good for diffusing light over a low area for paths and steps.

Floodlighting casts a more widely diffused light that's more blurred at the edges than spotlighting. It too can be used either to backlight an area from behind, lighting up the background plants and throwing foreground plants into silhouette, to flood a designated area. Lights are available for wall or post fixing and as spikes. The effect of the light comes partly from the bulb and partly from the way it is housed. Halogen bulbs are generally best for mains or low-voltage use, and must be fully waterproof.

designer's night garden

A garden takes on a magical, mysterious quality at night if it is carefully lit. The key is subtlety and restraint. Good, low voltage lighting extends the use of the garden, enhancing features, while safety lighting is invaluable along a path or beside steps. Portable lamps or candles are best suited for lighting the dining area.

▲ *The owners wanted a garden that would be low-maintenance and allow for evening entertaining or just relaxing.*

GARDEN DATA

location:	▦ New Jersey
climate:	▦ urban—temperate
soil type:	▦ clay
direction	▦ west facing
aspect:	▦ urban

Design brief

This garden is not used very much in daylight hours as the owners run their own business and often work at weekends. They want a pleasant, low maintenance space in which to enjoy summer evenings with friends and relax after work.

Design solution

The garden is fortunate in containing one of the loveliest of trees—an elegant weeping silver birch. This is a perfect subject for moonlighting, which will show off its delicate, fluttering foliage all summer. In winter the graceful, weeping branches and satiny white bark will provide an attractive focal point through dark evenings. On the other side of the garden we back-lit softly a contemporary stone sculpture. The dark shadowy angles and curves are dramatically heightened at night and while the white sculpture and white birch complement each other they are positioned far enough apart not to fight for attention. Having chosen our subjects we constructed two decks from which to view and enjoy the theatrical effects of the scheme. Four concealed safety lights were added beneath the front edges of the decks to complete this simple scheme and also prevent tripping over the deck.

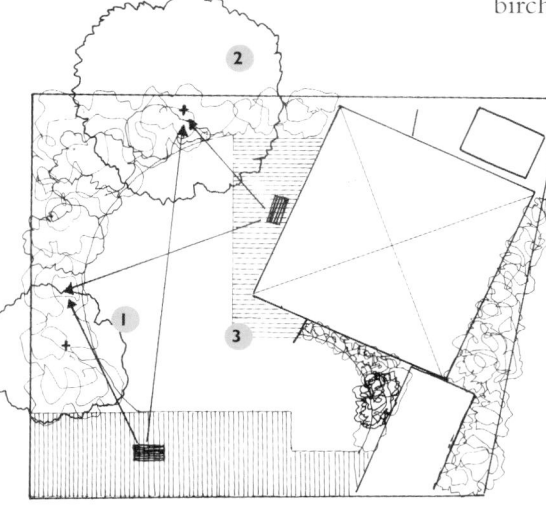

– 13m x 20m/45ft x 68ft –

▲ Modern sculpture is a central feature.

sculpture

up-lit tree

▲ White bark, lit from below, is stunning at night.

candles

◀ Candles elegantly placed on deck.

practical projects

Nighttime gardens can be havens of complete peace and tranquility. Forget boom boxes and all-night parties (and anyway these will make you a most unpopular neighbor). Instead concentrate on making a soothing environment where you can relax and find peace after a hard day's work.

Nighttime drama

For most people lighting is a crucial ingredient of a garden at night. Even if you intend to employ an electrician (to be recommended unless you really know what you're doing) you will want to know a bit about what is involved and what the options are (opposite).

It's best to think about lighting installation when planning the garden, because installation can cause major disruption. Cable routes need to be worked out with care and it makes sense to install cable for lighting and any water feature at the same time—and certainly before you put in any hard-landscaping.

The main point of outdoor lighting is to accent features of the garden with lighting, generally uplighting, aimed at plants or objects (as described on pages 138–139). This can be done by means of a small spot placed near the object or a more powerful one placed farther away. Spots can be focused on the same object from different places in the garden for high drama and of course you can also have different beams pointing in different directions from the same source. The light should point from where you will sit to what you will be looking at; think about whether there are various places where you will want to sit and consider the lighting from each.

▲ *Lighting need not be subtle or hidden but can be a feature in itself. This dramatic light sculpture takes central place in the garden.*

types of garden lighting

Here are some examples of the many types of lamps, lights, and candles available.

▶ *Accent lighting creates a dramatic effect. Remember that your ground surface may also be highlighted.*

▼ *A simple, lit candle staked securely in the ground is an elegant option for temporary lighting.*

▲ *Low-voltage lighting creates a subtle glow and this small light is hidden in long grasses.*

▲ *A light placed in a border is camouflaged from view, but at night will single out a chosen plant.*

▲ *This lantern holds a night light. It is safely away from children and is removed in daytime.*

▲ *Traditional lanterns attached to the wall are useful for barbecue areas and general lighting.*

night plants and planting

At nighttime a garden will develop hidden depths. As the colors fade in the dusk red takes on a deep, mysterious glow before it too is lost into darkness and just the palest flowers glimmer. Scents of the night arise after a warm day, and calm and tranquillity descend—this is a wonderful time to enjoy your garden.

Plants for nighttime gardens

Romantically minded people will think first of scented plants when planning out a garden for night. From the point of view of dramatic effect shrubs and trees light up well and create an atmosphere, and the foliage of a well-sited evergreen shrub will be welcome near the sitting area to make it feel sheltered and enclosed all year round. For a garden that will be used mainly at night you don't need to worry too much about detail—which will all disappear in the dark. Concentrate on well-shaped trees and shrubs and invest your money in a pleasing piece of sculpture. Incidental scent and pale patches in the dusk will come from annuals and biennials, and from long-lasting plants such as a favorite rose and lovely lilies. For a larger selection of spring- and summer-flowering scented plants see the list on pages 124–125.

Profile plants

Syringa vulgaris, white varieties
WHITE LILAC

Any white lilac is a gift to the nighttime garden. Its heady scent marks the transition from spring to summer—the time when we first start to enjoy being out of doors in the evenings—and the pale flowers

◄ Syringa vulgaris, *white lilac.*

ghost beautifully in the dark. 'Mme Lemoine' is a wonderful variety which has heavy heads of double flowers in creamy white. 'Maud Notcutt' has huge, single flowers in white, and the more compact shrub 'Vestale' has long, loose panicles of white flowers.

ht 3.6m/12ft

sp 3m/10ft

Soil and situation

Lilacs flourish best in a rich, fertile, and fairly moist soil, and a sunny situation. They do well on alkaline soils. Prune them every three years to maintain a well-rounded shape.

Dianthus 'Mrs Sinkins'
WHITE GARDEN PINK

Garden pinks and carnations are not difficult to grow as long as they have the conditions they enjoy, and with their sweet, clovey scent they are perfect for sniffing at night. Though long-lived, they generally weaken after a time and need to be replaced

◀ Dianthus *'Mrs Sinkins'*.

about every three to five years. Pinks are generally smaller than carnations; both come in single and double versions and both can be beautifully marked, eyed, ringed, or laced with a contrasting color. The gray foliage is part of their charm. 'Mrs Sinkins' is a lovely old-fashioned white pink— frilly, loose-flowered, and double, and with a longer life than many *Dianthus*. It's well known for its strong scent, making up for the fact that, like most old-fashioned pinks, it does not flower again (until next year) after its first flowering period, in early summer.

ht 38cm/15in

sp 30cm/12in

Soil and situation

Pinks and carnations need neutral, well-drained soil and will flourish on thin, chalky soil. They do best in a sunny position but where the summer is not too hot. A wet winter in cold soil does them no good but otherwise they are conveniently tolerant and hardy.

Matthiola incana 'Giant Excelsior'
BROMPTON STOCKS

Brompton stocks are deliciously scented biennials for late spring or early summer, flowering from seed sown the previous year, and are often bought as young plants ready for

▶ Matthiola incana *'Giant Excelsior'*.

planting out in spring. 'Giant Excelsior' are tall, bushy stocks generally grown as an annual and flowering in early summer. They have the soft, gray-green leaves common to the stocks and the long spikes of heavily scented flowers are in pale pink, deep red, cloudy blue, and creamy white. They may need staking if they grow too tall.

ht 70cm/28in

sp 30cm/12in

Soil and situation

Moist and fertile, well-drained, preferably lime-rich soil, and a position in sun or semishade. At their best in calm, warm weather.

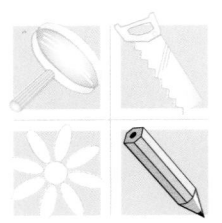

design alternatives

SKETCHES
Two alternative layouts
for this garden offer
different opportunities
for dramatic lighting. a
swimming pool, pergola,
or small water feature
are all suitable
subjects.

uplighter to light tree

downlighter angled to
'graze' sculpture and
climbing plants

path lights alongside edge
of deck

boardwalk continuation
of deck

Railroad ties walkway for
pond maintenance and
access to plants

formal pond in decking—
could be swimming pool
if preferred

downlighter concealed
just beneath over-
hanging edge of deck

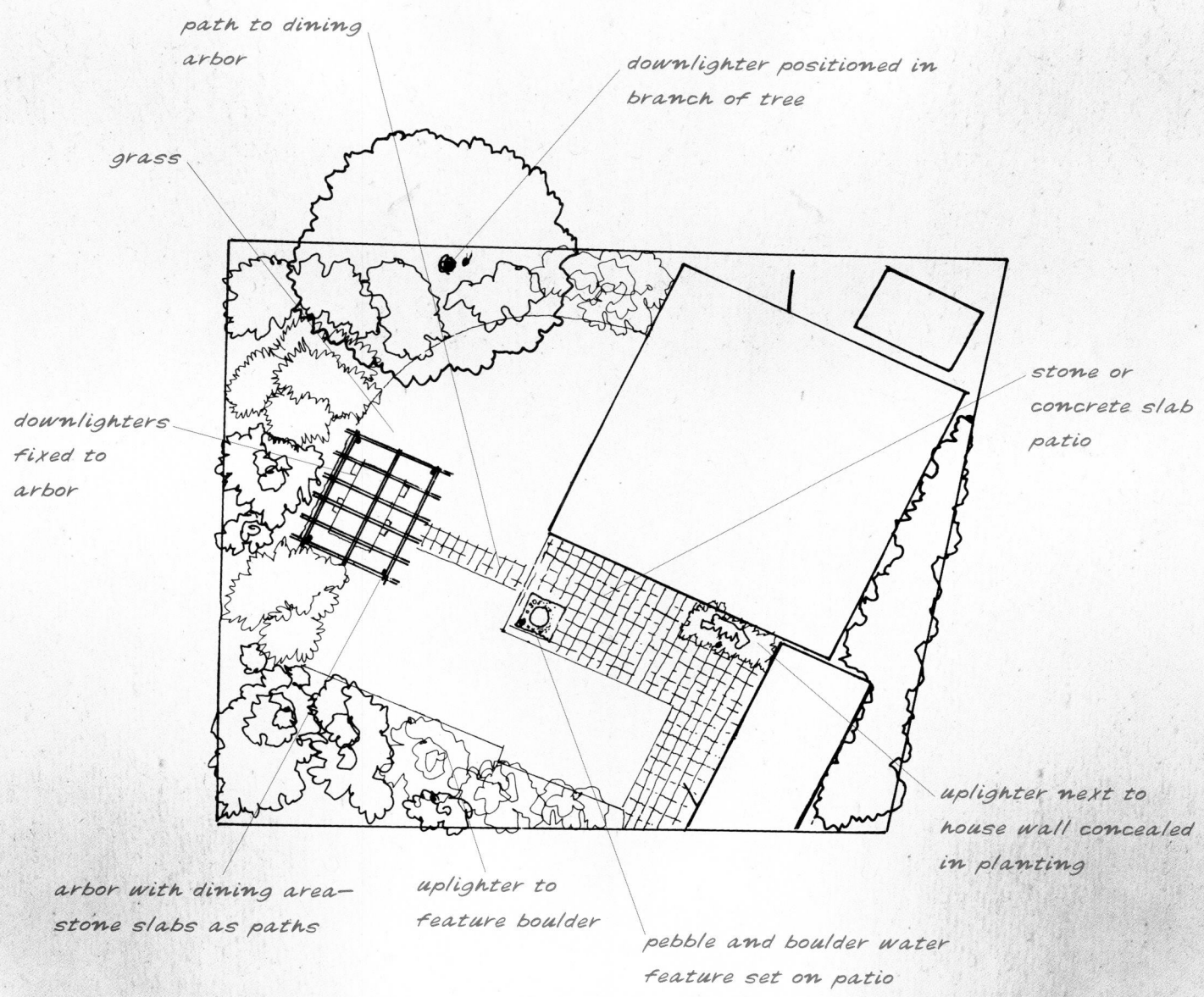

path to dining
arbor

downlighter positioned in
branch of tree

grass

downlighters
fixed to
arbor

stone or
concrete slab
patio

uplighter next to
house wall concealed
in planting

arbor with dining area—
stone slabs as paths

uplighter to
feature boulder

pebble and boulder water
feature set on patio

practical gardens

The gardens in this section answer very practical needs, the first to make a garden that's enjoyable for young children as well as their parents, and the second for people who for one reason or another have restricted movement and who want to be able to garden at elbow height. Gardens like these can offer a great deal to people who are interested in cultivating plants as well as to anyone who simply likes spending time and relaxing in a garden.

children's activity garden

A garden to be used by children should be a happy, fuss-free place. There is no point in cherishing delicate flowers and coddling tall-stemmed beauties here. Even your velvet lawn will have to be put on hold for now, as a much-used play area or mountain bike track is seldom smooth and green.

Blending interests

This doesn't mean that you have to deny yourself the pleasures and attractions of a garden if you have children—in some ways your interests will coincide. Most people want a sitting and eating area close to the house and if this is safely constructed and of ample size, it can double up as a daytime playing area for young children, somewhere they are under your eye or can be seen from the window of a room you frequently use. A small but shady tree makes sure that there won't be too much sun–exposure on sunny days. A safety rail is all that differentiates a play-deck from an adults' barbecue area, and shallow steps down if levels change make good sense for adults who'll be using the area at night.

Rather than having a bald and withered lawn, make over a large area to serious rough and tumble play by using a hard-wearing synthetic play surface. In a bold, curvy shape this area can later become a green lawn, a huge island bed for grasses or herbaceous plants, or even a garden pond when the children get older.

Adventure areas can be created with bought equipment such as chutes or swings or the wooden toadstools in our garden, and fantasy areas can be formed from exciting plants chosen for their toughness as well as their ability to make jungles or savannas.

▶ *A children's garden should be stimulating and colorful; these plastic twists reflect the light and bring color to the garden even in winter.*

People who are good at home improvement can make climbing frames and clambering posts, making sure the timber is smoothly planed and firmly and very deeply set in the ground.

Safe and sound

Especially if your children are young it's a good idea to fence your garden in securely so that you know they're safe. Plastic-coated mesh fencing is fine for this, taking up minimal space and letting through light for the plants, and it can easily be hidden by climbing plants. A sturdy, childproof gate is also a must. A soft ground surface is a good idea for adventure areas and a layer of finely shredded bark laid about 15cm/6in thick over a weedproof membrane is economical for this. Water is such a danger where there are young

▶ *Encourage your children to catch the gardening bug by allowing them a small plot of their own in which to grow plants or vegetables.*

◀ *An old-fashioned swing is tucked in a corner, while lawn space allows room to play.*

children that it is much better not to have a garden pond or permanent paddling pool, however much fun and interest these can offer. Instead use an inflatable paddling pool that is only brought out when someone is on the spot to supervise.

If your garden has a suitably strong tree it will be tempting to install a tree-house despite the cost, and these are increasingly appreciated and used by adults too. At ground level, instead of installing a permanent playhouse (costs money, takes up space), make sure that there is an open area that can be used for making a tent or wigwam,

which will be altogether much better for constructive child development. And if you have a sandbox make sure it's high-sided to keep the sand in—and remember the cat. Even if you have no cat yourself neighboring cats will enjoy this giant litter tray. This is not only unpleasant but also potentially a source of disease, so keep the sandbox covered when it's not in use.

Finally, many children have strong gardening instincts. If this is the case with your child, the thing to do is to select a small area where he or she can make their own garden. Find a position in the sun where many easy annuals and vegetables will grow well, and not too far from the water supply so that watering will not be difficult.

designer's children's garden

It may seem difficult to reconcile the idea of a peaceful green retreat with the exuberant activities of young children, but with careful planning there are many possibilities. Even a tiny garden can offer secret corners in which adults, too, can have their space for entertaining friends and relaxing, while the children have fun.

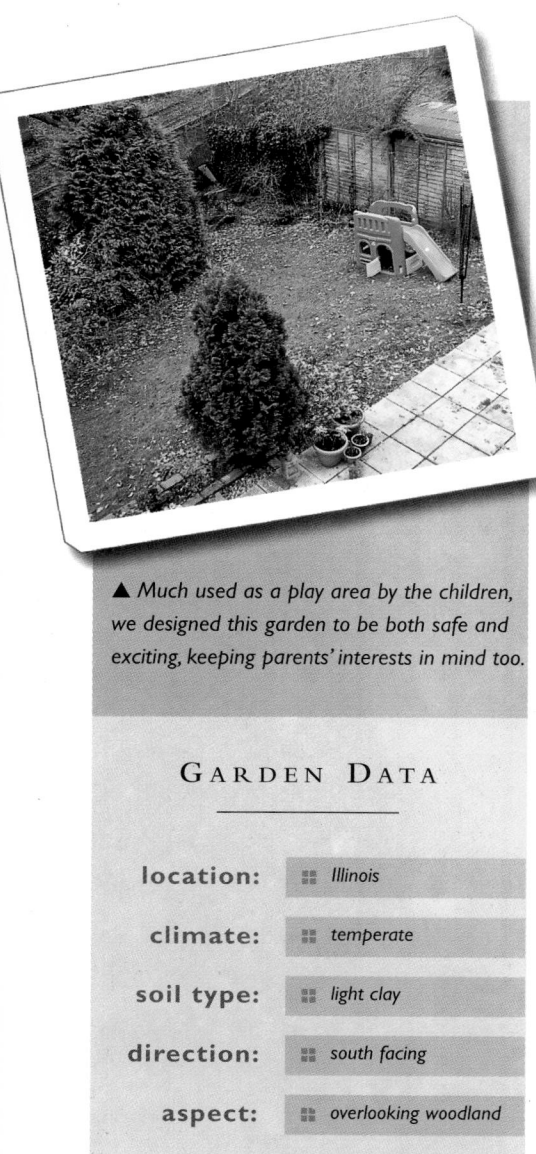

▲ *Much used as a play area by the children, we designed this garden to be both safe and exciting, keeping parents' interests in mind too.*

GARDEN DATA

location:	▦ Illinois
climate:	▦ temperate
soil type:	▦ light clay
direction:	▦ south facing
aspect:	▦ overlooking woodland

Design brief
The family comprises two small boys, aged two and four years and their parents. Dad enjoys gardening and both parents feel that plastic play furniture is unsightly and takes up too much space, but want to enjoy the outdoor garden experience and shared play activity with their offspring. Their small garden slopes gently away from the house but there is a drainage ditch at the end of the plot which is potentially hazardous for children.

Design solution
We divided the garden space into hard and soft landscaping, encompassing patio, play deck/barbecue area, soft play surface with sandbox, mown grass, and planted borders. The decked extension to the patio has safety rails and wide, shallow steps down to the play surface. Inverted, new, timber railroad ties at varying heights, offer climbing and hiding activity and there are grass dens, a woodland toadstool corner, and jungly plants which will withstand some bashing. A 1.2m/4ft high post-and-rail fence with plastic-coated wire mesh panels stapled to it provides a barrier in front of the drainage ditch.

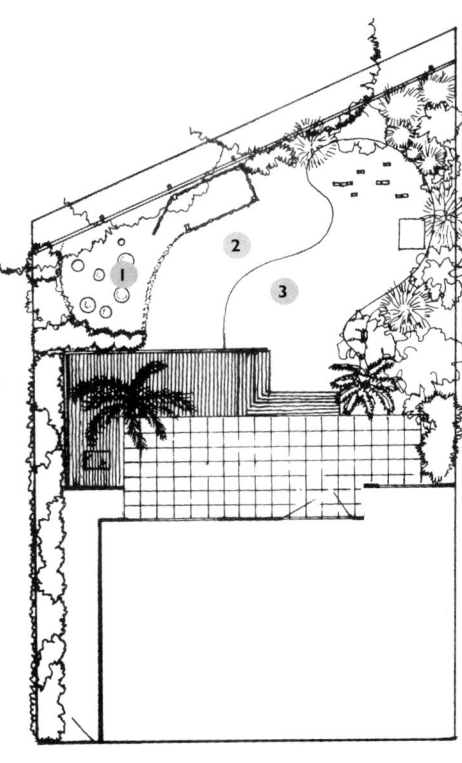

— *19m x 12m/60ft x 38ft* —

toadstools

▲ Handmade toadstools give a woodland feel.

play pen

▲ Den for the children.

safety play surface

▶ Synthetic play surfaces cushion knocks or falls.

153

practical projects

Of course there is lots of tempting equipment to buy for a children's activity garden, but there is also a lot that all but the most ham-fisted handyman or handywoman can make on a budget for the adventure play area. Equipping the play area will be fun for everyone.

▲ *This treehouse is simply but sturdily made. A removable canopy is used as roof canvas, and a rope is provided for safety.*

▶ *Adding a chute to this treehouse makes coming down all the more fun. A colorful plastic slide will not splinter or chip.*

Adventure area

No doubt a tree house is the dream of every child, but (a) you need a tree, and (b) they are expensive. If you do have a tree that's strong enough you could provide a rope ladder, a swing, or a tire on a length of rope as an alternative. Hammocks go down well, and will be equally popular with adults.

A very acceptable alternative to a treehouse would be a small garden shed made into a playhouse. (You can often buy secondhand ones from newspaper advertisements.) Paint it up and equip it with curtains and perhaps bean bags to sit on, with a small table, and it will make a wonderful den to escape to. If you have the talent you could consider making a raised decking platform (see page 197) for the shed to stand on, to make it more exciting.

A simple project to please a young child would be to make a proper sandbox, with a removable lid so that the sand will stay clean and dry when not being used. Use planed, pressure-treated softwood and make sure that it's ultrasmooth by sanding all exposed surfaces. Make the pit as big as you can so that other children can be invited to use it too. Be sure to buy proper sandbox sand rather than builder's sand which is not suitable. Special toys—spades and buckets—will add to the fun.

building a sandbox

The important thing to remember when building a sandbox is that it must be child-friendly. Before you begin assembling the box make sure that there are no rough edges and that the timber you use will not splinter easily. The box should be covered when not in use to prevent cats from using it as a litter tray.

▼ *All children love a sandbox, but look out for one with a close-fitting lid to keep out pets.*

1 Fix a block to each corner of the base of the box, either nailing it or screwing it through from the underside.

2 Screw the side pieces to the blocks, making sure they fit snugly.

3 Sand down the box carefully to get rid of any sharp edges. A few coats of an eco-friendly preservative or paint will keep it sufficiently watertight. Fill with sandbox sand.

DESIGNER'S TIPS

• There are lots of approved play surfaces in fun colors.

• Decking makes a warm, friendly surface for year-round play, as long as it is in an open, sunny position and is treated with proprietary nonslip finish.

• Make sure timber for decking, or any wooden surfaces, is planed, not rough sawn, to avoid nasty splinters.

children's plants and planting

You want your children to be able to play happily in the garden, but you don't want your own gardening efforts to be in vain. Your garden needs to be one that the whole family can enjoy, yet where aesthetic standards are met, and where you won't become a nag every time the bike comes out or friends come round to play.

Plant solutions

Probably the best planting solution in a garden where children play is to go bold, unless your garden is big enough for you to have an area away from the house that forms a separate garden room for quiet time only. Grasses are ideal for an adventure area and hardy bamboos can withstand a lot of active wear and tear.

Both cover a lot of ground and need little care once established.

Exciting-looking plants that take up a lot of space and need little attention are also useful: these would include a hardy palm or a foliage plant such as enormous gunnera (*rheum palmatum*) with its huge leaves. More delicate plants are best nurtured away from the play area.

Profile plants

Stipa arundinacea
PHEASANT'S TAIL GRASS

This is a wonderfully wild and wooly grass for a play area. Originating in New Zealand, it has rhizomes by which it spreads to form new tufts of strong green leaves which are tinted burnt orange in the summer, becoming orange-brown in winter. All summer long it whispers and moves in the breeze, with arching waterfalls of feathery flowers in a light purplish greeny brown.

ht 90cm/3ft overall

sp 1.2m/4ft

Soil and situation

One of the most tolerant of all the stipa species, pheasant's tail grass will grow in soils from heavy and fertile to light, poor, and dry, and in full sun or partial shade. Dead leaves can be removed in early spring.

◀ *The Japanese aralia has impressive leaves.*

▶ *Red-hot pokers have an instant appeal.*

▶ *Originating in New Zealand pheasant's tail grass is ideal for a children's garden. This playful mound waves gently in the summer breeze.*

Kniphofia 'Bees Sunset'
RED–HOT POKER

Red-hot pokers are fairly tough and resilient and make very striking plants likely to appeal to children. This variety is tall enough to match a small child and throughout the summer it has stiff spikes of flowers in a warm, strong orange, like fireworks rising up from the clumps of strong, grassy leaves. It attracts bees, which might foster an early interest in wildlife, though young children should be warned to take care. For other kniphofias for the garden, see page 242.

ht 90cm/3ft
sp 60cm/2ft

Soil and situation
Needs very well-drained but moist and fertile soil, preferably sandy, and will thrive in sun or partial shade. Although 'Bees Sunset' is hardy, it needs protection from frost.

Fatsia japonica
JAPANESE ARALIA

Strongly architectural, this is an evergreen shrub with large, lobed, leathery leaves on stiff stalks. Small,

spherical cream-colored flowers appear in late summer.
ht and sp 1.8m/6ft and over
Soil and situation
Fairly fertile well-drained soil, with some moisture and dappled shade suit the plant best. It tolerates city air and seashore situations as long as it has shelter from cold wind. The foliage can be damaged by frost but the plant will survive. The leaves may yellow in alkaline soil.

TALL GRASSES FOR THE GARDEN

Tolerate most soils and sun or shade unless otherwise stated.
Cortaderia selloana (pampas grass) tall, white, waving plumes (older children)
ht 2–3m/6 ½–10ft ('Pumila' is the smallest variety)
needs wind-shelter and a sunny position
Miscanthus sinensis slender leaves and feathery flowers
varieties include 'Gracillimus', 'Klein Fontane',

'Morning Light', 'Silver Feather', 'Zebrinus' (with yellow-banded leaves)
ht 1.5–2m/5–6 ½ft
Pennisetum alopecuroides (fountain grass) downy caterpillar flower heads
ht 1.2m/4ft
Stipa arundinacea (see profile plants)
Stipa gigantea (golden oats) blue-gray stems, oat-like flowers
ht 1.8–2.5m/6–8ft
needs a sunny position
Stipa splendens lofty, purple-tinged plumes
ht to 2.5m/8ft
See also Bamboos, pages 134–135

design alternatives

SKETCHES

These two designs explore alternative layouts and play possibilities, including space for highly active play such as cycling. Both use synthetic play surfaces instead of lawn.

multicolored proprietary play surface in rainbow ribbons of color

woven willow hurdle fencing—1.5m/ 5ft high

woven willow hurdle 'den' – approx. 1.5m/ 5ft high

willow fencing

'Dad's' garden

palm tree inserted into hole cut into play surface

'walk through' shed for storing bikes and toys, etc.

single level patio of terracotta tiles with 2 steps down to garden

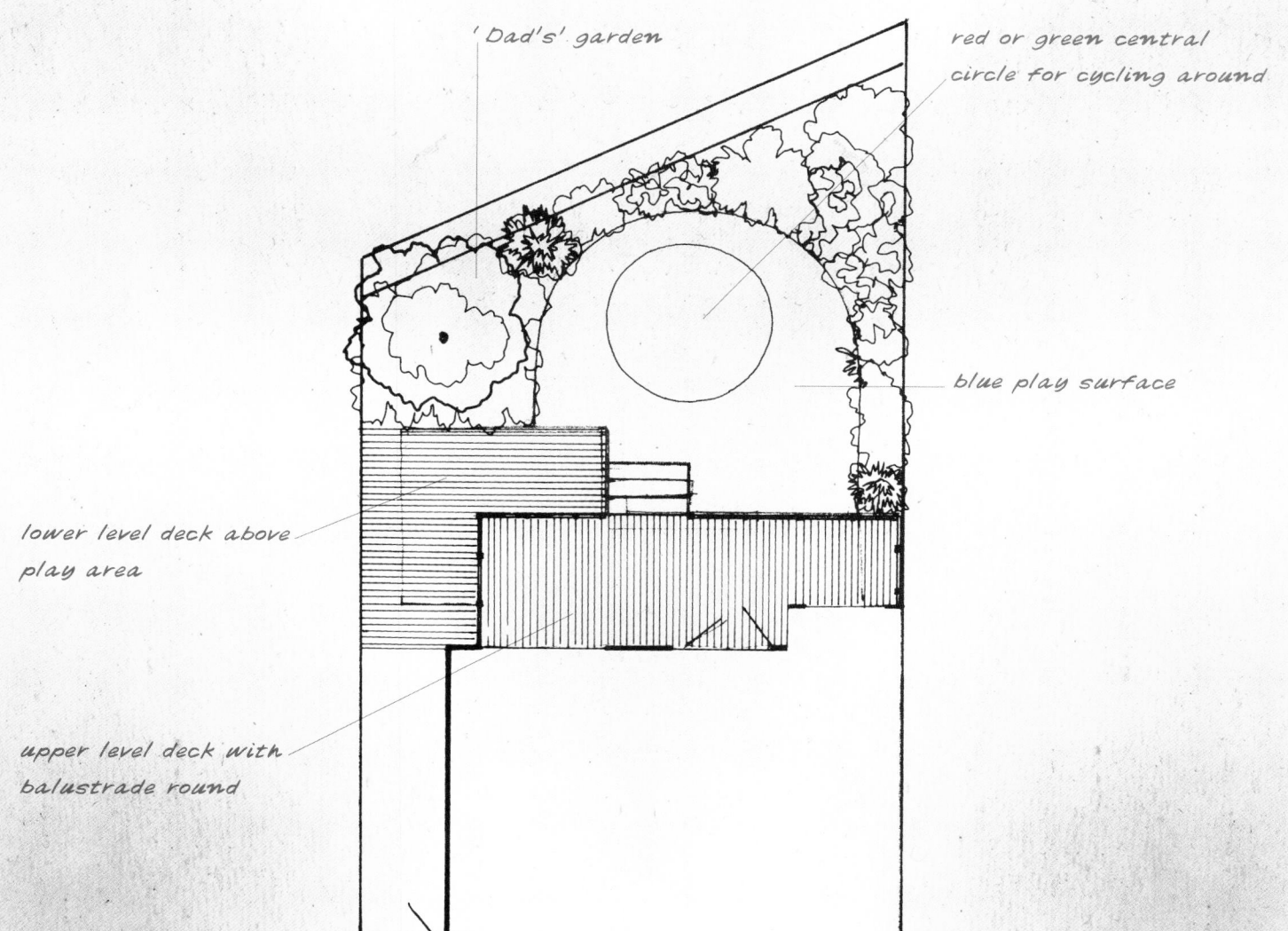

'Dad's' garden

red or green central
circle for cycling around

blue play surface

lower level deck above
play area

upper level deck with
balustrade round

easy-reach garden

In an easy-reach garden the planting areas must be accessible and high enough to be reached without bending—high-sided containers and raised beds offer all sorts of gardening opportunities. Allowing plenty of space and all-round access to the growing areas will make sure that these gardens can be used by everyone.

Key features

Many of the features of a garden that's easy to get at make it simple to maintain, and suitable for weekend gardeners or people who haven't got much time to spend on the garden. The only point to bear in mind is that if you use containers as an alternative to raised beds they will need more watering in dry weather.

A formal design best suits the requirements of gardens in this group as there needs to be a good deal of uncluttered open space. As a lawn for such areas demands too much attention and upkeep the wise solution is to use a hard, nonslip surface. This can be stone or stone substitute paving, brickwork, brick pavers, or rolled gravel, and the choice will depend partly on the style of the house and also on the budget available. It's worth investing in what you really want as this element of the garden is very visible at all times of year and will also have a very long life. Except in a very small garden it's usually more effective to vary the surface material, either as an all–over pattern or by using different materials in different areas, or the effect can be municipal and monotonous.

◄ *Strategically placed planters help add variety in a paved area, and the plants in them are readily accessible.*

Practical considerations

Except where they can be reached from all sides, raised beds or planting containers should be narrow enough for easy access (maximum depth 1.5m/5ft). The sides of a raised bed could also incorporate a seat and if let into the bed this could be used as a place to work on the plants as well as from which to enjoy them. Built features that create maximum effect, such as a rose arch or a long pergola, also provide a visually appealing way of growing plants that require little attention. You might also want to install a formal pool, with wide built-up sides deep enough to provide seating.

For watering, if you can afford the original investment, a built-in irrigation system in the form of a seep hose will be a wonderful aid. If not, the siting of the water supply

◄ *Raised water features are a possibility and ponds make a good choice. Broad edging provides informal seating.*

▲ *Setting seats into the raised beds will allow you somewhere to relax and enjoy the plants.*

needs careful consideration. It might be better to have more than one faucet, connected to short hoses, than to install one long hose.

With so much hard-landscaping it's a good idea to introduce softer material for elements. Instead of being built in brick, raised beds can be framed in timber, which should be pressure-treated to give it the longest possible life, and used in conjunction with heavy-duty plastic sheeting to line the inside of the walls and to retain the soil. A seat with an adjacent bench at the right height to be used as a work top while you are sitting would also be a useful feature for any garden.

designer's easy-reach garden

One of the most labor-saving gardens to maintain is one in which there are raised beds, no steps, and narrow borders. Raised borders are easy on the back, gentle ramps offer ease of movement around sloping sites, and nonslip surfaces can be varied in color and texture to complement the planting.

▲ *At present, the site is not practical for this elderly couple who wish to continue their hobby but have limited mobility.*

GARDEN DATA

location:	▪▪ Virginia
climate:	▪▪ mild temperate
soil type:	▪▪ light clay
direction:	▪▪ south facing
aspect:	▪▪ open, sloping to house

Design brief

Derek and Jean are retired and although they are keen gardeners they find that they no longer have the energy or suppleness for major maintenance work. They would like a garden that allows them to continue to garden well into old age, but that looks attractive as well as being functional. Their garden slopes slightly upward from the house and faces south, so is warm and sunny.

Design solution

We decided upon a simple, fairly formal layout, within which a large variety of plants and vegetables could be contained. A timber-decked ramp was sprayed with fine aggregate to make a nonslip slope up to the main garden. We used a combination of regular-sized, mortared slabs with a slightly gritty surface texture and firmly-rolled, self-binding gravel for the broad pathways. The borders are retained by new, railroad-tie walls, which are wide enough and low

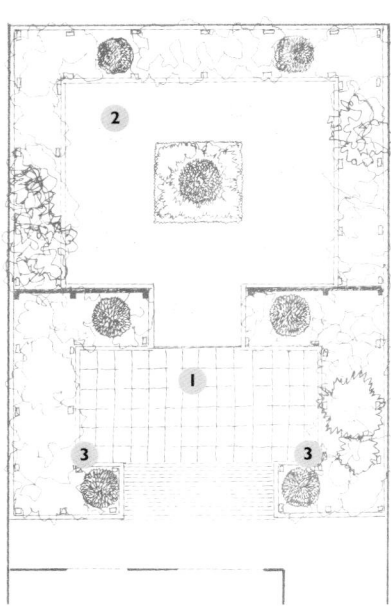

— 9m x 14m/30ft x 45ft —

enough to sit on. Brick or stone walls could be used if preferred, but timber makes a warmer seat. The borders are filled with colorful, fragrant and aromatic plants, and flowers for cutting. We added easy salad vegetables and a variety of herbs. All the planting, including the topiary, is low, both for ease of management and to let as much sunlight as possible into the garden.

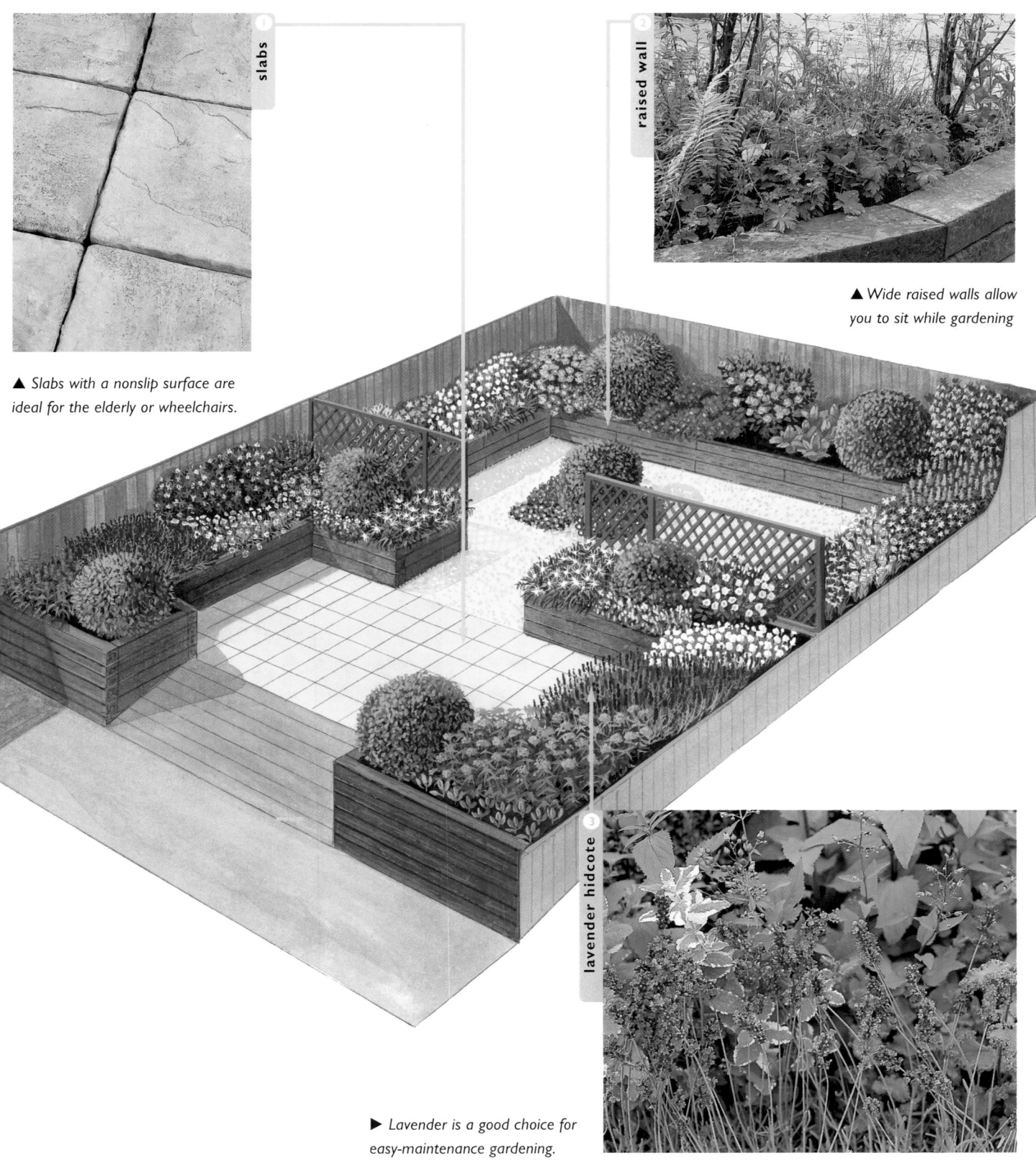

slabs ①

② **raised wall**

▲ Wide raised walls allow
you to sit while gardening

▲ Slabs with a nonslip surface are
ideal for the elderly or wheelchairs.

③ **lavender hidcote**

▶ Lavender is a good choice for
easy-maintenance gardening.

practical projects

Many of the features of an easy-reach garden can be adapted to any garden, and can be borrowed by people who want to make gardening easy for themselves. Nothing in our garden sacrifices the pleasures of a garden to convenience, yet still makes an attractive, low-maintenance space.

Making things easy

Designing for people who for one reason or another have restricted movement and who want to be able to garden at elbow height need not be a problem. Raised beds have many advantages but you would probably need to employ a specialist to build a stone or brick raised planting bed.

However, it is fairly simple to make a long-lasting wooden one, as shown on the opposite page.

You will need to give some thought to paths and changes of level. Many people find it more difficult to handle steep steps or sudden changes of level, so keep all steps broad and shallow and avoid

steep slopes by introducing terracing if necessary, with a series of broad, level areas between short flights of shallow steps. For wheelchair users install a ramp wherever possible. They need to be able to maneuver themselves about freely, so keep paths wide, avoiding sharp corners or awkward changes of direction.

PRACTICAL FEATURES FOR THE GARDEN

A simple rope provides guidance for those with limited vision, or a means of balance for anyone who is no longer confident on their feet.

Raised beds at seat height allow for relaxed gardening. Wheelchair users would also benefit from a low wall they can comfortably reach over.

A gentle curving path with even, smooth slabs and no planting between lawn and path, is an ideal design for wheelchair users as it allows them to maneuver with ease.

building a low retaining wall

You do need not need bricklaying skills to make a raised bed if you opt for reclaimed railroad ties. Check before you buy, however. Some have been treated with tar that can leach into the soil and harm your plants. Look out for new oak ties instead, which will not cause any problems.

1 Pile up the ties to the desired height, interlocking them at the corners. Drive a stake into the ground in the inside corners.

2 Screw the stakes to the ties, using long, rustproof screws.

3 To prevent excess moisture entering the ties from the soil, line the inside of the bed with heavy-duty plastic, nailed in position with rustproof nails. Fill the bed with soil and plant up.

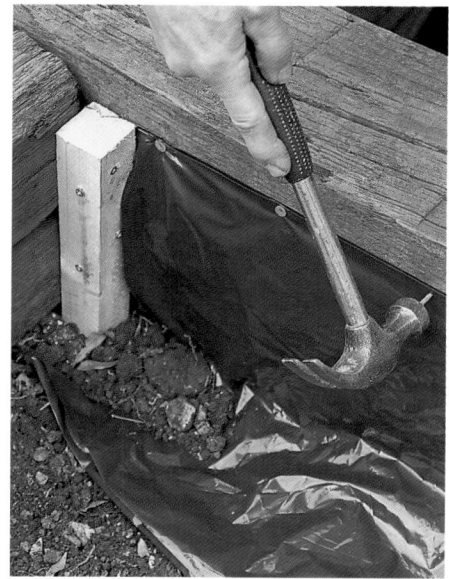

◄ *A low-retaining wall can look wonderful in old brick. The accompanying brick steps are shallow and wide for ease of use.*

easy-reach plants and planting

A large area of an easy-reach garden will consist of hard-surfaced circulation space; raised beds or planters will also comprise harder materials. Planting should aim partly to soften this effect, and full use should be made of plants that will billow and trail over the edges of the planting areas or form soft shapes.

◀ *The fragrant* Trachelospermum jasminoides.

Plants to grow

For people who find tending the plants difficult there are numerous ways of making the job easier, and planting low-maintenance plants and plants that perform well over a long period is perhaps the best start. These include small shrubs such as hebes and potentillas; shrubby herbs and aromatic plants such as lavender, thyme, and sage; perennials with a long flowering period or attractive leaves such as modern pinks, heucheras, and hardy geraniums, and ground-cover plants such as periwinkle (*Vinca major*) and epimedium (see Plant Directory).

For summer color, easy annuals such as California poppy (*Eschscholzia*), nasturtiums (*Tropaeolum*) and candytuft (*Iberis*) can be sown in odd patches where they are to grow. Climbers always add interest to a garden, especially when scented, and many of the best—honeysuckle

(*Lonicera*) and jasmine (*Jasminum officinale*) included—need little care. As in any garden the use of evergreen plants, such as box (for low hedging) and formally placed bay trees in pairs, emphasizes structure and acts as punctuation, as well as bringing form to the garden in winter.

CONTAINER PLANTS

Among the plants to make mounds and hide the edges of planters and containers are the smaller roses. Miniature roses only 30cm/12 in high include the pink moss rose 'Dresden Doll', 'Lavender Jewel' in pink and lavender, 'Stars 'n Stripes' with raspberry pink stripes on white, and the sunny 'Yellow Doll'. The continuously flowering dwarf polyanthas include 'Jean Mermoz' in deep china pink, 'Gloire du Midi' in orange red, 'Marie Pavie' in white, and 'Nathalie Nypels' in pink. All are 60cm/2ft or less in height.

Alpine plants revel in the well-drained conditions offered by a raised bed and can make a lovely tabletop-level display. Most herbs, including annuals and perennials also suit a raised container and are useful as well as scented or aromatic and good to look at.

▶ Lamium maculatum *f.* album *is a white-flowering member of the mint family.*

Profile plants

Lamium maculatum f. *album*
LAMIUM OR DEAD NETTLE

Lamiums—in fact members of the mint family—are excellent and undemanding plants grown mainly for their leaves. They will quickly spread to colonize an area and within the constraints of a container they can't get out of hand. They are perfect for people who don't want to spend too much time fussing over their plants, as they just need clipping after flowering. This is an attractive white-leaved, white-flowered variety.

ht 30cm/12in

sp to 60cm/2ft

Soil and situation

Lamiums are tolerant, but this variety does best in well-drained but moist soil and in a shady position. (See also page 242)

Jasminum officinale
JASMINE

With its heavily perfumed small white flowers and delicate, twining, evergreen foliage this is a lovely climber to plant near a seat. Capable of reaching a great height it can also be kept trimmed. Another *jasmine, J. angulare* is also a sweetly scented form, but with broader leaves, and from a different family there is the jasmine-like *Trachelospermum jasminoides*, which is also fragrant. Less vigorous, both are frost tender and need a very sheltered spot.

◀ *A colorful selection of thymes.*

ht and sp to 11m/36ft

Soil and position

Need moist but well-drained, fertile soil in sun or semishade.

Thymus species
THYME

Though thyme is known as a herb there are numerous species and many named cultivars that make attractive garden plants grown for their colorful flowers as well as their bushy growth and characteristic scent. Liking well-drained soil they are well suited to containers and raised beds and do well in fairly poor, alkaline soil.

ht to 30cm/12in

sp 40cm/16in

Soil and position

Needs very well-drained, gritty soil and full sun.

design alternatives

SKETCHES

These alternative schemes include the central concepts of raised retaining walls, nonslip surfaces, and open spaces that can be maneuvered around safely and easily.

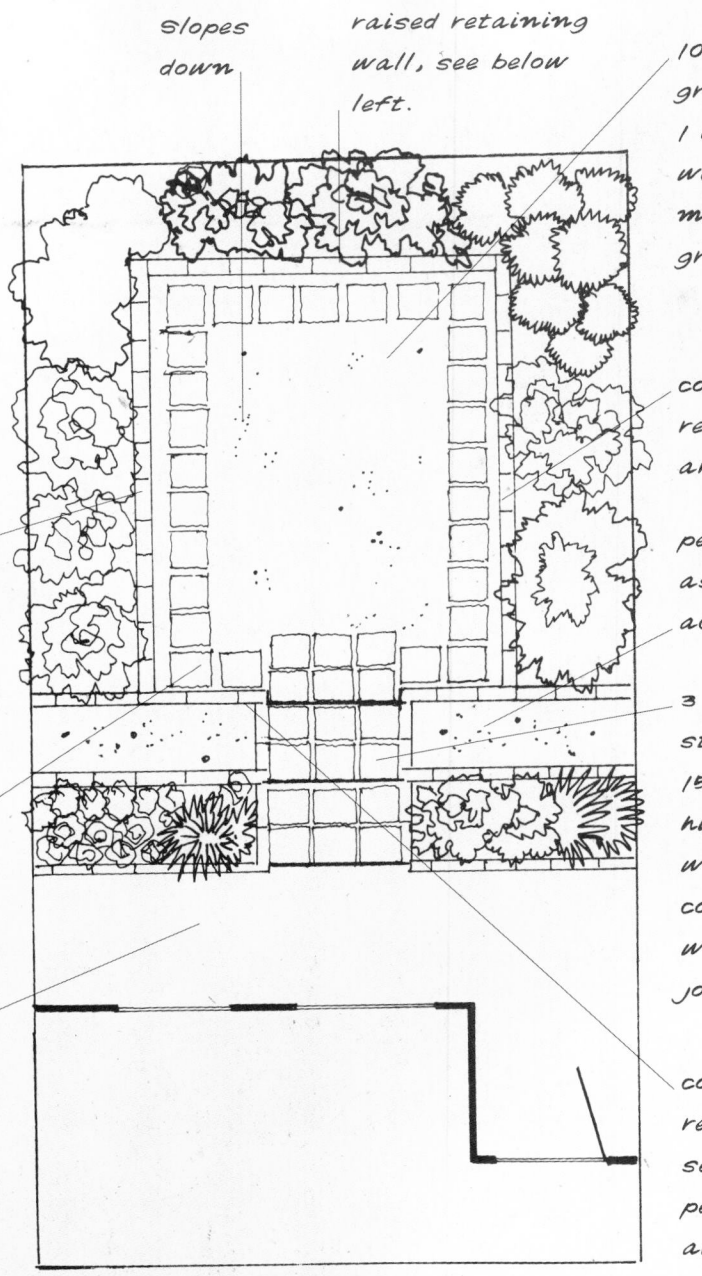

Slopes down

raised retaining wall, see below left.

10 mm/½in pea gravel laid 30mm/1 in deep over weedproof membrane, or grass if preferred

continuation of retaining wall around borders

pea gravel path as before for access to plants

3 shallow broad steps, each 150mm/6in high–surfaced with stone or concrete slabs with mortared joints

continuation of retaining wall set flush with pea gravel (to avoid tripping)

raised stone or brick retaining wall with brick or stone coping; height of wall up to 600mm/24in or as required

stone or concrete slabs (with mortared joints) set flush with gravel or grass

existing patio or continuation of stone or concrete slabs

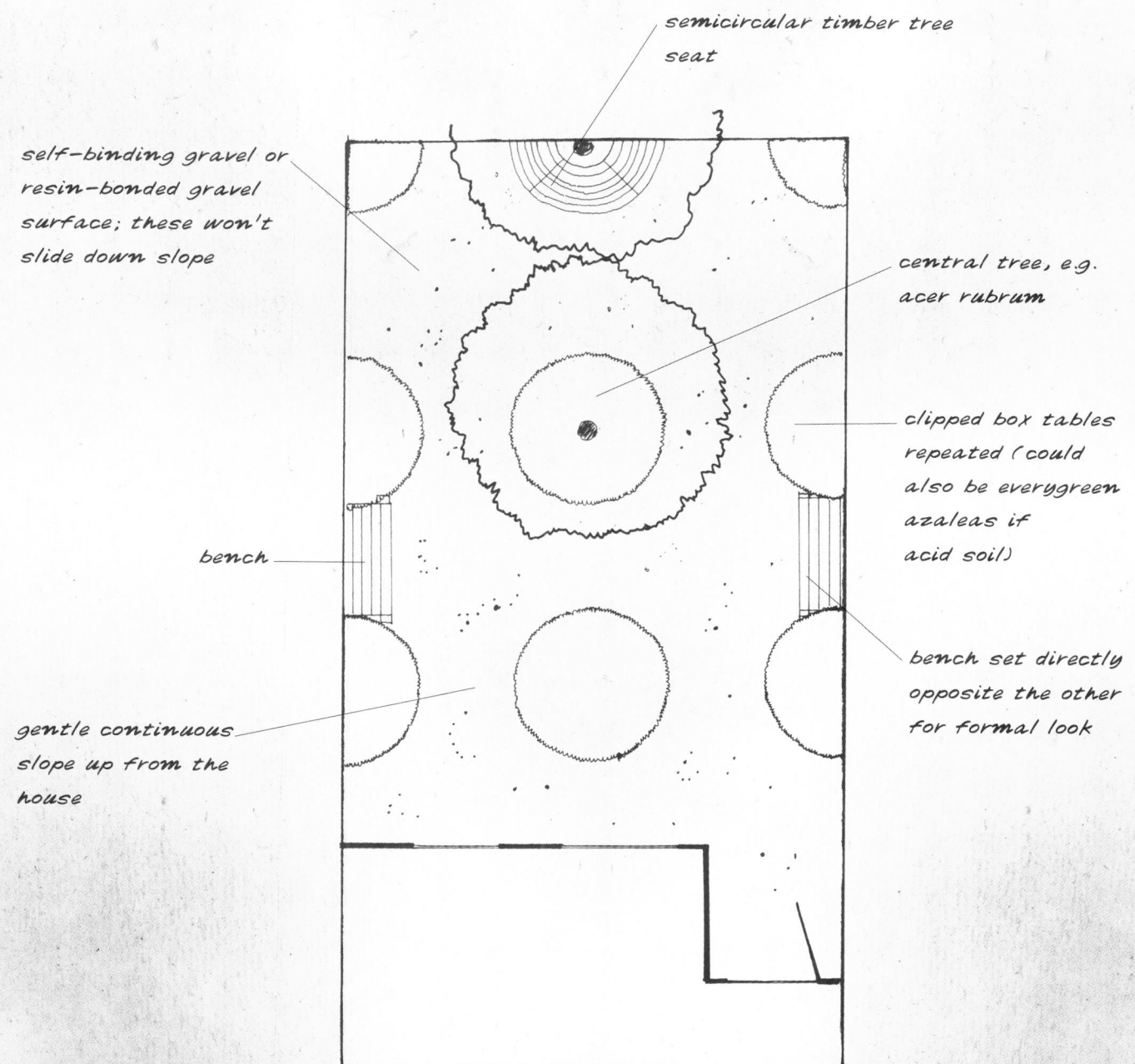

semicircular timber tree
seat

self-binding gravel or
resin-bonded gravel
surface; these won't
slide down slope

central tree, e.g.
acer rubrum

clipped box tables
repeated (could
also be everygreen
azaleas if
acid soil)

bench

bench set directly
opposite the other
for formal look

gentle continuous
slope up from the
house

specific location gardens

Every garden is of course unique and its character will be decided as much by the tastes and choices of its owners as by any other factor. Nevertheless, specific situations or contexts do impose certain constraints or offer unusual opportunities in planning and designing. What you can do or can't do in the given circumstances is always a very good place to start.

seashore garden

If you garden right by the sea you can't ignore it. Coastal winds can waft sea salt several miles inland, so even away from the sound of the waves you can be prey to seaside conditions. Coastal gardens offer a challenge and the first problem you need to address is usually that of providing shelter.

Seashore designs

A garden within sight of the sea is crying out for the full seashore treatment, complete with nautical ingredients and ideas from the sea shore: driftwood, sand, gravel and pebbles, shells, anchor chains, and even nets or ropes will all be at home here. A smooth green lawn would be almost impossible to maintain, and would look ill at ease in this setting, whereas hard surfaces are much more appropriate. Likewise the soil will be inhospitable to most plants, and you will need to concentrate on maritime species, and on creating a design through objects and materials as well as plants—although of course you can use containers and bought soil mix for those plants that demand more fertile soil.

Solid timber works well as a material of many uses in a real seashore garden, evocative of old boats and quay-sides, but it's best not to use tarred wood in proximity to plants as tarry poisons continue to seep out for many years—to the plants' distress. If you want to lighten new timber to give it a salt-sea look, the best treatment is to paint it with an opaque white wood stain, which is safe for animals and plants.

Dealing with exposure

One of the things a coastal situation has in common with rooftops (see pages 182-83) is exposure to the wind, and here the winds will be a nuisance not only because of their buffeting, but also because they carry salt with them from the sea. Luckily there are several salt-wind-resistant shrubs and trees that can be used to help to break the force of the wind, planted singly or grouped in key places (see our garden design on

◀ *Decking works perfectly in a seashore garden, especially if the timbers are treated for that salted, worn-away look.*

◀ *In a coastal garden, make sure you choose tough plants that can put up with sea spray, strong winds, and heavy rain.*

unpleasant view. Panels for fences and trellis screens are also, of course, readily available, and a great deal cheaper than the materials for walls, as well as being much easier to put together yourself.

As an alternative to a built boundary or enclosure a seaside hedge will filter the wind and give shade and shelter while being good to look at in its own right. While the hedge is getting established a temporary netting windbreak can be set up, stretched between posts on the windward side to give protection. See pages 178–79 for suitable shrubs that can be grown as hedging plants for coastal areas.

pages 174–175). A strong screen in the form of a fence or wall that is perforated to let through light and reduce the wind's strength without creating turbulence is sometimes preferable, especially to give privacy in a small area. A fence need not have a straight top and can be painted to enhance the garden scheme rather than left as it is. In the bright coastal light bold colors (other than matt white) work well, while pale ones can look insipid, unless placed in an area of shade, where they look cool.

For total privacy a stone or brick wall will provide complete shelter but a solid barrier does cause wind turbulence. Furthermore, a solid wall

has the disadvantage that you can't get a glimpse of the view through it if there's a good one. Despite these disadvantages, if you live in an area where stone is the natural local material, a low stone wall, traditionally built, can be very attractive, particularly where you are creating a courtyard-style garden immediately next to the house. Generally, however, a pierced wall or fence, or heavy-duty trellis is more effective as a windbreak, and works well if you want to hide an

▶ *Natural objects bring a seashore garden to life; this old rowing boat looks as though the sea has carried it straight into the garden.*

designer's seashore garden

Gardening by the sea can be a challenging task, but is less so if you create a basic design that does not try to compete with the elemental landscape of sea and sky. There are wonderful pieces of twisted bleached driftwood, shells, and beach cobbles that can all find a place in your seashore landscape.

▲ *This coastal site seems problematic but is easily turned into an attractive, low-maintenance garden.*

GARDEN DATA

location:	▪▪	*Massachusetts*
climate:	▪▪	*temperate*
soil type:	▪▪	*chalky*
direction:	▪▪	*west facing*
aspect:	▪▪	*open to seafront*

Design brief

The L-shaped garden of this holiday home opens directly on to a stony beach along part of its boundary and is exposed to salt-laden gales. Topsoil is virtually nonexistent and is replaced by shifting shingle and sand. The garden needs a primary shelter belt and must be simply planted for low maintenance, as the owners visit only at weekends.

Design solution

We chose reclaimed oak planking for the deck and for the planked walkway toward the beach. An informal but sturdy "fence" is provided by similar oak planks inserted deeply into the shingle at varying heights. Lengths from old telephone poles would do just as well. The "fence" not only marks the boundary and helps break the force of the wind, but also helps anchor the shingle. We shaped the existing grass sward into a natural wave shape and added some large boulders for variety of texture.

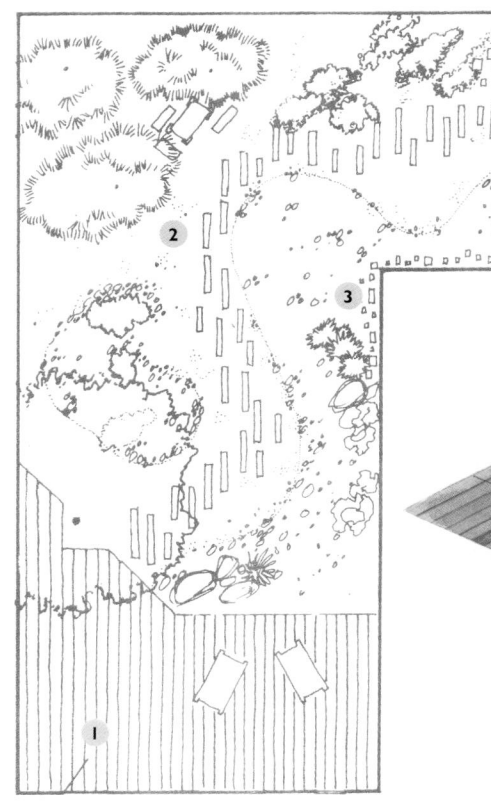

–37m x 10m/112ft x 32ft –

Planting is confined strictly to a few low-maintenance species that can cope with the extreme conditions. These are grouped boldly around and between the boulders to form strong focal points.

deck chair

◄ *The sitting area is well sheltered from wind.*

windbreak

shingle

▲ *A slatted fence makes a good windbreak.*

◄ *Cobbles and shingle mark a natural path to the beach.*

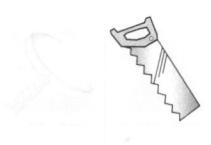

practical projects

The soil is almost always poor in coastal areas, and you are often faced with exposed and windy conditions, even if there is sun. Design to face these challenges by making over a large area to a timber-floored dining and sitting space and building a wooden palisade to act as a windbreak.

A nautical air

In a seaside garden you may enjoy seafood barbecues, do some undisturbed sun worshiping, and take advantage of the local micro-climate to grow something exotic and unusual without having to spend too much time coaxing unwilling plants. Building a palisade fence will help to turn a sunny coastal plot into a more sheltered seaside garden, making it more conducive to planting despite the otherwise exposed situation—the perfect place for growing sun-loving plants and basking in the sun.

This sort of windbreak has a homespun look and there is no need to worry about careful measuring. An uneven top to the fence ties in with the garden's rustic furniture and decking. The decking laid directly into shingle gives a nautical look and the theme is continued throughout. Controlled irregularity is the look you are aiming for and natural materials are best.

DESIGNER'S TIPS

• Remember it may be illegal to remove stones, boulders, pebbles or cobbles from their natural setting, so check first.

• Try to use only native plants and local materials. Anything alien to your seascape will look just that.

• Position driftwood, boulders, and plants to lie directionally along the invisible line of the prevailing wind and weather.

• Gauge the direction of weather fronts from the way that surrounding shrubs and trees grow to lean away from the wind.

◄ *Seashore dwellers are bound to have lots of visitors, so these gardens benefit from an area for entertaining and feeding that sea appetite.*

building a rustic seashore windbreak

A rustic-looking windbreak is easily made. If you live by the sea, the timbers will soon weather attractively, but if you garden inland but want that distinctive seaside look, try staining them to the appropriate bleached color—a soft whitish gray is best.

1 Dig a trench to a depth of up to a third the length of the longest timber.

2 Line the base of the trench with pebbles or coarse gravel for good drainage around the base of the timbers.

3 Cut the timbers to length. For a really rustic look, make sure the lengths are uneven. Stain the timbers if necessary.

4 Knock the timbers well into the ground using a mallet and a piece of timber held horizontally over the top.

5 Leave a gap between each timber to filter the wind. The uneven topline will break the wind further and look less rigid.

seashore plants and planting

There are many plants for coastal areas. Despite the gales, at least the coastal climate is generally frost-free, and it may even be balmy. Most seashore gardens are exposed to high levels of sunshine and dry conditions from spring to fall, so drought-tolerant, salt-wind-proof sun-lovers are generally required.

SHRUBBY PLANTS FOR COASTAL AREAS

Artemisia absinthium (wormwood)—mound-forming shrub with silvery-gray leaves
ht 90cm/3ft
Cytisus scoparius (common broom)—bright yellow flowers on bright green branches
ht to 2.5m/8ft
Escallonia species—glossy-leaved evergreen for warmer areas; white, pink, or red flowers
ht 1.5–2.5m/5–8ft
Elaeagnus pungens—(see page 246)
Fuschsia magellanica—hardy fuschsia with crimson and purple hanging flowers
ht 1.2–1.8m/4–6ft
Genista hispanica (Spanish gorse)—golden yellow flowers on tough, spiny branches
ht 60cm–1.2m/2–4ft
Olearia x *haastii* and *O. cheesmanii* (daisy bush)—evergreens with white flowers; glossy green leaves have white, felty backs
ht 1.8m/6ft; 3.6m/12ft *(O. cheesmanii)*
Juniperus communis (juniper)—weather-resistant evergreen (dwarf forms available)
ht to 3m/10ft

For plants for sunny, dry areas
see pages 198–199

Plants for the seashore

Plants for hot, dry, sunny places give away their sun-loving, or sun-tolerant nature partly by their leaves, as it's through its leaves that a plant loses moisture. To reduce water loss these plants have small or very narrow leaves, hairy leaves (as in silver- and gray-leaved plants) or waxy leaves. Succulent plants also are adapted to dry conditions, and this includes not only the true succulents (the cacti) but also fleshy-leaved plants such as sedums and houseleeks (*Sempervivum* species). Many flowering plants from bulbs and corms, such as the hardier agapanthus, alliums, and crocosmia can also do well by the sea, given some shelter.

Beating the wind

Wind-resistance is a key feature, as seaside places can suffer gales from fall until late spring and strong winds

▶ *California poppies are bright and adaptable.*

even in summer. The solution is partly to provide shelter, but also to look out for wiry, spiky plants that sift the wind and resist water loss, and low-growing plants whose natural habitat is cliffs and rocks. Even a screen as low as 50cm/20in gives adequate shelter for low-growing plants, and plants themselves can form a screen. Phormiums, elaeagnus, and several olearias (the daisy bush)—see panel opposite—all cope well.

Profile plants

Eschscholzia californica
CALIFORNIA POPPY

These brightly-colored but delicate looking poppy-like annuals are just right for gray pebbles and blue skies. California poppies love the sun and their petals close on cloudy days. They are very easily grown from seed, sown in succession from early spring onward for a continuous display. The characteristic color is orange, but mixtures with flowers in cream and yellow are available.

ht 20–30cm/8–12in

sp 10–15cm/4–6in

Soil and situation

Must have well-drained, poor soil (suitable for sandy and stony soils), and a sunny position.

▶ Rutus graveolens, *common rue.*

◀ *Flowers of the* Cynara cardunculus.

Cynara cardunculus
CARDOON

Related to the globe artichoke cardoon has the same statuesque, thistle-like magnificence and these are very attractive plants with their wooly grayish white stems, spiny gray leaves and purple thistle flowers which attract bees all summer long. Cardoons are best grown from seed. The leaf stalks and midribs can be blanched for eating.

ht 1.5m/5ft

sp 1.2m/4ft

Soil and situation

Well-drained, reasonably fertile soil in full sun, but with shelter from strong winds.

Ruta graveolens
COMMON RUE

Rue is a bushy herb with pretty blue-green leaves and small yellow flowers in summer. It was taken by the Romans to their colonies and is still an ingredient of the fiery Italian grappa. The leaves have a very distinct scent when crushed. It is used more as a decorative plant than as a culinary herb today. **Can cause blisters on sensitive skin.**

ht to 90cm/3ft

sp 75cm/30in

Soil and situation

This species is at its best in hot, dry places, in poor, well-drained or sandy soil and a sunny position.

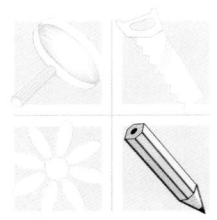

design alternatives

SKETCHES

Our designer's alternative plans retain the use of organic materials and stong, hardy grasses for planting. They are very simple, low-maintenance designs that make the most of the natural beauty of coastland.

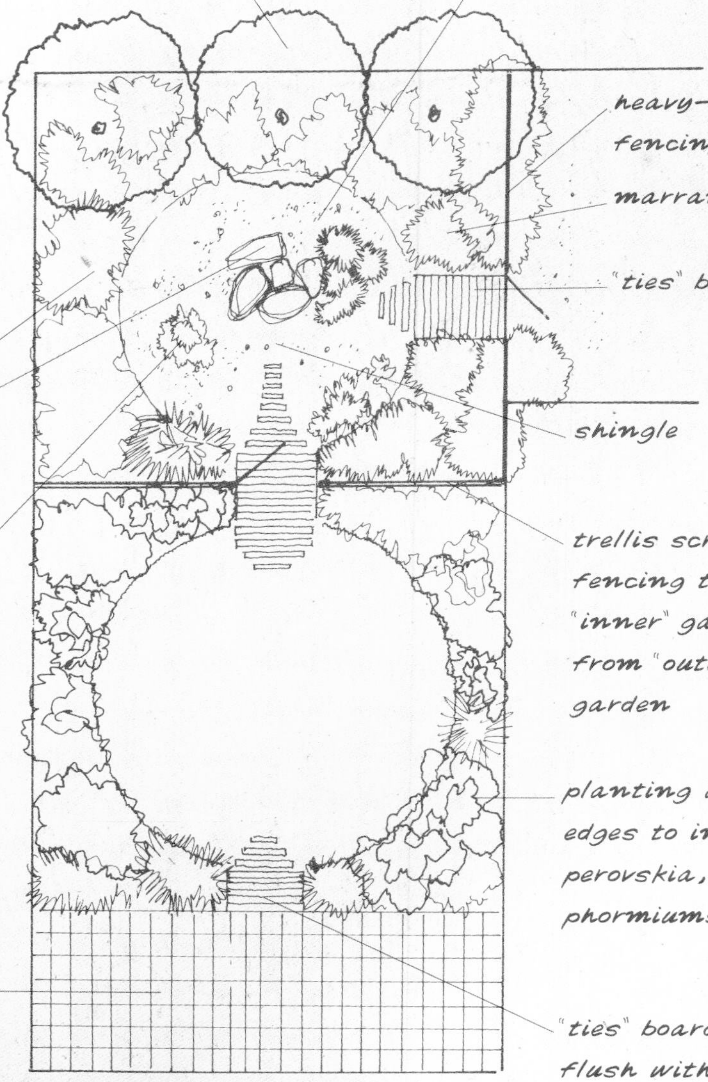

"stone" pines

"exposed" area—open to seashore except for fencing

heavy-duty trellis fencing

marram grass

"ties" boardwalk

sea buckthorn hedging

standing stones up to 2m/6ft high and down to 1.2m/4ft

seakale and grasses planted in shingle

shingle

trellis screening fencing to divide "inner" garden from "outer" garden

planting around edges to include perovskia, lavender, phormiums

terracotta tile terrace

"ties" boardwalk set flush with grass for easy mowing

a very exposed garden

raised jetty style
boardwalk onto beach

standing stones or
boulders

marram grass

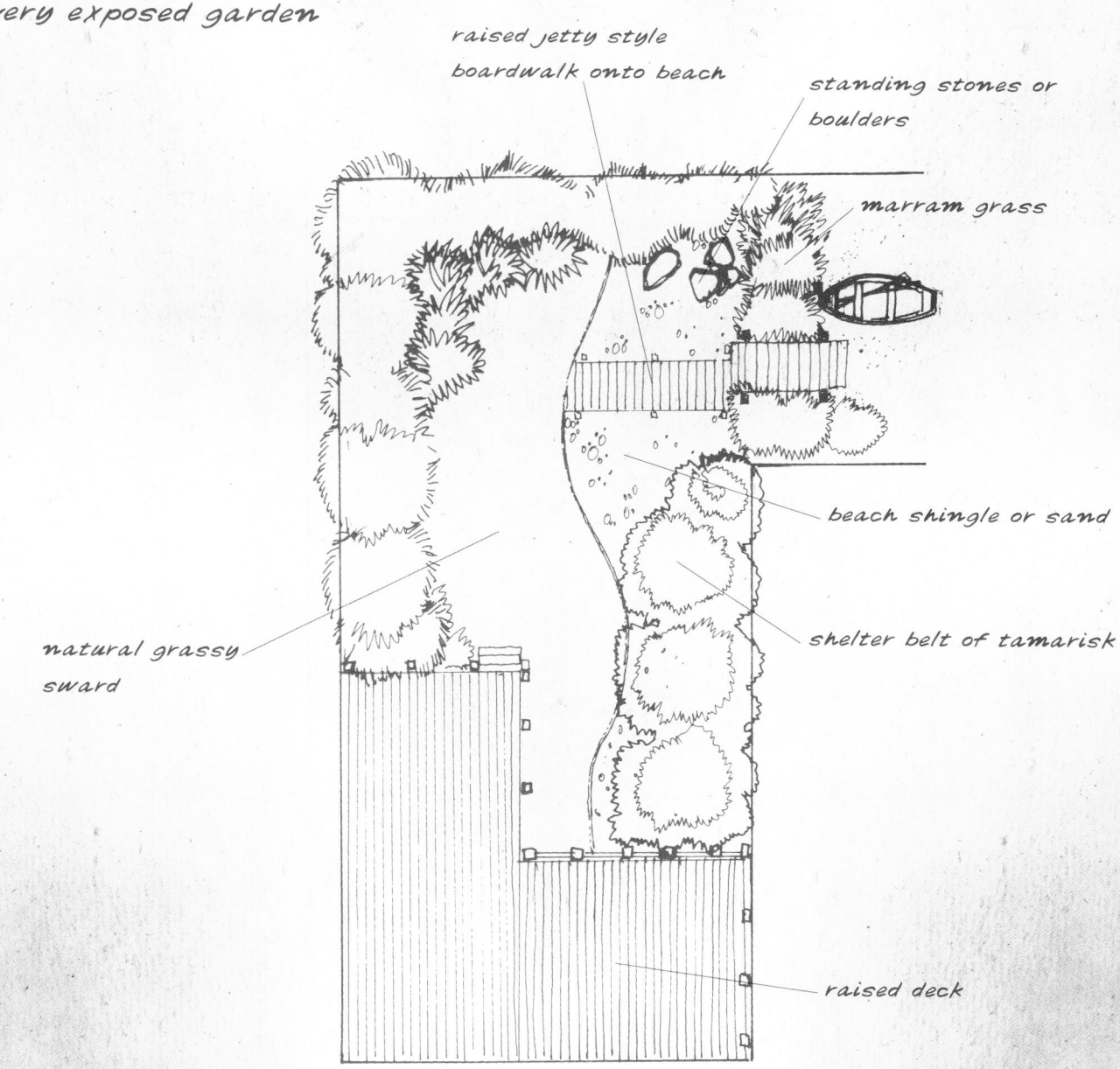

beach shingle or sand

shelter belt of tamarisk

natural grassy
sward

raised deck

roof garden

Some of the most exciting modern gardens are those designed for roofs where, with fewer precedents as a starting point, the imagination can take off. And with many problems to face, your ingenuity is called into play to find a multitude of brilliant solutions in terms of plants and overall design.

◄ *A roof-top garden can be as innovative as you like, as this modernistic design shows.*

Problems to be solved

The problems associated with roof gardens are manifold: safety, the challenge to the strength and water-resistance of the roof, and the exposed position being at the top of the list. Before you start there is the question of whether the roof can take the strain and bear the weight of a garden. This is something that must be resolved by a qualified surveyor. Roofs tend to be exposed to the wind, and often also to others' view if there are higher buildings around. Unless you are lucky enough to have a decent parapet to which you can fix a windbreak you will have to take advice about this matter too. Then there is the question of access, which makes bringing plants and materials to the site quite a challenge. The materials used on the roof will almost certainly have to be lightweight and easily portable, partly in order to convey them there and partly because there will probably be weight restrictions in force. When laying a surface you will have to make sure that rainwater can still run off the roof and drain away as before, and that it will not get trapped and cause damage (for example, it is not a good idea to fix decking bearers crosswise against the "fall" or incline of the roof where they will impede the run-off of rainwater).

Lightweight solutions

Light asbestos slabs (perfectly safe), lightweight decking in pressure-treated timber, gravel or stone chippings are all possible materials for the roof surface in preference to heavy stone or concrete paving. Screening for privacy, enclosure, and shelter should be strongly constructed and heavy-duty to withstand the buffeting of the wind

▶ Balconies have comparable problems, and solutions, to roofs on a smaller scale.

and must be securely fixed and bolted to the walls to insure your safety. A built-in store for tools and barbecue equipment will be welcome to save hauling things in and out. A convenient water supply will be necessary as planting soil mix will dry out quickly in this situation—it may be possible to install a rainwater tank on the roof, against a wall to take the weight, but automatic or semiautomatic irrigation will be necessary.

Plant containers can be fiberglass, plastic, or aluminum, as well as timber, and if necessary they can be bracketed to the perimeter wall so that their weight isn't transferred to the roof surface. Because of weight limits lightweight soil mix will be needed for planting.

Enjoying your position

If, as often in older houses, the roof is at second-floor level over a back extension, with the house wall behind it, a patio can be created by building a timber frame bolted to the wall. Plants can be grown over this frame to make a green shady place to sit beneath.

Basking on a roof can make you feel rather smug—a bit like being on horseback and talking down to people on foot. Getting a bird's eye view of the neighborhood is bound to make you feel one-up. So when possible, enjoy this by maintaining a sense of height and keeping the view, if only in part, by using strong, open trellis. And if you place plant containers along the top of a parapet wall they must be securely fixed to the parapet and carefully watered to make sure there is no danger of their falling off and injuring, or dripping onto, anyone below.

◀ Screened for privacy and shelter, this roof makes good use of lightweight timber for decking and fitted seating.

designer's roof garden

A roof garden is the perfect get-away-from-it-all solution for city dwellers. Relatively private, it can be a pleasant retreat for weekend breakfasts, summer sunbathing or drinks parties. Or it can be a simple space for a few containers positioned just outside a window where you can reach them for watering.

▲ *This small roof-top needs work and a good safety rail, but its stunning view over the countryside lends the area great potential.*

GARDEN DATA

location:	▪▪	New Jersey
climate:	▪▪	mild temperate
soil type:	▪▪	n/a
direction:	▪▪	north facing
aspect:	▪▪	open rooftops

The brief

The offices of a small family-owned company are two floors above ground level in the center of a busy coastal town. Although it's exposed to strong salt-laden winds the staff decided to utilize this small flat roof as a garden space, to be enjoyed from inside the building and to add variety and interest to the views of the town roofscape and country beyond.

The design solution

We chose tough, woven, polyethylene netting to form a perfect lightweight windbreak that allows light through to the plants but protects them from strong winds. A "crazy log" floor makes a perfect decorative surface for this roof and lets air circulate beneath the containers. Galvanized buckets make great planters—we drilled holes for drainage, painted the buckets the steely blues and greens of the nearby sea and grouped them around the roof space. They were then planted

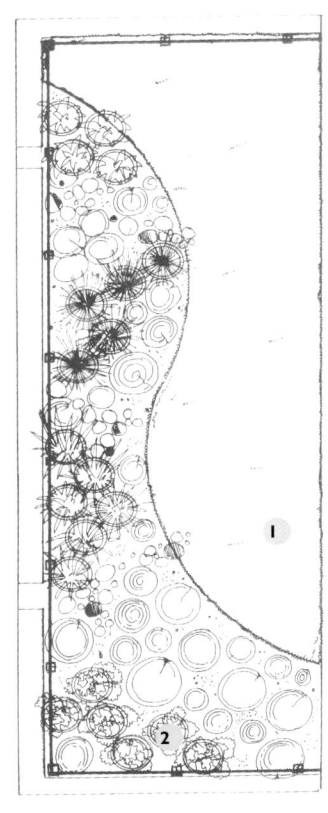

– 9m x 4m/30ft x 12ft –

with phormiums, eryngiums, seakale, easy-care grasses to catch the breeze, and sedums. We set the containers among scattered white beach cobbles. For summer flowering we included white pelargoniums and for fun, you could add a windsock or flag.

▲ *Plastic or galvanized buckets make smart and lightweight containers.*

▲ *Artificial turf provides light, hard-wearing flooring.*

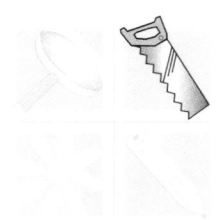

practical projects

Most roof gardens are likely to be exposed and windy. They are also by their nature "built" gardens to be used as outdoor rooms—very private spaces that are as much used for living as for gardening. Providing shelter as a windbreak and to give you privacy will be a key priority.

▲ *A bamboo, hazel, or willow screen will help camouflage safety rails as well as providing an effective and attractive windbreak.*

Boundary materials

Your windbreak should be at least 1m/3ft high and firmly fixed with wire or staples to stout posts which must be bolted to the roof parapet. Black or green net creates the least visual impact for neighboring buildings. If you fancy something wacky and the town planners don't mind you can use barrier netting of the type seen on construction sites. Bamboo, hazel, or willow screens make extremely attractive windbreaks, with sufficient support, but need to be replaced every five years or so.

Surfaces

Make sure there is a slight slope away from the building to a drainage gully, which must be kept clear of debris and which should run to a stormwater downpipe. Now use your imagination. Make a grassy roof with artificial turf, or play-surface matting which comes in a range of bright colors. It can be cut to fill the space or to make patterns and glued to the roof. A simple, elegant surface is easily made with modular decking tiles laid amongst pale stone chippings, no more than 5cm/2in in depth. The ultimate roof garden has a

BUYING ADVICE

If you buy plants at the garden center or nursery, there are a number of things to look out for. Check the leaves for signs of pests or disease (left), avoid plants that have moss growing on the container because they have been in it for too long, and if possible check that the roots are healthy (right).

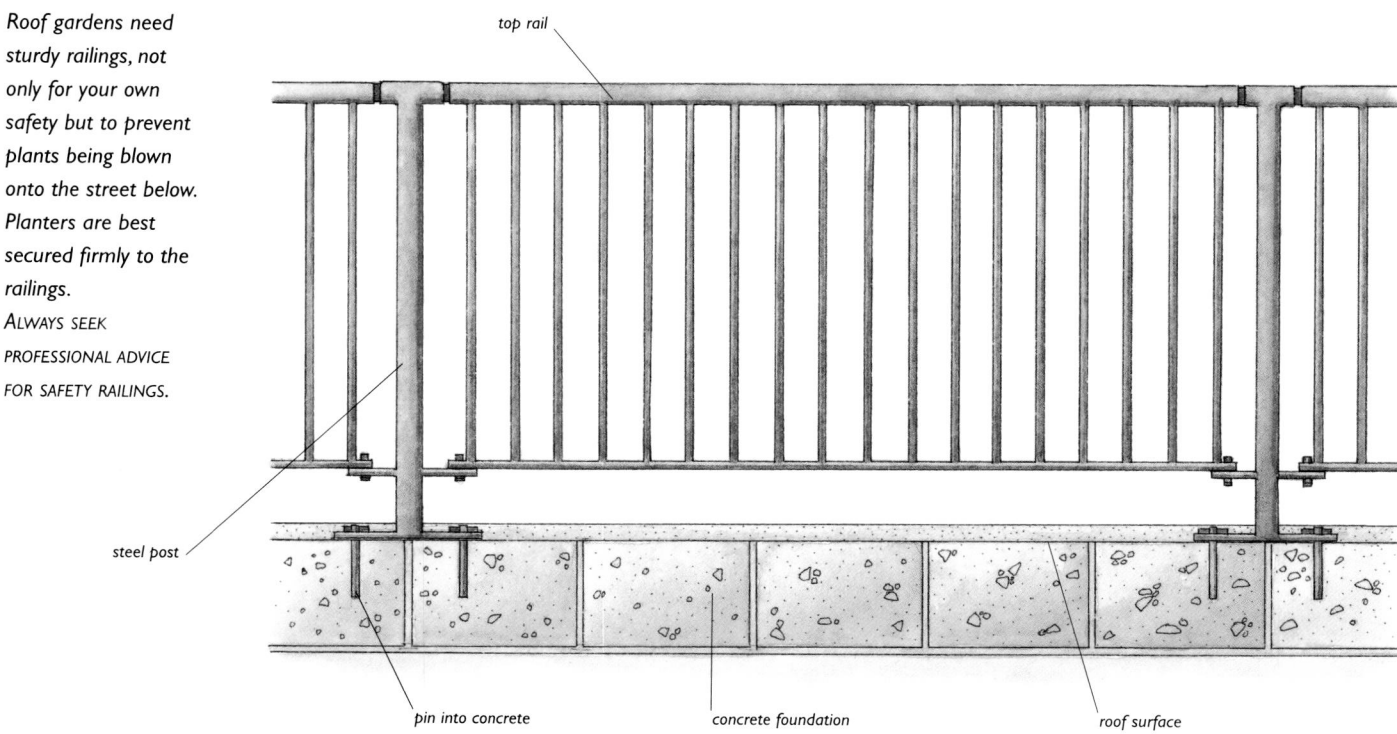

Roof gardens need sturdy railings, not only for your own safety but to prevent plants being blown onto the street below. Planters are best secured firmly to the railings. ALWAYS SEEK PROFESSIONAL ADVICE FOR SAFETY RAILINGS.

top rail

steel post

pin into concrete

concrete foundation

roof surface

real turf surface that grows wild flowers, but this requires professional assessment and installation. You also have to be nifty with a pair of scissors, to keep it shorn.

Now choose your containers. Ideally these should be of plastic or galvanized metal, rather than heavy terracotta or stone which may also be susceptible to cracking in icy weather. Choose plain, simple shapes. Select larger pots than you think each plant will need. This allows room to line the insides of the pots with moss before planting, to help keep the roots cool during hot weather. Add perlite to the soil mix to reduce weight.

DESIGNER'S TIPS

- A good windbreak protects plants over a distance at least five times its height.

- Choose lightweight, but strong materials. Buy a lightweight soil mix specially designed for roof and balcony gardens. Trees are OUT!

- Make sure you can reach your plants to water them. Better still, install automatic irrigation, so no one has to take on the job of plant monitor.

- Light your office roof garden to cheer up dark winter afternoons. One or two uplights are enough for a small space.

◄ *Safety railings are essential for all balconies and roof gardens. This simple metal wire rail fits in perfectly with the balcony's metallic design.*

roof plants and planting

A roof-top site is likely to be exposed to every kind of weather. So, even with a windbreak, a choice of resilient plants will be a priority. And the roof will probably be open to the sun too, so include some sun-lovers and plants such as grasses, which respond beautifully to breezes on sunny days.

Plants for sun and wind

Resourcefulness is required when planting a roof garden. You want to make the most of what is usually a small and inaccessible space and you are likely to want low-maintenance plants so that you can spend more time sitting in the garden than tending plants. Whatever you choose it's as well to accept from the outset that you will probably have to do more replacing of plants here than in any other type of garden.

Many herbs enjoy an open, light and sunny spot. Thymes, lavenders, rosemary in particular thrive in such a position. Plants for dry and well-drained soils, including some grasses, broom or gorse, are also ideal. Plants that are too tall will catch the wind except in a sheltered corner so it's best to choose lower-growing varieties rather than risk top-heavy plants toppling over (light grasses, however, such as *Stipa gigantea* should be safe as the wind is filtered through them). The best way to make variations in height is through planters of different sizes or standing on stepped stands, and these should be placed mainly around the roof edges unless you are sure the structure is sound enough to bear the weight of pots placed centrally.

SUITABLE ROOF PLANTS

Allium flavum—low-growing, yellow, summer-flowering allium
ht 30cm/12in
Buddleja davidii varieties (buddleja)
(see page 245)
ht to 3m/10ft
Crambe maritima (seakale) (see page 239)
ht 75cm/ 30in
Kniphofia (red hot poker) (see page 242)
ht 90cm–1.8m/3–6ft
Santolina chamaecyparissus (cotton lavender)
gray-green mounds with buttony yellow flowers
ht 50cm/20in
Pleioblastus pygmaeus var. *distichus* (pigmy bamboo)—short, very leafy green bamboo
ht to 90cm/3ft
Sedum spectabile (sedum or ice plant)
(see page 244)
ht 45cm/18in
Stipa gigantea (giant feather grass)
(see pages 156–157)
ht 1.8–2.5m/6–8ft
See also plants for seaside gardens,
pages 178–179

◀ Eryngium x oliverianum, *sea holly.*

188

▶ Pennisetum alopecuroides 'Hameln'.

Profile plants

Eryngium × oliverianum
ERYNGIUM

Eryngiums or sea hollies are excellent plants for a roof garden as their architectural, branching stems filter the wind and the spiky bracts which surround their cone-shaped flower heads look good in strong light. *Eryngium × oliverianum* has particularly frosted-looking stems, bracts, leaves, and flowers in silvery blue, sometimes purple-tinted. Flowers during the whole summer.

ht 90cm/3ft
sp 45cm/18in
Soil and situation
Poor, well-drained soil, sunny situation.

Pennisetum alopecuroides varieties
FOUNTAIN GRASS

These grasses have many varieties suitable for roof-tops because of their dense, low, mound-forming growth and undemanding nature. The feathery bottle-brush flowers rustle over narrow arching leaves all summer. In 'Hameln', a compact form, the flowers begin in early summer and the leaves become golden yellow in the fall as the flowers turn from white to a soft grayish brown. 'Bunny' is another variety to look out for.

ht 60cm–1.5m/2–5ft
sp 60cm–1.2m/2–4ft
Soil and situation
Light, well-drained but fairly fertile soil, in a sunny situation.

◀ Phormium tenax, *a hardy, strong plant.*

Phormium species
PHORMIUM

Given a sunny, warm situation phormiums are tough as old boots and there are several good, smaller species of this striking architectural plant. *Phormium cookianum* is the mountain flax, normally with yellowy green coloring, but the hybrid 'Maori Sunrise' has apricot and pink stripes and bronze outer edges to its leaves. The species *P. tenax* itself is something of a giant, but 'Bronze Baby' is a dwarf hybrid with bronze-colored leaves which turn downward at the tips. 'Dazzler' has leaves striped red, orange, and pink.

ht and sp to 2m/6ft;
75cm/30in ('Bronze Baby')
Soil and situation
Well-drained but fairly fertile soil in a sunny situation.

design alternatives

SKETCHES

Roof gardens are ideally suited for strong, innovative designs. Here our designer has employed different surface materials, and foliage-interest plants.

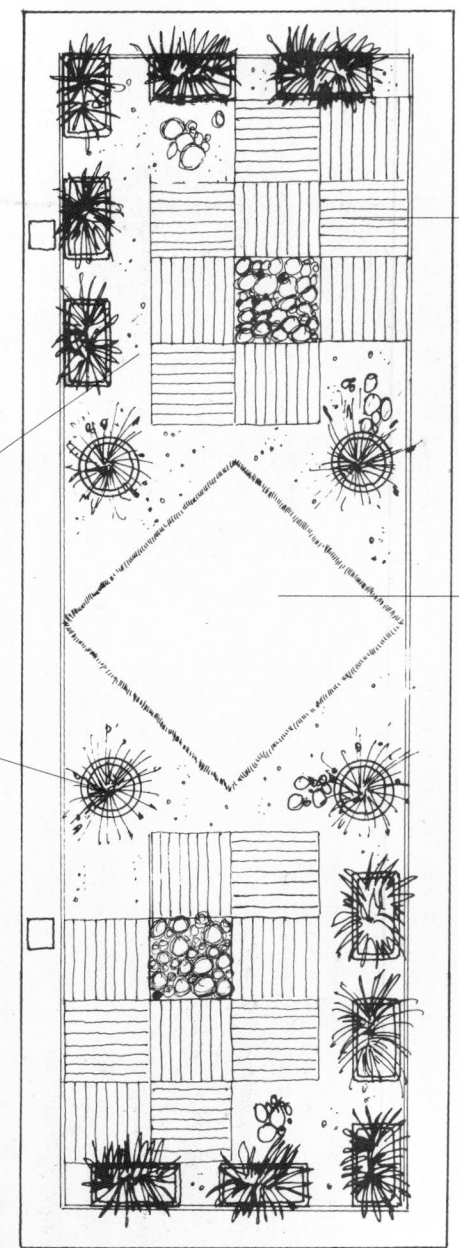

modular decking boards (available from building supply stores)

20mm/¾in stone chippings with scattered beach cobbles

artificial turf

matching containers planted with a variety of grasses (automatic irrigation needed)

*a minimalist
garden for a
shady roof space*

fine raked gravel or
additional shade plants

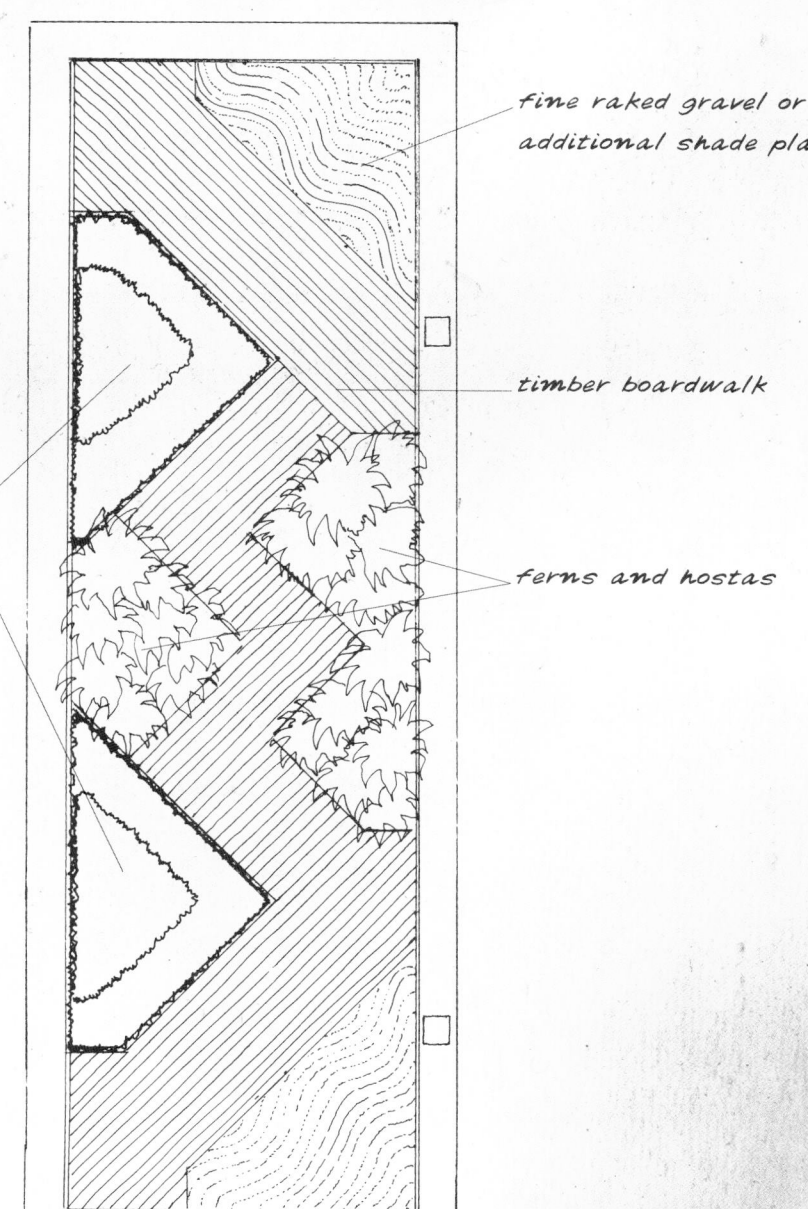

timber boardwalk

"tables" of clipped box or yew,
400 mm/15 in within higher
protective hedges:
600mm/24in

ferns and hostas

patio garden

A patio is not necessarily an enclosed garden, but is best if sheltered for privacy and protected from drafts. There is no reason for a patio to be at the back of the house. If the front garden is warm and sunny, and you enjoy some privacy from the neighbors, why not make that your outdoor room?

Outdoor living

Ideally the patio garden will be right next to the house, preferably situated so that you can spill out on to it and use it as an extension to a living room or dining room. Because you want to use it for sunbathing and for outdoor eating it will have a great deal in common with a sunny seashore garden and with sheltered courtyard gardens. You don't have to devote your whole garden to a patio, but if the plot is small this may well be an ideal design solution.

A patio garden is perfect for people who are too busy to spend a great deal of time on the garden and who want to use it mainly as living space. The area should have a firm surface, and at least part of this should be suitable for furniture. A pebbled patio is not usually very successful as chairs and tables can't stand on it properly. The best choices are paving, brickwork, or timber decking, which makes a pleasant surface for sunbathing and is less unforgiving when plates and glasses are dropped on it. Whatever you choose, the surface is going to be a major investment in this type of garden, and it's wise to consider carefully which is best for you. In a large area you might like to vary the materials used, and provide planting space between stone slabs or bricks, or in gravel to avoid too hard a look.

◄ *Providing places for plants in the patio will soften the overall effect of this garden which can easily be dominated by the hard patio materials.*

◄ *Established planting at the front of the house provides shelter from wind and prying eyes.*

Equipping your patio

Enjoy planning your barbecue equipment and patio furniture. In the long run it is generally best to make a serious investment and get well-designed tables and chairs that look good and will last well. If you buy hardwood, cast-iron, or good-quality aluminum furniture you can leave it out in all weathers. Wood will need oiling every year and metal furniture may need painting occasionally, but both will enhance your garden and age well. If you buy plastic you will need somewhere to store it during the winter—and it doesn't have the same style. Resin café tables and chairs are a possible alternative and pack away neatly for winter storage.

Cooking outdoors

If you expect to be having frequent meals outdoors, consider building a barbecue into a wall on the patio as part of the design. This may be a job for a qualified builder. However, a

free-standing barbecue, in materials that blend with walls or floor surfaces, is within a confident home improver's scope. The essential ingredients are a back and two sides, with a burning rack raised above ground level so that air can feed the fire, and a cooking rack above it. The

rack should be about 90cm/3ft high for comfort, and should be wide enough to have areas at each side that are not directly above the fire, so that cooked food can be pushed to the side to keep warm. The side walls should be wide enough to hold utensils, food supplies and perhaps plates. A shallow pit below the burning area will help to prevent ashes blowing about the patio. However, a fixed barbecue may be unsightly in winter.

Whatever the design of your barbecue, it should not be placed beneath overhanging trees, or close to shrubs or flowers, which might catch fire. Ideally it will be close to the kitchen so that supplies can be kept refrigerated until they are needed and easily conveyed to the cooking area.

Lighting will enhance the patio at night (see pages 142–143 for more information). And, without spoiling the atmosphere, it's a good idea to make sure that the area around the barbecue and the path to and from the kitchen are well lit for safety. These safety lights can always be turned off for romantic dining by candlelight or lamplight.

◄ *A patio can provide privacy or a romantic retreat. This tucked away corner is an example of a covered patio space.*

designer's patio garden

A front patio makes an instant statement about a house and its owners. It is the setting in which visitors first view the house and welcoming area. It is also usually less private than the back garden and should therefore be simply designed, in harmony with the style and materials of the house, secure and easily maintained.

▲ *This front patio garden leaves much to be desired, especially as there is no back garden to compensate.*

GARDEN DATA

location:	▪▪ *Connecticut*
climate:	▪▪ *temperate*
soil type:	▪▪ *neutral*
direction:	▪▪ *east facing*
aspect:	▪▪ *partially shaded*

The brief

This small space, bounded by low brick walls, typifies the size of many front gardens on housing estates. In this instance the developers have used cheap materials and mixed several different colors, shapes, and textures together to make an uninspired and unwelcoming garden, which does not relate at all to the attractive mews-style house it fronts. Although there is not much of it, the existing planting is unharmonious and out of scale with the house. As there is no back garden this tiny area must double for its owners as somewhere to sit and relax.

The design solution

We liked the gray stone setts that are used to pave the private roadway to this small development and decided to echo them by using similar small unit setts to replace the existing concrete slabs. Instead of paving wall to wall we left a generous border for planting and varied the surface

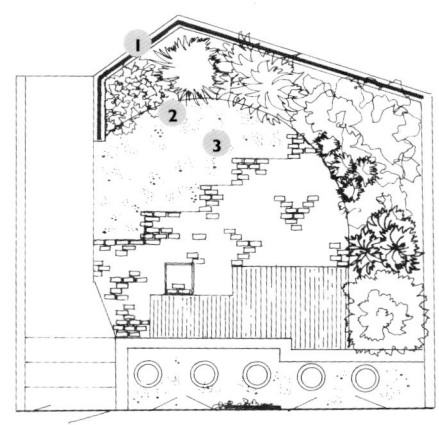

— 7m x 6m / 22ft x 19ft —

texture by introducing creamy white stone chippings. These also define the shape of the paved area. Close to the house we laid a timber deck, which provides a small seating area bounded by brightly-colored plants in containers. In colder weather it can be used as a stage for winter-flowering violas and heathers in carefully grouped containers. We erected neat, timber, picket fencing along the front boundary wall, to afford some privacy without casting dense shade. The planting is simple—fragrant, white flowering climbers and lush, leafy, evergreen foliage, with vivid splashes of hot color.

fence

▶ Hostas thrive in a
shady area.

hostas

▲ Planting helps create privacy.

chippings

▶ Stone chippings
complement the pale paving.

practical projects

Timber decking is a versatile and practical complement to many garden styles. It looks at home in formal and informal situations and can be contemporary or traditional, depending on how it is used. It mixes well with many other materials and is a sympathetic foil to planting.

Types of decking

The simplest decking is made from planks supported by joists, themselves resting on bearers of timber or brick. Ready-to-assemble kits are available, as well as framed squares that can be simply bedded on sand.

Raised decking must be very strongly constructed and is not a construction job for the inexperienced. Built on joists over foundation posts secured to concrete pads it can be attached to the house wall by a timber wall-plate.

Use pressure-treated softwood, which can be painted or stained and varnished. Always use timber which is suitable for your garden design, which comes from renewable sources, and is produced with minimal harm to the environment.

PICKET FENCING

To assemble your fence place the arris rails on a flat surface and lay the pales over them. Make sure that the pales are evenly spaced and nail them to the rails. Now nail to the supporting uprights (set about 1.9m/6ft 6in and 2.7m/9ft apart), driving in two nails per arris rail. Use a level to check rails are horizontal.

To form a right-angled corner fix the rails so that one side of the corner overlaps those on the other side of the corner. Then drive a long nail through the overlapping rail to the end of the overlapped rail so the join will not part.

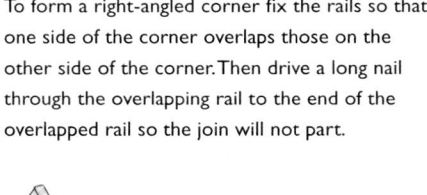

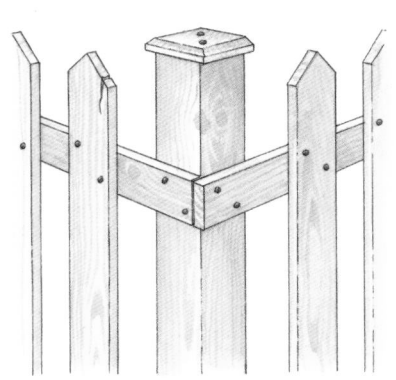

Below are four common styles of pales.

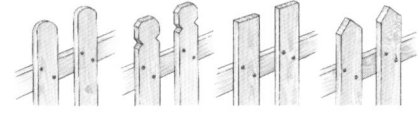

building a deck

A raised deck attached to the house makes a seating area for adults or, with a safety rail around it, a play area for children.

1 The posts which support the deck must be set in concrete. It does not matter if the ground is uneven, as the posts can be cut to different heights to insure that the finished deck is level. Correct spacing is important, however, if the weight is to be spread evenly. Place the concrete pads in position and bolt down the metal plate and socket fixings.

2 If the deck is to be secured to the house, attach a timber wallplate to the wall, bolting it securely to the masonry. The plate should be notched to the correct size at regular intervals to take the ends of the deck joists.

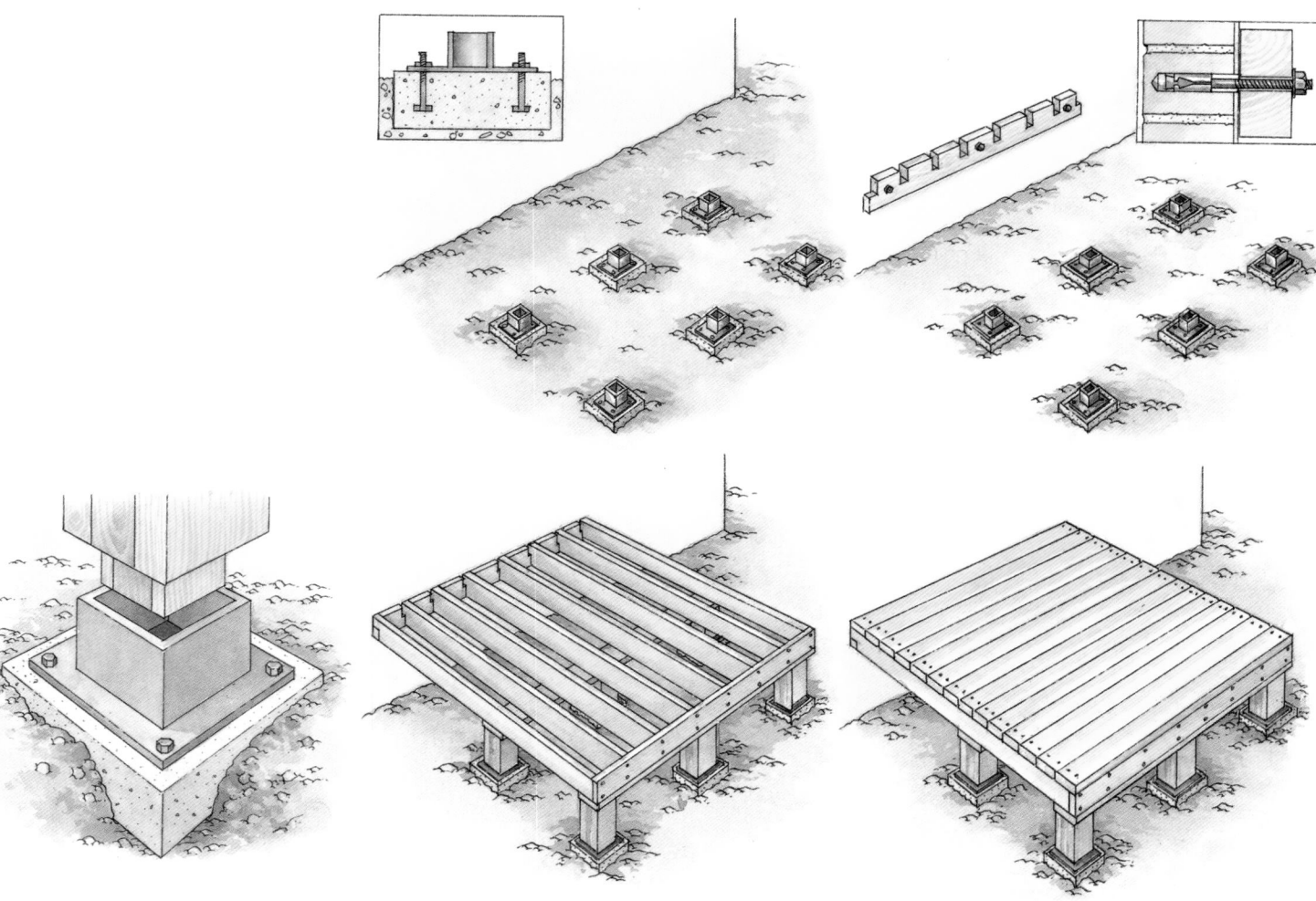

3 Insert the posts into the metal shoes. The base of each post should be cut to fit snugly into the sockets. Shorten the posts to the desired height, if necessary.

4 Attach the outer joists, butt joining them at the corners. Trim the intermediate joists to length and cut notches at one end to fit into the wallplate. Nail or screw them into position.

5 Lay the decking timbers, cut to length, over the joists, with suitable gaps between them of 8–10mm/3–4in to allow excess rainwater to drain through (but not wide enough to cause a hazard). Nail or screw them down using hot-dipped galvanized nails or brass screws. Finish the deck with exterior woodstain.

patio plants and planting

For a good-looking, low-maintenance patio that enhances the house invest in the building and construction, choosing the best materials you can afford, in keeping with the house. Then invest some more in long-lived, evergreen plants that will give shape and interest throughout the entire year.

Plants for form and flowers

Even in a sunny patio, a choice of evergreen shrubs will provide you with shaded areas, and an underplanting of shade-loving plants such as the leafy hostas (see pages 114–115) and ferns (see pp 28–29), and winter- or spring-flowering helle-bores (see page 241) will fit the bill nicely. Foxgloves *(Digitalis purpurea)* will self-seed in semishade, while patches of lady's mantle can spill over on the hard surfacing in sunny areas.

Summer-flowering plants, such as pelargoniums or nasturtiums grown from seed, can be grown in pots near the house for shelter and ease of care and climbing plants such as clematis and jasmine can be grown on trellis up the walls of the house. Most patios will get plenty of sun (or you wouldn't choose to have them where they are) and there are many plants that thrive in these conditions. Plants for roofs and seashore gardens will be suitable for sunny patios too (see pages 178–179 and 188–189).

Profile plants

Choisya ternata
Mexican orange blossom

This is a very glossy evergreen shrub with beautifully scented small white flowers over a long period in late spring and throughout summer, giving it the appearance and fragrance of an orange tree in blossom. The leaves release a pleasant aromatic scent when crushed. Preferring warmth and shelter, but extremely tolerant and needing little or no pruning, these are excellent plants for providing year-round structure and interest. A golden-leaved cultivar, 'Sundance' is also available.

◄ Choisya ternata, *Mexican orange blossom.*

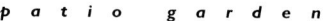
◀ Ilex aquifolium *'J.C. van Tol'*.

Ilex aquifolium 'J.C. van Tol'
HOLLY

When choosing a holly tree for a small garden you need one that is shapely, not too large, and self-fertile so that it will produce berries without a partner. 'J.C. van Tol' is obliging in all these respects and is particularly generous with its bright red berries. It has smooth, beautifully glossy leaves from dark purple stems and a variegated variety, 'Golden van Tol', with yellow-edged leaves is also available. The tree is slim in shape and very hardy, so that it can be used to provide shelter for less robust plants.

ht 3–5.5m / 10–18ft
sp 1.8–3m / 6–10ft
Soil and situation
Ordinary garden soil, preferably with some moisture, and any position, in sun or shade. The variegated form needs sun for best coloring. Tolerates polluted city air.

---

ht to 1.8m / 6ft
sp to 2.5m / 8ft
Soil and situation
Ordinary, well-drained garden soil, and a position in sun or partial shade. In colder areas *Choisya* does best against a sheltering wall. Cutting off any frost-damaged shoots in spring encourages new shoots to grow.

Mahonia × media 'Charity'
MAHONIA

The mahonias are useful low-maintenance plants well suited to a patio garden and rewarding anyone who plants them with lily-of-the-valley-scented flowers in winter or early spring, depending on the variety. 'Charity' flowers all winter, with long racemes of small yellow flowers in plentiful bunches. Glossy, dark-green, rather holly-like leaves make the plant attractive when it's not in flower and blue-black berries follow on from the flowers.

ht to 3m / 10ft
sp to 2.5m / 8ft
Soil and situation
Although tolerant, mahonia prefers humus-rich, moisture-retaining soil and a position in light shade; the plant will brave some wind and winter exposure.

▶ *Winter-flowering* Mahonia x media *'Charity'*.

PLANTS FOR SUNNY PATIOS

These plants all like dry, sunny situations. Those marked * can be grown between paving stones or in gaps in brickwork to soften the hard surface.

Armeria maritima (sea thrift)—tufts of grey-green leaves; bright pink summer flowers ht 20cm/8 in
Cortaderia 'Gold Band' (syn. *C.* 'Aureolineata')—grass with gold-margined leaves; ht 1.8m/6ft
Euphorbia characias (see page 240)
Lavandula species* (see page 242)
Kniphofia caulescens (see page 242)
Phormium cookianum ssp. *hookeri* 'Cream Delight' and *P. tenax*—tough, sword-like leaves ht to 1.8–3.6m/6–12ft
Santolina species* (cotton lavender) – silver-grey leaves and tiny yellow flowers ht 30-80cm/12–32 in
Sedum spectabile (see page 244)
Yucca filamentosa and *Y. gloriosa* (yucca) sword-like leaves ht to 75cm/30 in

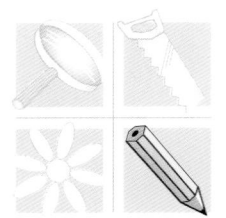

design alternatives

SKETCHES

These two alternatives make use of mixed shrub and perennial planting. We chose materials for the hard-landscaping and retaining walls that complemented the brickwork and architectural style of the house.

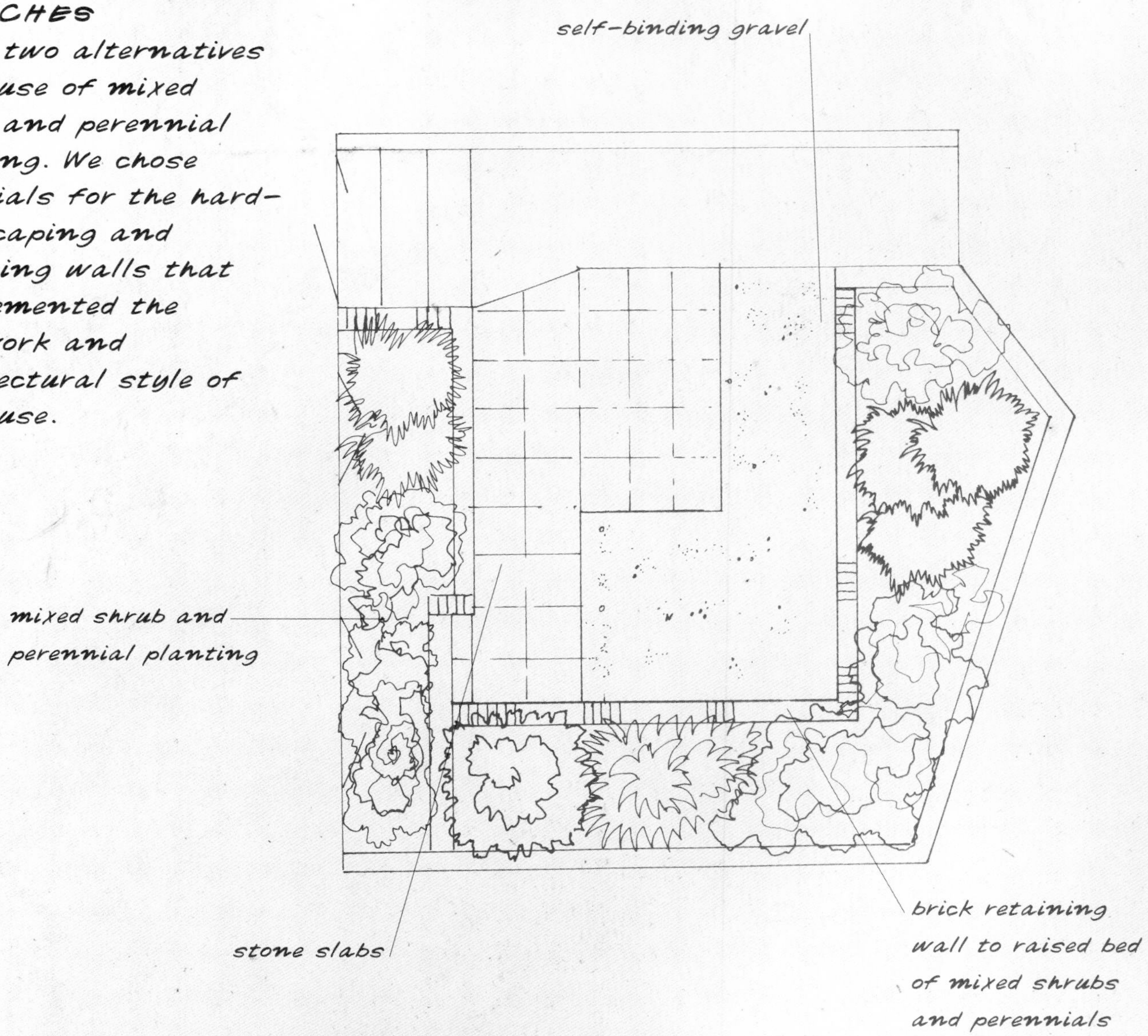

self-binding gravel

mixed shrub and perennial planting

stone slabs

brick retaining wall to raised bed of mixed shrubs and perennials

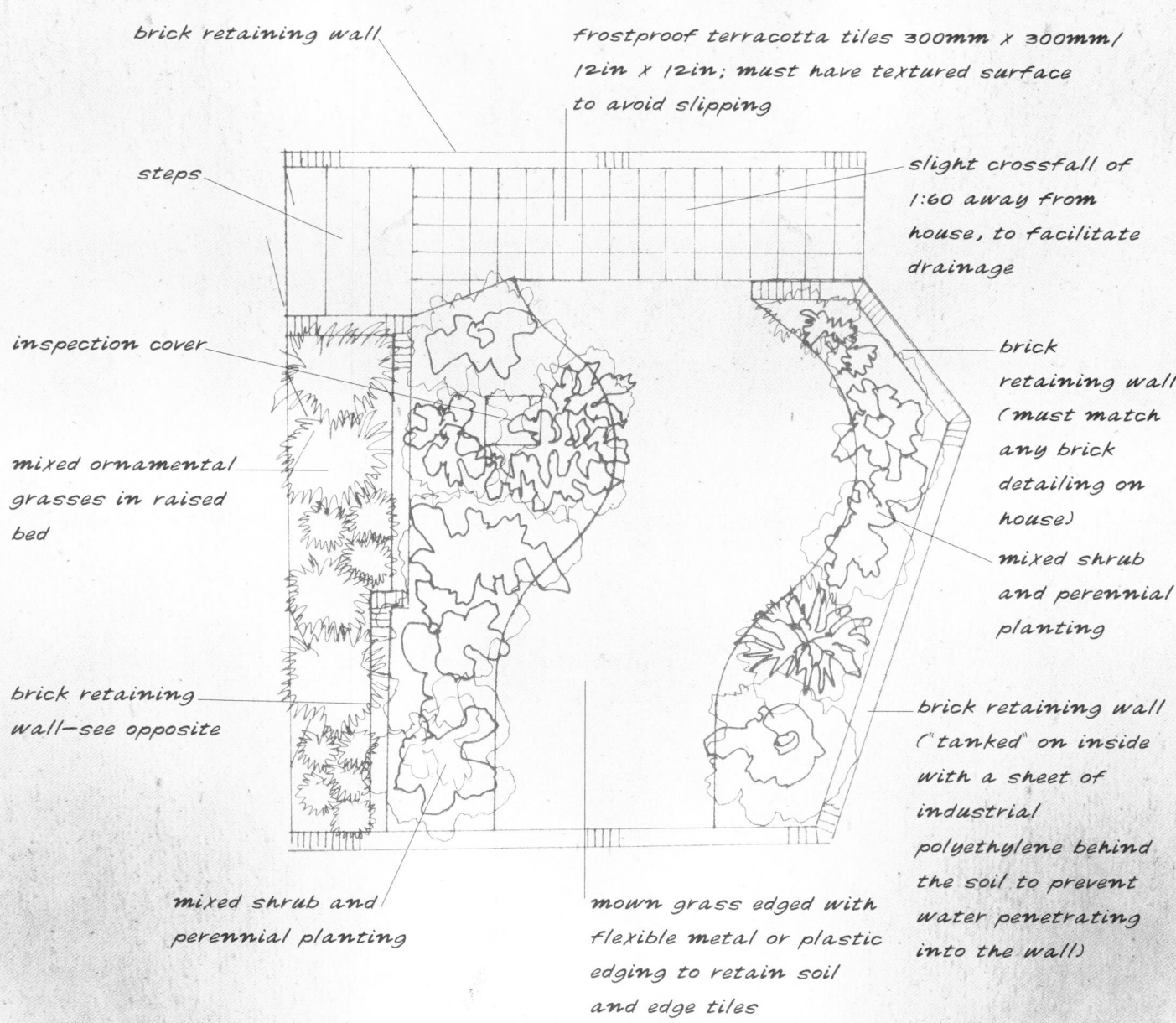

brick retaining wall

frostproof terracotta tiles 300mm x 300mm/
12in x 12in; must have textured surface
to avoid slipping

steps

slight crossfall of
1:60 away from
house, to facilitate
drainage

inspection cover

brick
retaining wall
(must match
any brick
detailing on
house)

mixed ornamental
grasses in raised
bed

mixed shrub
and perennial
planting

brick retaining
wall—see opposite

brick retaining wall
("tanked" on inside
with a sheet of
industrial
polyethylene behind
the soil to prevent
water penetrating
into the wall)

mixed shrub and
perennial planting

mown grass edged with
flexible metal or plastic
edging to retain soil
and edge tiles

seasonal gardens

Gardening is partly about enjoying the seasons. And while winter slips mysteriously into spring, spring into summer, and time never stands still completely, there are still marked pauses—in summer and in winter—when for a season we can enjoy a garden that is almost unchanging.

summer garden

Most gardens are at their best in summer, but unless they are well planned their glories can be surprisingly fleeting. And while there is a riot of summer-flowering plants on offer you need to be disciplined in using them if your garden is not to look like a not very exciting patchwork quilt.

◄ *The majority of plants flower in summer, insuring that the garden will be a rainbow of color and scent.*

A garden for summer

There could be many good reasons for choosing to make a summer garden—apart from wintering abroad. When you first move into a house you may want to give the garden you inherit a year to see what it has to offer—in terms of plants and general advantages and disadvantages—before laying in with a spade or weedkiller. You may be on a budget and have very little to spend on perennial plants and shrubs. You may want to lay out the basic structure of the garden bit by bit as you can afford it and fill in with temporary color meanwhile. Or you may simply be a sun-loving person who chooses to hibernate in winter.

If you have a sunny garden your choice may be to concentrate on making it a blaze of color during the summer in "hot border" style. In other situations a gentle blur of softer

◄ *Summer gardens can be full of color. Whatever your taste, there is a huge choice of summer-flowering plants to choose from.*

chippings, or paving. Pots and containers can stand on such surfaces to give extra interest and contribute solid shapes to the scheme.

At the end of the season you can have a great clear-up, digging or forking over the areas between any permanent plants, putting into store any containers that are not frost-proof and any bulbs that are not hardy. Spread bought or home-made compost or manure on the soil, especially around shrubs; plant out wallflowers and biennials; take in your pelargoniums; plant bulbs outdoors and in containers; and put the garden to bed for the winter.

colors may be your aim. In either case, since buying plants can be expensive, consider growing annuals and biennials from seed. Most of the plants we buy as bedding plants can be grown relatively easily at home in a small greenhouse or mini-greenhouse against a house wall. Many traditional favorites can be sown directly into the ground, either in spring as the earth warms up, or in the fall for an earlier display and stronger plants the following year. Biennials, or plants grown as such (such as the aquilegias and verbascums in our summer garden), are usually sown in the summer of the year before they flower, and renewed every year. In a summer garden you will be able to plant them out in the same fall as you tidy up the garden for the end of the season and the start of winter.

A place to sit

Using your garden mainly in summer may also mean devoting a great deal of it to a patio or sitting area, and this also cuts down on the work of gardening. A patio by the house still has advantages of convenience if you want to use it for cooking and eating, but a sheltered place to sit and read, doze, or dream somewhere farther away will be an asset in summer. A sitting area that gets the morning or evening sun is ideal.

For the sitting area it's best to use hard surfaces, as the lawn soon gets thin and brown if it's over-used. And although a green lawn is a good foil for summer borders, plants that enjoy conditions in a dry garden generally look better surrounded by gravel,

▶ *Spires of pale foxgloves in a shadier, patio area will bring a cool note to the color scheme of a summer garden.*

designer's summer garden

A summer garden sacrifices year-round color and structure in order to be at its glorious best for just a few months of the year. Sumptuous flowers and fragrances assail the senses only briefly, but provide memories of long summer days spent lazing in the garden that will sustain you through the dark winter evenings.

▲ *This small garden must exploit its natural attributes, brick walls and a strawberry tree, with the minimum economic requirements.*

GARDEN DATA

location:	East Long Island
climate:	mild/temperate
soil type:	neutral
direction:	east facing
aspect:	open

Design brief

This tiny garden belongs to first-time home owners who are furnishing and decorating their home on a shoestring budget. It is an almost empty plot but has two valuable features: a 1.5m/5ft brick wall which, although neglected, encloses and shelters the garden, and a young *Arbutus unedo*, 'strawberry tree'. This beautiful tree is evergreen, has sensational, coppery, peeling bark, clusters of white, scented flowers and edible fruits. We recommend that in any summer garden you do not abandon evergreen planting altogether, because a large, bare patch of earth can look very dreary unless it is supported by some strong shapes of trees or shrubs.

Design solution

We chose very simple, geometric shapes that would allow the garden to be constructed as economically as possible. Unfussy lines define the broad flower borders without

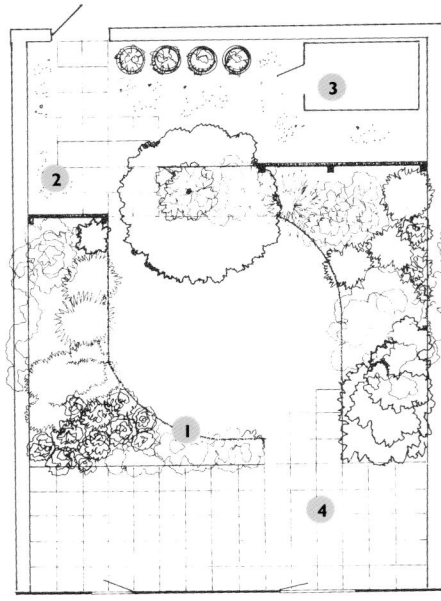

– 10m x 7m / 32ft x 22ft –

distracting from their show of color. We used basic materials: regular sized, natural colored paving slabs laid to exact measurements, to avoid cutting; tanalized timber trellis, and stone chippings to match the paving. The walls were repointed where necessary and coated with masonry paint in a shade of warm cream. The planting is in rich reds, yellows, orange, creamy whites, and blues, with silver-gray and green foliage.

tomatoes ②

▲ *This sunny corner is ideal for tomatoes.*

summerhouse ③

▲ *A summerhouse is a perfect retreat.*

border ①

patio ④

▶ *A low-level summer border allows views of the lawn.*

▶ *Patio has room for table and chairs.*

207

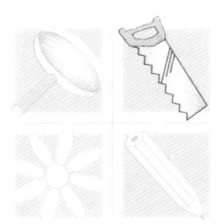

practical projects

Once the paving has been laid, the walls painted, and the screening fixed, our summer garden relies a great deal for its effect on annuals and short-lived plants, grown from seed. Container planting is also a major feature, with summer plants from pelargoniums (geraniums) to tomatoes, flowering shrubs, herbs, and bulbs.

If you enjoy being in the garden on a winter's day, turning the compost pile, and catching up with jobs left over from the fall, including the digging, these are among your projects for a summer garden. You will also be justified in spending evenings in front of the fire, selecting seeds from the catalogs.

When spring comes, it's time to sow annuals as the earth warms up, and then turn your attention to containers. Buy the best you can afford, as cheap terracotta flakes in the frost and needs to be replaced, and cheap plastic looks cheap. A mixture of sizes in a limited range of types usually works better than a jumble or too many pots the same size. You will have to water at least once a day in hot, dry weather—the smaller the container, the more frequently it will need watering. Clay containers lose moisture to the air, while plastic can overheat the roots. Wooden troughs or barrels keep their contents reasonably damp, especially if lined with moss. All containers should have plenty of drainage. Be generous when planting. Three, five, or seven plants of the same kind and color in a medium-sized pot make more impact than the same number of mixed colors.

At the end of the summer remove plants that won't survive the winter and put the potting mix onto the garden or the compost pile. Clean out the container and store for winter. Alternatively, plant with winter-flowering plants or bulbs for spring. Plants which need warmth and shelter can be brought indoors in containers.

▲ *To grow seedlings simply place them in moist soil mix. Cover the tray with glass or clear plastic and leave somewhere light and warm.*

planting a summer container

Planted up in late spring, a container can provide interest throughout the summer if you use long-flowering plants such as pelargoniums, fuchsias, and bedding plants. Be sure to set them off with some reliable foliage plants, such as small-leaved ivies or the trailing *Helichrysum petiolare*.

1 Line the base of the container with crocks, pieces of broken pots or cobbles. You can further improve the drainage by adding a layer of gravel or horticultural grit.

2 Add the soil mix, to about two thirds of the pot's depth. You can lighten the mix by forking in perlite or vermiculite. To cut down on watering later, add water-retaining crystals.

3 Begin to plant the pot with your choice of plants. For the best effect, cram them in. Fill up around each plant with more soil mix. To allow for watering there should be a gap of around 25mm/1in between the top of the pot and the surface of the compost.

4 Add slow-release fertilizer. This is best applied in pelleted form: the nutrients are released gradually over the summer, making further feeding unnecessary.

5 Water the container well. Water regularly throughout the summer, even if you used water-retaining crystals. Containers look best when grouped together rather than dotted singly around the garden.

summer plants and planting

A large part of a summer garden will be used as an outdoor room. The aim is to make the surrounding areas a riot of color—or a gentler haze, depending on the aspect and on your taste—to please the eye. Some permanent planting using shrubs, small trees, or evergreens will help to give a more composed look.

Using summer color

In full summer there are lots of hot or striking colors for drama and excitement in the garden. Strong reds, oranges, and yellows look good in bright light and have a completely different effect when used together than when dotted lightly about. But the effect, though exciting and exotic, can be almost too strong unless you make contrasts or use shades of green, and plants with silver foliage, to tone it down. For this reason it helps to have a lawn to act as a green foil for a hot border. Green from foliage plants helps both to calm what might otherwise seem too bright and to make the transition between colors that don't look good side by side.

Annuals and bedding plants

Growing your own summer plants instead of buying them in trays from the garden center or supermarket not only saves you money—it also gives you the chance to grow superior plants in colors of your choice instead of the standard mixtures. Petunias, impatiens (busy lizzies), tobacco plants, snapdragons, and

◀ Crocosmia 'Lucifer' *is a real eye-catcher.*

many less familiar bedding plants, including lavatera, can all be grown quite easily.

Annuals like the lovely opium poppy (*Papaver somniferum*) don't take kindly to being moved, and need to be sown where they are to grow, and others (including calendula or marigolds) are difficult to buy as plants yet incredibly easy to grow. Biennials such as the verbascums and sweet williams (*Dianthus barbatus*) in our garden are also quite easy to raise from seed. Pelargoniums can be tricky and are probably best raised from plugs (available from garden centers and by mail order).

► *The strawberry tree has attractive fruit.*

Profile plants

Crocosmia 'Lucifer'
MONTBRETIA OR CROCOSMIA

Crocosmias are summer flowers from corms, with flowers like miniature lilies in vibrant oranges and reds and strappy green leaves, revealing their close cousinship with irises. Originating from South Africa crocosmia cultivars now grow in temperate climates all over the world. 'Lucifer' is a deep, bright, fiery red and will quickly form strong, healthy clumps that can be thinned in the fall if they get too big. Their normal height is at the lower end of the scale.

ht 1–1.5m/39in–5ft

sp 8cm/3in

Soil and situation

Crocosmias do well in any well-drained soil, in a sunny position; they like heat and light but must not dry out completely.

Arbutus unedo
STRAWBERRY TREE

The strawberry tree is a rounded, evergreen shrub or small tree with reddish-brown bark and clusters of cream-colored, waxy, bell-shaped, pendent flowers in the fall. The round, bumpy-surfaced fruits redden as they ripen. This takes a year, with fruits maturing as new flowers appear.

ht 4.5m/15ft sp 3m/10ft

Soil and situation

Fertile garden soil preferably and in a warm, sheltered position.

Aquilegia longissima
AQUILEGIA OR COLUMBINE

This elegant version of the country columbine or old maid's bonnets is a lovely pale lemon yellow, and the flowers have unusually long, bright yellow spurs. The flowers are fragrant and the leaves are delicate and ferny. Although it is strictly a perennial it is best grown as a biennial for fresh plants each year.

Aquilegia is fairly easily grown from seed, which should be sown during the fall months.

ht 60–90cm/2–3ft

sp 45cm/18in

Soil and situation

Well-drained soil, including poor

◄ *The long-spurred* Aquilegia longissima.

design alternatives

SKETCHES

Due to the amount of time spent outside in summer, our alternative schemes make good use of patio and seating areas, as well as mown lawn for relaxing. Remember these gardens act as an additional "room" so do not let your planting overtake available space.

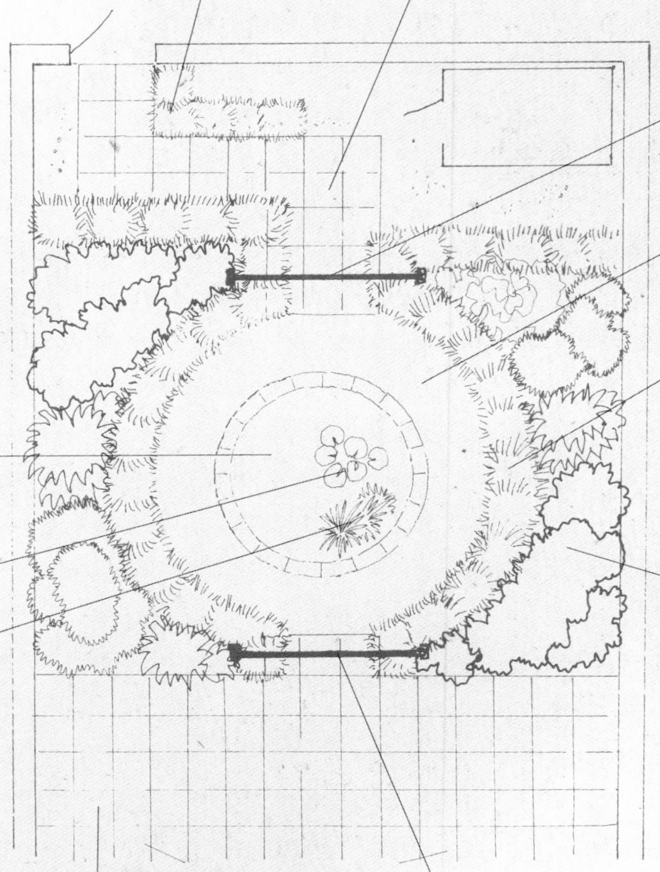

lavender

stone slabs, as below

purchased metal arch

grass

low lavender hedge, approx 400mm/15in high

mixed herbaceous planting—can mirror the planting opposite or move from color to color around the circle

circular pond with stone slab surround

water lilies

Pontederia cordata

regular-shaped stone slabs set as patio, pale cream in color, 450mm x 450mm/18in x 18in

purchased metal arch

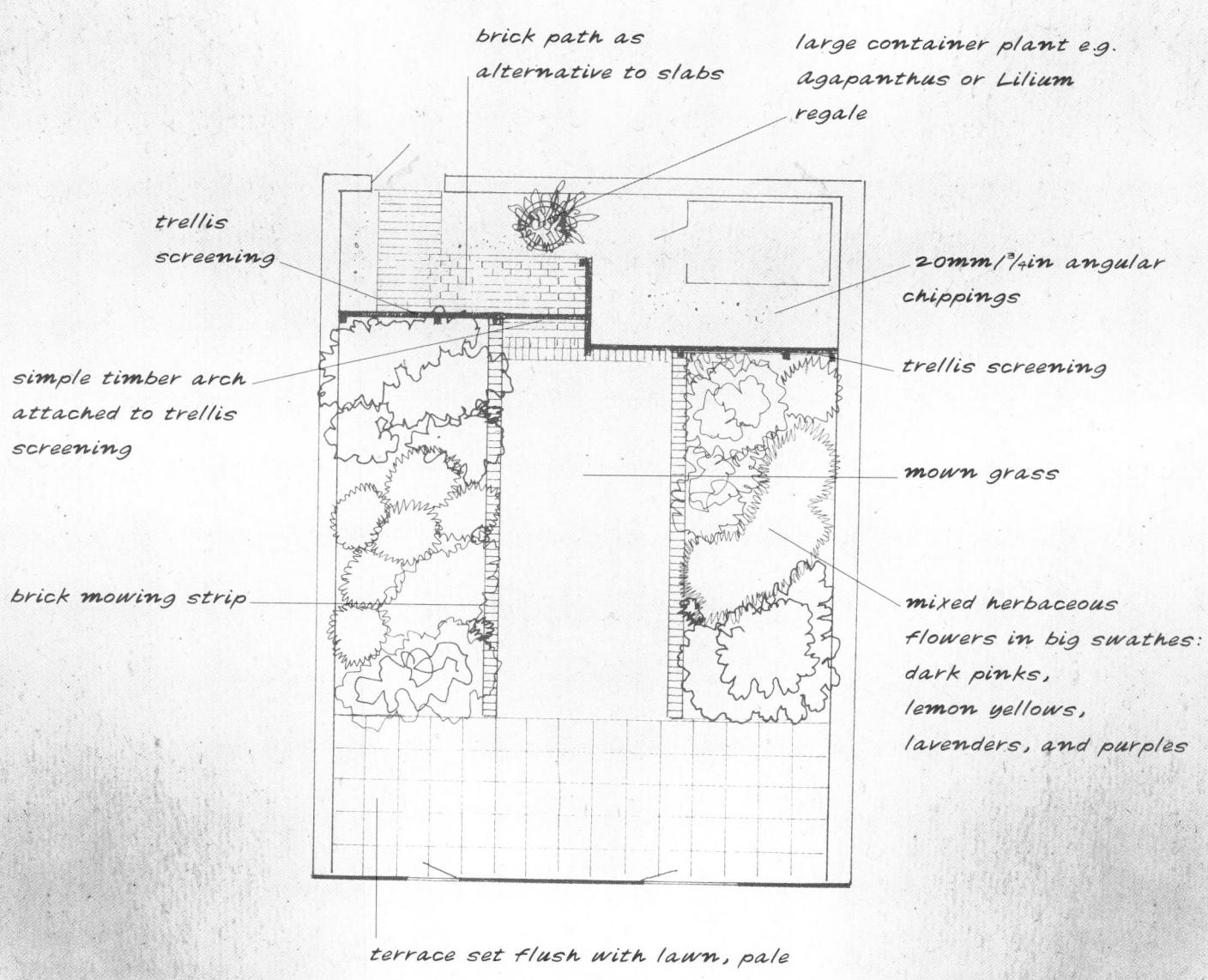

brick path as
alternative to slabs

large container plant e.g.
Agapanthus or Lilium
regale

trellis
screening

20mm/³⁄₄in angular
chippings

simple timber arch
attached to trellis
screening

trellis screening

mown grass

brick mowing strip

mixed herbaceous
flowers in big swathes:
dark pinks,
lemon yellows,
lavenders, and purples

terrace set flush with lawn, pale
creamy regular slabs, 45cm x 45cm/
18in x 18in

winter garden

Winter reveals the essence of your garden. With all the growth of spring and summer stripped away and nothing but the bare bones left there can still be much to please—visually, for example, or from scented plants. Creating a garden for winter can be satisfying and rewarding.

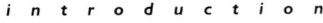

◀ A light covering of snow brings a beautiful change to the garden. Shapes of leaves are highlighted against the cold, blue winter sky.

Designing for winter

Making a winter garden need not be such a challenge, but it does demand more decisiveness from the start than the summer garden because you will need to form a permanent structure that is pleasing in its own right, while in the summer garden you are distracted by temporary color and camouflaging foliage. You can easily make instant changes in summer by moving plants about or adding pot plants where color is needed, and you can always do something different next year.

A winter garden will rely for its structure partly on the layout of paths and any hard-surfaced areas, and the materials used for these can add color and texture. Warmly colored old bricks, for example, will be welcome in the winter light, echoing the shining reds and gentle browns of bare bark. Evergreens are also a key to expressing structure, and an evergreen hedge forms a contrasting backdrop to border plants at any time of year. The beauty of white-stemmed trees such as silver birch is highlighted by an evergreen background, too, as is the color of winter-flowering heathers.

Formality, because of the importance of structure, is at home in a winter garden. While an ivy-covered trellis or well-clipped yew hedge will mark the outline of the garden, other evergreens can make pleasingly formal patterns within it. Box, tightly clipped, may be used as in grand formal gardens to make low hedges in geometric patterns defining planting areas, and rounded bushes of box or bay, or single-stemmed standardized bay trees form strong exclamation marks to emphasize the overall structure.

▶ *Hard-landscaping, topiary, and sculptures become the dominant features in winter, when much of the garden is bare.*

Enjoying winter sun

Keep in mind the direction of the sun's low rays and plan to make the most of any area that gets the brief midday sun. On sunny winter days a sheltered place to sit can be appreciated to the full, if only for an hour. Try to insure that sunlight will be falling onto features such as colorful dogwood stems and dry winter grasses (and, at the same time, that delicate winter-flowering camellias are not sited where they will be hit by early sun as this can cause damage on frosty mornings). Structural planting and the built ingredients in the scheme must act as a backdrop, rather than preventing the precious winter light from shining on plants that need it for

their effect or, indeed, into the house.

Walls, fences, trellis, gates, and pergolas are on display at this time of the year, unless hidden by ivy or evergreens, so need to be chosen with care. Handsome containers come into their own now, as do well-positioned sundials, garden statues, or sculptures—center-stage is often best for winter gardens, which will be mainly viewed from indoors.

Winter visitors

Don't be in too much of a hurry to tidy the garden before the winter. Grasses, seed heads, and architectural plants look magically transformed when picked out with hoar frost or a thin layer of snow, and many provide food for hungry winter birds too. A birdtable in your garden will allow you to appreciate winter visitors from your warm home.

◀ *The attractive railings that surround this garden become an even stronger feature when summer plants die down.*

designer's winter garden

A winter garden shows off structure, texture, and form perhaps more than any other garden. The shapes of plants take on a mysterious beauty when rimmed with hoar frost and you notice the extraordinary skeletons of seed heads and the delicate tracery of branches across a wintry sky.

▲ *Strong shapes, evergreens, and careful planning will be needed if this garden is to make an impact in winter.*

GARDEN DATA

location:	▦ Massachusetts
climate:	▦ mild
soil type:	▦ neutral
direction:	▦ east
aspect:	▦ open

The design brief

The owners of this traditional country cottage want their east-facing front garden to be at its best during the long winter months. Their sitting room overlooks the garden and they envisage cosy log-fire days during which they can observe and enjoy the garden from indoors, or wander out to feed the birds. The site is level and roughly triangular.

The design solution

The garden is shaded during the short winter afternoons but benefits from morning sunshine. To add color we used old brick for the paths, although crazy paving or flagstones would be equally appropriate. We chose strong architectural shapes and some warm colors for the planting, which will be backlit by morning sunlight. The design adopts a more formal approach than we would employ for the larger and more private back garden. The layout counterbalances the strongly

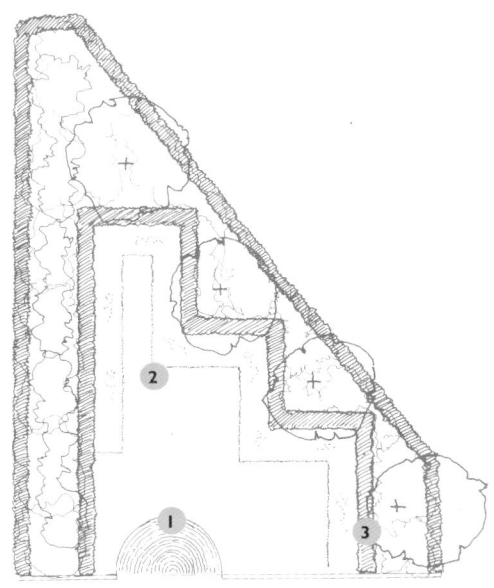

— *18m x 14m/58ft x 46ft* —

triangular shape of the site and incorporates dramatically contrasting planting of tightly clipped evergreens with looser, breezy grasses and perennials. These are selected for their interesting seed heads that are less likely to collapse in a mild and wet winter. We added a bird feeding station, positioned where it can be viewed from indoors.

brick patio

▲ Old bricks make a warm patch of color.

bird table

▲ The birdtable will be a focus of interest.

box hedge

▶ The low box hedge is tightly clipped.

practical projects

For any of a host of reasons you may want to concentrate your gardening efforts and produce a garden mainly for winter, to be enjoyed as you walk through it on your way in and out of the house, and to be viewed mainly from indoors. If so, aim to make a well-structured garden, with plenty of well-used hard materials.

Hard surfaces

If you have lengthy summer vacations away from home, or spend summer weekends walking, swimming, on sailing, or decorating the house, you won't have too much time left over to admire, or work in, the garden at this time of year. Summer gardening may not be for you, so instead spend a weekend or two in the summer setting up the hard-landscaping for your winter garden.

For paths and other hard surfaces it pays to buy the best materials you can afford. In our garden we used carefully laid bricks to make a feature in its own right. Whatever your design, the surface is always going to be on view so good materials are worth the expense.

As for the work involved, care and attention to detail are important: laying hard surfaces takes time, but no over-demanding skills are required, and what you save by supplying your own labor you can spend on the materials.

PLANTING TREES

Fall to spring is the best time to plant. Start by digging a hole large enough to take the root-ball with space to spare for well-rotted manure and compost.

Using a stick laid across make sure the root-ball is level, then knock in the stake without damaging the roots. Add the soil, firm well with your boot, then water.

Secure the tree trunk to the stake with an adjustable tie so that the tree won't rock in the wind. Remember to check growth regularly and loosen the tie.

If your design has straight lines make sure they really are straight. If a geometric feature (such as our circle of bricks) is used be sure of your geometry, and if you use curves in an informal scheme make sure the curves are pleasing (try them out using a hosepipe filled with water, doing this on a warm day, when it will be easier to manipulate).

Bricks and crazy paving need to be carefully and neatly laid but neither needs to be set in concrete. They can be laid on a level bed of sharp sand over a layer of firmly compacted, weed-free earth some 10cm/4in deep. Laying a water-permeable membrane between the earth and sand will help prevent weeds from growing through gaps.

laying a brick path or patio

Brick paths are easily laid, but it is important to use the right kind of bricks. House bricks look attractive initially, but are unsuitable, since they tend to flake and crack in freezing weather. Use paviors, sometimes called pavers, that are specially designed for pathways, available from garden centers, home improvement stores, and builders' merchants.

1 Level the ground and tamp down to compact it. Cover with a layer of sharp sand, and tread this down firmly. Check the level. Set the bricks in position, butting them tightly together.

2 Brush more sand over the surface of the bricks to fill the gaps and to prevent movement between them.

3 Place a length of strong board over the path and tamp down the bricks with a lump hammer. Brush more sand over the top to fill any remaining gaps.

winter plants and planting

There is plenty of glowing, sun-catching color from bark, stems, and even leaves, for the winter garden, and almost all the winter-flowering shrubs have a wonderful fragrance as well as being surprisingly easy to grow. Most of them also provide excellent material for cutting for the house.

Flowers, bark, and evergreens

Evergreens are a key feature of a successful winter garden. The formal design on pages 216–217 uses the classic box and yew, which clip neatly to shape. For a less formal garden the common laurel (*Prunus laurocerasus*) is excellent, shade-tolerant, and vigorous, and garden birds often nest among its broad, leathery leaves. Various conifers, including gold, blue, and pale green junipers, bring color in winter, as well as contributing their interesting shapes, and the good old garden privet in green or gold (*Ligustrum ovalifolium* and *L.o.* 'Aureo-marginatum') is a useful standby for garden hedging.

Dogwoods (*Cornus* and *Salix* species) are outstanding for their winter stems, in reds and oranges, lively light browns, yellows, and lime or olive green. Silver birches (*Betula* species) have pale silver-white or orange-red stems and the strawberry tree (*Arbutus unedo*) has bright, peeling, cinnamon-red winter bark. Many maples (*Acer* species), especially those known as the snakebark maples, are also grown for their bright, peeling winter bark. Fragrant flowers are part of winter's bounty, and these include the delicately perfumed snowdrop (*Galanthus nivalis*) and blue and purple-blue short-stemmed winter-flowering iris, *Iris reticulata*. (See the panel on the right for more examples.)

◄ Erica carnea *has excellent winter foliage.*

Profile plants

Buxus sempervirens
BOX

With its small and neat evergreen leaves and dense growth, box is a wonderful hedging plant for a low or medium hedge, as well as being *the* plant for topiary. Young plants 20–30cm/9–12in high are used for hedges, planted 30–40cm/12–16in apart, and one third of the growth must be clipped back in the first spring to encourage thick, bushy growth.

ht 3m/10ft unless clipped lower
sp to 1.8m/6ft
Soil and situation
Thrives in any ordinary garden soil in sun or partial shade.

Erica carnea
WINTER HEATH

Ericas are almost indistinguishable from heathers; this species has many named varieties which all make a wonderful display in winter, with masses of pink, purple, red, or white flowers over the springy mounds of needle-like foliage. *Erica carnea* is a particularly useful species in that it will tolerate alkaline—chalky or limy—soils if given good drainage (most heathers sulk if not in peaty or acid soils). Among the many varieties to choose from, 'Aurea' is a gold-leaved form with pink flowers, and 'Vivellii' has bronze leaves and deep magenta flowers.

▶ *Hellebores have exquisite winter flowers.*

▶ Salix britzensis *have colored stems.*

ht 30cm/12in
sp 60cm/24in
Soil and situation
Well-drained garden soil and a light position. Heavy soils can have sand dug in to lighten them.

Prunus serrula
FLOWERING CHERRY

This particular ornamental cherry is especially attractive in winter because of its shining, mahogany- or coppery-colored, peeling bark. In spring it produces slim, willow-like leaves and clusters of small white flowers. The leaves turn yellow in the fall and the tree takes on a pleasing, rounded shape.

ht 8m/26ft
sp 5.5m/18ft
Soil and situation
Ordinary well-drained garden soil, particularly if it is somewhat limy, and a light position. The tree should be staked until it is growing well (see page 218 for more on staking).

design alternatives

SKETCHES

These alternative schemes employ strong architectural shapes and feature a selection of box, grasses, Salix, Cornus, and Erica for winter planting.

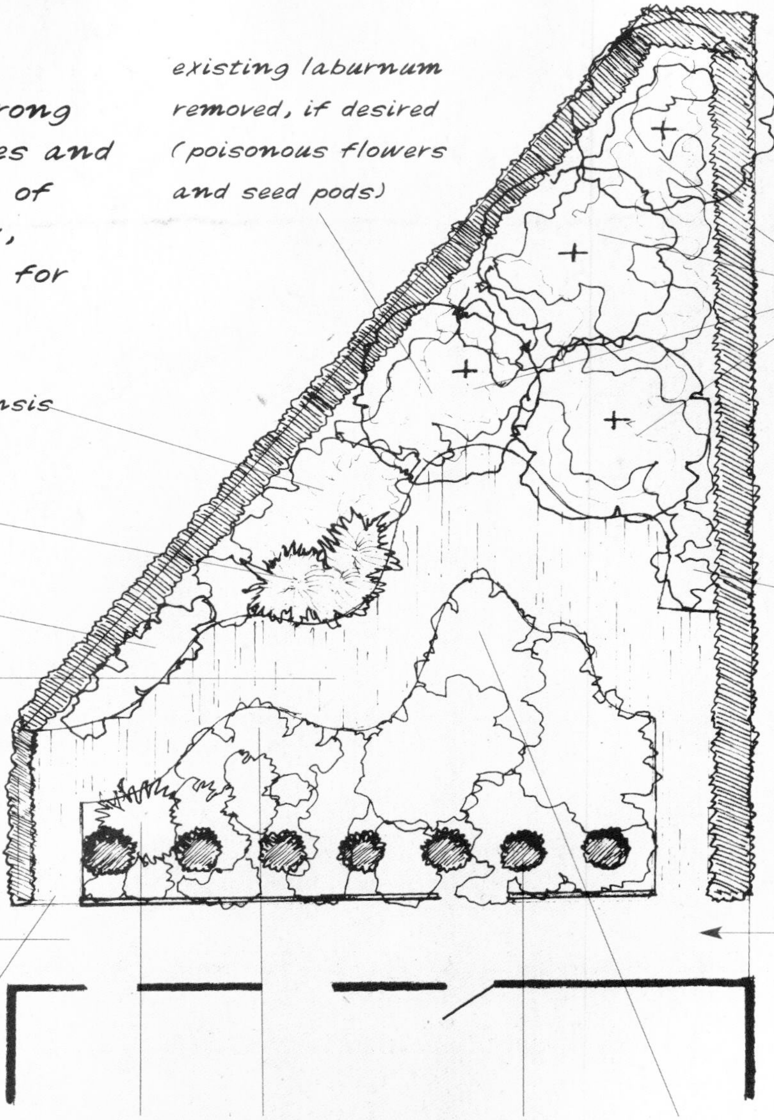

Cornus or Salix britzensis

big grasses

perennials

serpentine brick or grass path—note direction of brick

entrance

existing laburnum removed, if desired (poisonous flowers and seed pods)

four Prunus serrula underplanted with Cornus stolonifera 'Flaviramea', with plum-colored hellebores in front

Cornus 'Midwinter fire'

entrance to garden through gate

single step down to path

grasses

Erica carnea aurea

formal clipped box

mixed heathers with Erica carnea aurea featured

222

Colors in winter gardens:
lime-yellow, purple, blood red,
buff, bleached almond, and
dark green

topiarized clipped box

existing laburnum

topiarized, clipped box
or box hedges, clipped
straight

perennials

box hedge (or
yew) clipped
straight

Cornus or
Salix

mixed
grasses and
perennials
from list

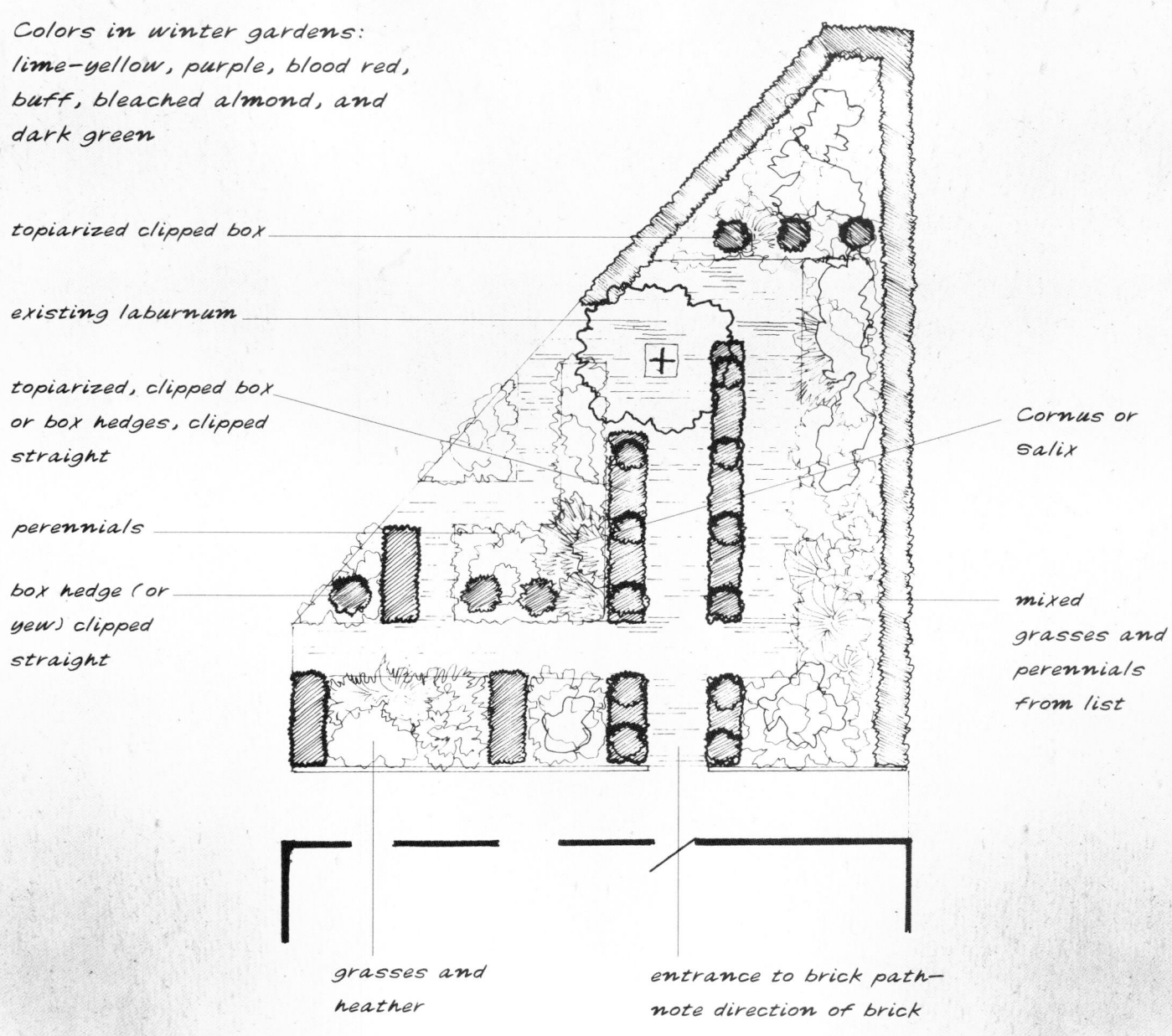

grasses and
heather

entrance to brick path—
note direction of brick

starting a garden

To get the best from your garden, you need to put in a bit of spade-work as well as thoughtful planning. Understanding your soil and situation helps you to select plants that will thrive. Any time you devote at the beginning to preparing the ground and making a gardening plan will be repaid many times over.

◀ Rhododendrons are among the plants that are particular as to soil pH. They should be planted in acid soil in order to thrive.

Understanding the soil

Essentially you need to know whether your soil is light or heavy, acid or alkaline. When it's wet, pick up a handful and squeeze it. Light, sandy soil will feel gritty and leave your hands fairly clean, while heavy soils feel muddy and slimy, and will cling to your hands and be difficult to clean off.

Light soils are good because they are well drained and quick to warm up in spring. But they need lots of organic material to supply and retain nutrients. Some light soils contain peat, rather than sand, which makes them warm, well-drained, and rich in nutrients already.

Heavy clay soils crack in summer and form a cold, wet mass in winter, preventing air from reaching the plants' roots. Their nutrients are unavailable to the plants unless the texture is improved to aerate the soil.

Heavy soils are also cold so that seeds don't germinate and get off to a good early start. Chalk soil is similar in many ways but also lacks nutrients. This is the poorest of all soils, and it is also highly alkaline.

Acid and alkaline soils

Alkaline soils are found in areas of chalk and limestone. They are usually lighter in color than acid soils. It is often believed that clay soils are always acid, but this is not necessarily the case—these types of soil can be strongly alkaline too.

Acidity and alkalinity are measured in pH, on a scale from 1 to 14. Anything lower than 4 is strongly acid and anything higher than 8 is strongly alkaline. For most plants the absolute ideal is a pH of 6.5—just slightly acid, as pH 7 is neutral—but between 4 and 8 most plants are

PLANTS FOR ALKALINE SOIL

buddleja (*Buddleja*)
campanula
Mexican orange blossom (*Choisya ternata*)
clematis
hardy geraniums (*Geranium*)
hellebores
lilac (*Syringa*)
mock orange (*Philadelphus*)
pinks and carnations (*Dianthus* species)
potentilla
red-hot poker (*Kniphofia*)

ACID SOIL

Most plants are happy on acid soil but the following plants demand it:
azaleas and rhododendrons
camellias
heathers, except *Erica carnea*
lilies, with some exceptions (see page 237)

IMPROVING THE SOIL

Improve the drainage of heavy soil in localized areas by digging in grit at the rate of one bucketful per square yard/meter. It is best to avoid limestone chippings if you wish to grow acid-loving plants.

All soils are improved by the application of organic matter, and this will raise the fertility of poor, dry soils. Use garden compost, well-rotted farmyard manure, spent mushroom compost (usually alkaline) or hop waste.

happy as long as the soil's texture and organic content are good. There are many plants that thrive in alkaline soil and a very few that must have acid soil (see box above).

Kits are widely available for testing the acidity or alkalinity of the soil, either giving the actual pH, or using a color chart as an indicator. Follow the instructions carefully and take readings in different parts of the garden. If your soil is alkaline it is best to go with it and choose plants accordingly. The main aim is to improve the structure so that plants can get air, food, and warmth.

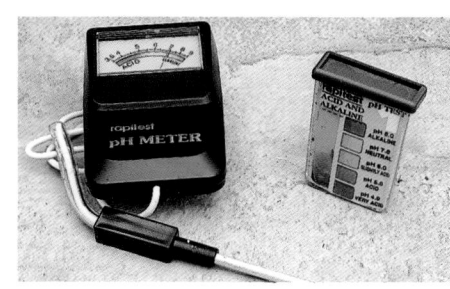

▲ *To make the most of your garden's natural advantages, you can test the pH of your soil either with a meter (left) or chemical kit (right).*

Improving the soil

Incorporating manure or organic matter helps any kind of soil. (You should not use peat for this because of the devastation it causes to the areas where it's extracted.) Organic material such as home-made compost or leafmold, farm manure, mushroom compost, and wood chippings improves

◄ *You will need a range of tools to make and maintain a garden. Try to keep them clean.*

◄ *Foxgloves are natural woodlanders that will thrive in a woody shady garden, though they are also tolerant of some direct sunlight.*

and becomes incorporated. Digging (with a spade) is particularly important to break up heavy soils, and is best done during September through November.

The simplest way is to dig out a trench a spade deep, keeping the spade vertical (putting the soil to one side) then to fork over the lower layer of soil and fork in the organic material. Dig a neighboring trench and throw the top layer of soil over the forked soil in the first trench, leaving it in rough clods to be broken down by the winter weather (the surface will now be higher than originally). Carry on like this over the whole area, finally using the soil from the first trench to top the last one. In the spring you simply need to fork the whole area over again to break up any large particles.

Understanding the situation

While most garden plants need good light, some positively flourish in shade and others—coming originally from deciduous woodland—need partial or dappled shade. If you are lucky your garden will be able to offer a variety of positions so that you can meet requirements from full sun to full shade. In addition some plants do best in an open position, while others require shelter from the wind. Open positions usually go with exposure to the sun, but shelter does not necessarily mean shade (some plants need sun and shelter).

Many plants will be unhappy exposed to strong winds, and specially tough and resilient plants are needed for such situations, whether there is sun or shade. You

soil texture, adding moisture-retentive bulk to sandy, gritty, and other well-drained soils and opening up heavy clay soils and making them warmer. It also adds nutrients (the amount and type varies depending on the particular material), and encourages earthworms and other creatures whose activity in the soil helps to break it down and make it more hospitable to plant roots.

Organic material can be incorporated by digging or forking but it can also be used as a mulch, scattered around individual plants while the soil is wet in spring. (Wood chippings are best used this way.) This helps to conserve moisture in the soil while it slowly breaks down

MEASURING UP

To mark out a path or flower bed, drive a stake or tent peg into the ground and attach a length of string to it.

Pull the string taut and tie to a second stake. You can move the stakes at will to alter the angle or placement.

▶ *Taking time over planting pays dividends. Plants will establish more quickly and grow more strongly. Remember to label your plants.*

need to bear all these requirements in mind when selecting plants. The plants listed in the directory on pages 228–249 have been selected as being generally tolerant of a wide range of conditions, even though many have preferences and some have special requirements, which are also listed.

Buying plants

The simplest way to stock your garden is to buy container plants from nurseries or garden centers. This enables you to see the plant at its best, and container plants can be planted at any time of year as long as you're prepared to water them well to get them established if it doesn't rain. Choose a nursery which is thriving and where the plants in

general look strong, healthy, and cared for. If it grows on its own so much the better as the plant will have been well looked after from the start. Some nurseries specialize in certain kinds of plants, which will usually be those that grow well in the locality, and the owners are also often happy to pass on advice and information.

Look for plants with strong stems, healthy leaves and plenty of buds. Reject plants if roots are coiled round the top of the pot or protruding from the holes at the base—this means they have been too long in the pot and have become pot bound. Also reject any plant with signs of disease

◀ *Most bulbs are best planted when dormant and should be buried to twice their own depth in suitable soil conditions.*

(mildew, for example) or insect infestation. Before planting, water well, ease the plant out of the pot and tease out the roots with your fingers or a small fork. Make sure the planting hole is bigger than the root ball, fork a little compost or general fertilizer into the soil at the bottom of the hole, place the plant in, replace the remaining soil, firm, and water.

Some plants, especially roses and small trees, may also be bought as bare-root plants (often from specialist nurseries or by mail). These are available in the appropriate planting season (whether fall or spring). It's important to keep the roots moist if you are unable to plant at once, either by placing the plants all in one hole and piling earth over the roots or by wrapping them in wet burlap.

plant directory

ANNUALS AND BIENNIALS

Annuals and biennials are short-lived plants usually grown for one season only. After flowering they die down and only rarely survive the winter. Annuals come into flower within 12 months of the seed being sown. Biennials usually flower in the second flowering season of their lives. Both can be raised quite easily from seed and bring color and variety to the garden.

Alcea rosea
(syn *Althaea rosea*)
HOLLYHOCK

Hollyhocks are lovely old-fashioned flowers with large rosettes or (in the double form) pompons of flowers towering above the leaves in spires, best grown as a biennial although they may last. The flowers come in a range of colors which all blend well together, from deep crimson, maroon, and violet purple to white, pink, and chalky yellow. A real cottage garden plant, hollyhocks grow quite happily against a house wall or through cracks in paving and also look good in a sunny border where their height can be appreciated. They flower from late summer onward, attracting butterflies and bees. *A. r.* 'Chater's Double' (tall) and *A. r.* 'Majorette' (short) are double forms, the latter flowering a little earlier and being particularly good in a mixed grouping.
*ht 1.8m/6ft or more (tall),
60–90cm/2–3ft (short)
sp 60cm/2ft
Soil and position*
For well-drained and even stony, but fertile, soils in a light, sunny position. In all but sheltered places they will need staking.

Bassia scoparia
(syn. *Kochia scoparia*)
SUMMER CYPRESS
OR BURNING BUSH

This green-leaved bedding plant looks like a miniature conifer,

◀ Alcea rosea (syn Althaea rosea) *hollyhock.*

adding shape and solidity to a planting scheme. Well used it can be a useful foliage plant, bringing a temporary mound of bright new green into the garden. You can grow it in a pot instead of topiary, or line the plants up to make a summer-long "hedge". In the fall it colors up to a glowing bronze-red before succumbing to harsh weather. A non-reddening variety, 'Evergreen,' is also available.
*ht 90cm/3ft
sp 45cm/18in
Soil and position*
Almost any, though light soil and open position are best.

Bellis perennis
ENGLISH DAISY

English daisy is a little garden daisy that flowers in late spring in shades of pink, red, and white—some bicolored, and each with a yellow center. Grow these neat little plants as a biennial from seed the previous summer, or buy as small plants. 'Carpet Mixed' and Pomponette Series are a good choice.
*ht to 20cm/8in
sp 15cm/6in
Soil and position*
Well-drained soil in sun or partial shade.

Brachyscome iberidifolia
SWAN RIVER DAISY

The Swan River daisy produces masses of daisy-like flowers in shades of blue or pinkish purple, sometimes with an inner ring of white. Can be grown easily from seed sown in spring but does best in a sunny spot. In warm, sheltered places it will even seed itself into cracks in stone walls. Good for hanging baskets and

containers; flowers from early to
late summer.
ht 23–45cm/9–18in
sp 30cm/12in
Soil and position
Very well-drained soil in a sunny,
sheltered position.

Calendula
CALENDULA/POT MARIGOLD
Calendula or pot marigold is a
good old-fashioned garden
flower, easily grown from seed.
The bright orange petals of the
plant originally grown in plots
and gardens, *C. officinalis*, were
dried and used in winter stews.
There are now many attractive
cultivars in shades of bright
orange, orange-yellow, and
cream, with lance-shaped, pale
green leaves. *C. officinalis* Pacific
Beauty Series includes a large,
warm yellow marigold with the
name 'Lemon Queen' as well as
many others with unusual and
subtle shades.
ht 30–60cm/1–2ft
sp 30–45cm/12–18in

Soil and position
Likes even poor soil, as long as
it's well-drained, and seeds itself
merrily in a warm, sunny
position.

Centaurea cyanus
CORNFLOWER
The familiar cornflower is at
home in informal schemes and
will flower for a long period as
long as you cut off stems as the
flowers die. Seeds can be sown
in spring but the plants are
stronger and earlier to flower
if you start them off the previous
fall. Mixed shades of pink, white,
and purple are available
as well as the original blue. Can
be grown in pots or containers
for a patio display. Need the
support of twiggy sticks in less
sheltered positions.
ht 20–75cm/8–30in
sp 15cm/6in
Soil and position
Do best in ordinary well-drained
soil and good light. Will tolerate
some drought.

Clarkia
CLARKIA AND GODETIA
Easy plants to grow from seed,
Clarkia elegans or clarkia has
cheerful, salmon-pink flowers
bustling up the stems (also
purple and lavender pink
shades). *C. amoena* or *godetia* has
silky, tissue-papery, more delicate
flowers, mainly in shades of pink
and white, some with interesting
markings. All flower during the
main summer months after a
spring sowing outdoors. A fall
sowing will produce earlier-
flowering plants the following
year. (*Clarkia elegans* is now
properly called *Clarkia
unguiculata* but the name is not
widely in use.)
*ht 30–90cm/1–3ft depending on
variety*
sp 20–30cm/8–12in
Soil and position
Clarkia need well-drained,
slightly acid soil with protection
from full sun—often flower best
in dry, poor soil.

Consolida ajacis
LARKSPUR
Larkspur, the poor man's
delphinium, has flowery spikes of
spurred flowers in blue or mixed
shades of pink, ruby red, white,
and violet, and finely cut leaves.
This plant is very much at home
in an informal border. The seeds
can be sown in the open in early

▲ Centaurea cyanus *or cornflower, ideal
for informal gardens.*

spring and the plant will usually
self-seed. Giant Imperial Series
are particularly strong and well-
branched.
*ht 90/cm/3ft (dwarf varieties
30cm/12in)*
sp 25cm/10in
Soil and position
Undemanding as to soil, as long
as it is well drained.
CAUTION: LARKSPUR SEEDS
ARE POISONOUS.

Cosmos bipinnatus
'Sensation Mixed'
COSMOS OR COSMEA
The airy, daisy-like flowers of
cosmos have a delicacy that is
enhanced by their feathery
foliage, and the plants flower
from mid- to late summer until
the first frosts from seed sown
indoors in spring. The common
variety 'Sensation Mixed'
produces tall flowers in white
and lilac-y pinks and purples.
Individual shades are available
from within the Sensation Series.
ht 90cm/3ft
sp 45cm/18in
Soil and position
Reasonably fertile, moist but
well-drained soil and a sunny
position.

Dianthus barbatus
SWEET WILLIAM
There are many garden dianthus,
including pinks and carnations.

◀ *The purple flowers of the Swan River
daisy,* Brachyscome iberidifolia.

▲ Salvia splendens, *salvia flowers throughout the summer.*

D. barbatus are the fuzzy, bright-colored sweet williams that have an old-fashioned appeal and are best grown as biennials from seed sown early the previous summer and planted out in the fall, or bought as bedding plants in spring. There are many varieties. Most are banded or bicolored with a central eye and have a sweet scent. Cutting the plants back after the first flowering early in the summer will usually encourage a second crop of flowers. Plants can be left to chance their luck over the winter and may develop into good clumps in the right soil conditions.
ht 45cm/18in
sp 25cm/10in
Soil and position
Well-drained, fertile soil, preferably slightly alkaline, and a bright, sunny position.

Digitalis purpurea
FOXGLOVE

Foxgloves need no introduction.

Grouped together in a semi-shady spot they add tranquillity to any garden, and of course are useful for their height as well. As well as the purple shade that gives the plant its name, foxgloves now come in shades of cream, apricot, and pink. Excelsior Hybrids are in shades that blend well together and are tall-growing. *D. g. f. albiflora* is a pure white-flowered form. Because of their height they need staking in all but the most sheltered spots.
ht to 2m/6ft 6in
sp to 60cm/2ft
Soil and position
Tolerate all but extremes but prefer humus-rich soil and dappled shade. They are excellent in light woodland, and will seed themselves where suited.
CAUTION: ALL PARTS OF THE PLANT CAN BE HARMFUL IF EATEN.

Erysimum cheiri
(syn. *Cheiranthus cheiri*)
WALLFLOWER

It would be hard to manage without this beautifully scented bedding plant in late spring. The flowers may be simple and not very large but the velvety petals have wonderfully intense colors, from deep blood red and crimson to bright eggyolk yellow. The single-colored varieties 'Blood Red' and 'Cloth of Gold' speak for themselves, and 'Persian Carpet' gives a good mixture of shades. They can be grown from seed sown the previous spring but are readily available as young plants in late fall. Plant close together for the best effect. *E.* 'Bowles Mauve' is an evergreen perennial, but without the wallflower scent. It flowers throughout the year.
ht to 45cm/18in
sp to 30cm/12in

▶ Helianthus annuus, *annual sunflower.*

Soil and position
Well-drained, fertile, fairly alkaline soil in a bright position.

Euphorbia marginata
GHOST WEED

Also known as 'snow-on-the-mountain', this hardy annual euphorbia adds a touch of class. Although the plant does flower, its white-marked foliage is what appeals. Given the right position it will flourish all summer grown from a spring planting outdoors. It's also a good plant for patio pots or containers.
ht 60–90cm/2–3ft
sp 30cm/12in
Soil and position
Needs a light, well-drained soil and an open, sunny position.
CAUTION: THE SAP CAN CAUSE IRRITATION TO THE SKIN.

Gomphrena globosa
GLOBE AMARANTH

Globe amaranth is unusual and colorful and fairly undemanding. Its robust clover-shaped flowers come in shades of red and pink; its bushy shape makes

it a good border filler. The flowers can be dried for indoor use. Flowers all summer from seeds sown indoors in spring.
ht 30–60cm/1–2ft
sp 40cm/10in
Soil and position
Needs well-drained, fairly fertile soil and a sunny position.

Helianthus annuus
ANNUAL SUNFLOWER

In recent years many new forms of the cottage garden sunflower have been produced, so dwarf plants as well as towering giants are available. Flowers are in shades of yellow and orange and the central disk develops into the heavy seed head which will attract birds when ripened. 'Pacino' is a good reliable, traditional variety; dwarf varieties include 'Music Box' and 'Teddy Bear'.
ht to 5m/15ft (tall); 45cm/18in (dwarf); 70cm/28in ('Music Box'); 90cm/3ft ('Teddy Bear')
sp to 60cm/2ft
Soil and conditions
Well-drained, humus-rich soil,

◄ *The tobacco plant,* Nicotiana, *suits well-drained soil in sun or partial shade.*

including alkaline soil and soil that is fairly dry. The plants need a warm summer to do well.

Ipomoea
MORNING GLORY

Morning glory is an annual climber with twining stems to be grown from seed sown in late spring. It has heart-shaped leaves and singly borne flowers in flattened trumpet shapes, wide and flaring, usually in a bright, clear blue. Each one lasts only a day, but the plant is covered with flowers all summer. A few plants together will quickly grow up a fence or climb up a wigwam. The variety *Ipomoea purpurea* has flowers in pink, pinkish blue, purple, and white. *I. tricolor* (syn. *I. violacea*) has white-centered, sky-blue flowers.
ht 3m/10ft
sp 30cm/12in
Soil and position
Well-drained, but fertile soil in a sheltered, sunny position.

Lathyrus odoratus
SWEET PEA

Members of the pea family, sharing the wiry tendrils by which pea plants cling to a support, sweet peas have wavy-edged flowers in a very wide range of pastel colors, with some in bright, deep reds, and darkest purple. Not difficult to grow from seed sown outside in the fall or indoors in late winter or early spring, they can also be bought as small plants in pots in late spring and will flower from early summer until the fall. Delicious scent (in most varieties) and luscious colors make them delightful cut flowers as well; the more you cut the more the plants produce. Plant out in groups and provide netting, tall twiggy sticks or other supports. 'Jet Set Mixed' and 'Knee High' are dwarf varieties suitable for patio pots.
ht to 2m/6ft 6in to 2.5m/8ft; 1m/39in ('dwarf' varieties)
sp 15–25cm/6–10in (the plants grow into each other planted at these intervals)
Soil and position
Fertile, deeply dug soil that is moist but well-drained, and a light, sunny, but sheltered position.

▶ *Sweet pea,* Lathyrus odoratus.

Lavatera trimestris
ANNUAL GARDEN MALLOW

This annual garden mallow makes a shrubby, flowery plant that belies its ease of growth. One of the commonest varieties is the pink-flowering 'Silver Cup', which is showy and cheerful but a bit too pink for some tastes. Try 'Mont Blanc' for a snowy white. Seeds can be sown directly outside in spring.
ht 75cm/30in
sp 40cm/16in
Soil and position
Light, well-drained, fairly fertile soil and a sunny but sheltered position.

Limnanthes douglasii
POACHED EGG PLANT

Poached egg plant forms a low and spreading mass of eggy yellow-centered flowers that are very attractive to bees and ladybugs (which devour greenfly). Flowering in mid-summer, they can be sown in early fall or mid- to late spring. Where the plant feels at home it will self-seed for the following year.
ht to 23cm/9in
sp 15cm/6in
Soil and position
Needs a well-drained, but fairly moist soil and an open, sunny position.

Lunaria annua
(syn. *Lunaria biennis*)
HONESTY

Also known as 'money plant' because of its round, flat seed heads, *Lunaria annua* most commonly has purple flowers. *L. a.* var. *albiflora* has white flowers, *L. a.* 'Variegata' has white-splashed leaves, and *L.a.* 'Alba Variegata' is blessed with both. The plant usually self-seeds. Mature plants grow from the seedlings of the previous year's spring sowing.
ht to 90cm/3ft
sp 30cm/ 12in
Soil and position
The plants are undemanding.

◀ Nigella damascena, *love-in-a-mist.*

Meconopsis cambrica
WELSH POPPY

Not immediately recognizable as a poppy, Welsh poppy is a bright, clear yellow and somewhat shorter than most annual poppies. It shares the silky petals, hairy stems, and nodding flower buds of other poppies and frequently pops up in just the right place. Similar, but even more unusual, is *M. grandis*, the Himalayan poppy, with flowers of a stunning blue.
ht 38cm/15in
sp 20cm/8in
Soil and position
Almost any reasonably well-drained, but not dry, soil in partial shade. Hot dry summers do not suit this plant.

Moluccella laevis
BELLS OF IRELAND

Bells of Ireland has spikes of unusual greenish flowers which can also be dried for winter flower arrangements. What appear to be the flowers are really green calyces that look like elfin caps, almost hiding tiny, slightly scented white flowers. The plant flowers in late summer. Seeds can be sown indoors in early spring or outdoors in late spring, where the plants are to flower.
ht 60–90cm/2–3ft
sp 20cm/8in
Soil and position
Needs fertile, well-drained soil and a sheltered position.

Nemophila menziesii
NEMOPHILA

This is a spreading, low-growing flowering plant for rockeries and border edges. The pretty, light green foliage is almost hidden by the masses of small, pale-blue, white-centered flowers in the best-known variety 'Baby Blue Eyes'. A classy black and white version, 'Penny Black', and the pure white 'Snowstorm' give the gardener plenty of choice. The plants, which flower throughout the summer, can be grown from seed sown outside in late spring.
ht 20cm/8in
sp 30cm/12in
Soil and position
The plants like well-drained, fertile soil but need some moisture, and thrive in part shade as well as full sun.

Nicotiana
TOBACCO PLANT

The tobacco plants widely on sale for summer planting are usually Domino Series cultivars and come in various colors from red and deep pink to white, cream, and lime green, mauve and purple. These are very cheerful and have some scent, but if fragrance is what you're after the taller *Nicotiana alata* is worth looking out for. The milky white or lime green flowers are especially well scented at night. A rather different species, the tall *N. sylvestris* has heads of strongly scented, pendent flowers, long, narrow and tubular, from branching stems above broad, tobacco leaves. All are normally grown as biennials and flower from early to late summer.
ht 30cm/12in (Domino Series); 2–3ft (N. alata); 4–5ft (N. sylvestris)
sp 30cm/12in; 60cm/2ft (N. sylvestris)
Soil and position
Fertile, well-drained, moist soil and sun or light shade.
CAUTION: THE FOLIAGE CAN BE A SKIN IRRITANT.

Nigella damascena
LOVE-IN-A-MIST

Love-in-a mist does have a misty look, because of its mass of wispy foliage and misty blue flowers. The inflated seed pods are an extra attraction. This annual is a cottage garden favorite that looks at home in many other situations too. A mixed strain is available in a range of moody blues, pinks, and purples, and white (Persian Jewels Series mixed). Purists, however, like to stick with 'Miss Jekyll', in beautiful blue. The seeds are best sown where they are to grow as doesn't like being transplanted.
ht 40–45cm/16–18in
sp 23cm/9in
Soil and position
Moist, fertile, well-drained soil and a sheltered sunny spot. Does best in fairly cool summers.

Papaver
POPPIES

Every flower garden is enhanced by annual poppies. They have a long flowering season, wave about in the breeze and catch the light beautifully, are tissue-paper fine and fleeting and come in lovely colors. *P. rhoeas* Shirley Series, the Shirley poppy comes in single and double varieties in watercolor shades of pinks, light purple, white, and occasionally orange and red. *P. somniferum*, known as opium poppy, has various shades of sultry pink, purple, and occasionally white or red, and bluish leaves, seed heads and stems.
ht 90cm/3ft (P. rhoeas); to 1.2m/4ft (P. somniferum)
sp 30cm/12in
Soil and position
Reasonably fertile, well-drained soil in good light.
CAUTION: CAUSES POISONING IF EATEN.

Rudbeckia hirta
RUDBECKIA

Rudbeckia hirta, sometimes known as coneflower, are perennials that are grown as annuals, casting a warm glow in the garden in later summer and early fall. The flowers are large, single petaled and daisy-like, in shades of warm yellows, reds, and reddish-browns, with conical centers of purple-brown, and are borne on sturdy, branching stems with a mass of simple, darkish green leaves. Among the best are 'Rustic Dwarfs' in a good range of dark-zoned and flecked colors; 'Goldilocks' with double or semidouble golden flowers, and 'Marmalade' with large,

bright yellow flowers. 'Becky
Mixed' is a dwarf variety in a
mix of colors. Cut the stems
after flowering to prolong the
flowering period.
*ht 60cm/2ft; 25cm/10in
('Becky Mixed')*
sp 30–45cm/12–18in
Soil and position
Fertile, well-drained soil and a
position in full sun.

Salvia splendens
SALVIA

This is a perennial grown as an
annual bedding plant, flowering
during the whole summer and
surviving even the early frosts.
With their vibrant flowers they
are widely used in park bedding
schemes. There's no need to stick
to red salvias as the spikes of
tubular flowers now come in a
range of pinks, purples, and

muted orange as well. 'Blaze of
Fire' speaks for itself; Cleopatra
Series are violet purple; others to
choose are *S. s.* 'Phoenix Mixed',
S. s. ' Phoenix Purple', and
'Sizzler Mixed' in the Sizzler
Series.
ht 30–40cm/12–16in
sp 25–30cm/10–12in
Soil and position
Needs a soil with good drainage
and a light position with plenty
of sunlight.

Scabiosa atropurpurea
PINCUSHION FLOWER

Pincushion flower or sweet
scabious has lilac blue flowers
carried singly on narrow, wiry
stems all summer. The loose,
wavy petals surround a
'pincushion' center and the
flowers attract butterflies and
bees. They are best grown in

small groups in an informal
border. Short-lived perennials,
they are usually treated as a
biennial (with seed sown the
previous spring) or annual.
'Double Mixed' and 'Dwarf
Double Mixed' have flowers in
shades of white, pink, and
purple, as well as blue.
*ht 90cm/3ft; 45cm/18in (dwarf
types)*
sp 20cm/8in
Soil and position
A well-drained, fertile, limy or
even chalky soil is best and an
open, sunny position.

Tropaeolum
NASTURTIUM

Nasturtiums are easy annuals that
are very well worth growing for
their bright, velvety, spurred
flowers and round, flat, grayish
green (and edible) leaves. Most

make bushy, low-growing little
plants but some are climbers that
quickly scramble up a fence or
trellis, or over another plant.
Many named hybrids are
available, in single colors (scarlet,
orange, mahogany, yellow, and
cream), or with white-splashed
leaves. Alaska Series has leaves
that are marbled with cream and
pink. Look out for blackfly,
which tend to gather on the
backs of the leaves.
*ht 30–60cm/1–2ft;
1–3m/3–10ft (climbers)*
sp 45–60cm/18–24in
Soil and position
Flower best when grown in poor
but well-drained soil, and in a
sunny position.

▼ Meconopsis cambrica, *Welsh poppy,
is small with bright yellow flowers.*

◀ Allium christophii, *allium.*

BULBOUS PLANTS

Bulbous plants produce a huge range of flowers, not just in spring but at almost every time of year, and for every situation from well-drained rockeries to moist meadows and pondsides. Allowing the foliage to die down naturally after flowering enables them to build up their resources for the following year, and when they feel at home they thrive. This list includes plants grown from bulbs, corms, and rhizomes—all being food-storage organs which enable the plant to survive the dormant period.

Agapanthus africanus
AGAPANTHUS OR
AFRICAN LILY

In late summer agapanthus has drumheads of bell-shaped or trumpet-like flowers on tall, stately stems, usually in shades of blue although some varieties are white. This striking plant has a mass of long, spear-shaped leaves, and is excellent for containers as well as in garden beds. In all but the most mild and sheltered areas needs protecting with a thick mulch in winter.
ht 60–90cm/2–3ft (a few varieties much taller)
sp 45–60cm/18–24in
Soil and position
Must have a light, well-drained but moist soil or potting soil mix, and needs a very light position.

Allium christophii
ALLIUM

This member of the onion family produces lilac-colored globes of star-shaped flowers on tall stalks, and strappy gray-green leaves, making an architectural plant. There are many different species of allium, producing flowers from spring to fall and in a wide range of heights from dainty to stately. *Allium christophii* flowers in early summer. *A. giganteum* is a giant version with dense round heads of purplish flowers in summer.
ht 60cm/2ft (Allium christophii);
1.5–2m/5–6.5ft (A. giganteum)
sp 15cm/6in (both)
Soil and position
Not fussy as to soil, as long as it is fairly well-drained. Needs a sunny position.
CAUTION: THE JUICE FROM THE BULBS CAN CAUSE SKIN ALLERGIES OR A RASH.

Anemone blanda
WINDFLOWER

Flowering in early spring in shades of heavenly blue, bluish pink, pinky purple, and pure white, this daisy-like anemone, with its deeply cut leaves, is a lovely plant for a semiwild "woodland" area or rock garden, and will soon spread widely if it feels at home.
ht 15cm/6in
sp 10cm/4in
Soil and position
Well-drained soil that is not too dry, in a position in sun or partial shade. Grows well under deciduous trees as it flowers before the leaves open.

Arum italicum
LORDS AND LADIES OR
CUCKOOPINT

Closely related to the wild woodland plant, the garden arum has very glossy leaves in winter and early spring, from the center of which springs up a sturdy spike of minute flowers surrounded by a sail-like spathe in creamy green. In late summer the spike becomes a head of bright red beady berries. The variety *A.i.* 'Marmoratum' (syn. *A. i.* 'Pictum') has marble-patterned, variegated leaves. The less hardy *Arum pictum* has narrow, white-veined leaves.

ht 30cm/12in
sp 15cm/6in
Soil and position
Humus-rich but well-drained soil in any position from full sun to shade.

Chionodoxa
GLORY OF THE SNOW

In early spring chionodoxa produces bright, wide-open, starry flowers amid shapely mid-green leaves. *Chionodoxa forbesii* (sometimes sold as *C. luciliae*) is the species usually grown; its flowers are a clear blue with white centers, or, in the variety 'Pink Giant', a lovely soft pink. Chionodoxa is a good plant to grow in a rockery or under trees, where it will seed itself and spread freely.
ht 10–20cm/4–8in
sp 2.5cm/1in
Soil and position
Well-drained soil with adequate moisture, in sun.

Colchicum
COLCHICUM OR
AUTUMN CROCUS

These delicately colored early fall-flowering crocus-like plants have acquired the name 'naked ladies' from the fact that their broad, most un-crocus-like leaves appear at a completely different time from the "naked" flowers. Some are rare and sought-after (and expensive to buy) but *C. autumnale*, the meadow saffron, and *C. speciosum* are both quite widely available. Both come in several varieties, in white and rosy lilac-pink.
ht 10–15cm/4–6in
sp 8cm/3in
Soil and position
Fertile garden soil and an open, sunny position.

Crinum × Powellii
CRINUM

Crinums are lily-like flowers from South Africa and many of them

▲ Agapanthus africanus, *African lily.*

don't like a cold climate. But *Crinum × Powellii* is surprisingly hardy and bears its hanging pink or white trumpet-shaped flowers well into the fall. Each sturdy stem bears six to eight flowers and the bulbs form clumps, with broad, strap-shaped leaves. Protect with a thick mulch in winter in all but very mild areas.
ht 90cm/3ft
sp 30cm/12in
Soil and position
Well-drained soil, with moisture, and a warm, sheltered spot.
CAUTION: ANY PART OF THE PLANT CAN CAUSE SEVERE STOMACH UPSET; THE JUICES CAN CAUSE SKIN IRRITATION.

Crocus
CROCUS

Spring-flowering crocuses are a must in any garden, planted under trees, in a rockery, or in pots on the patio or corners of

the border. Among the earliest to flower are *C. tommasinianus*, in delicate shades of amethyst blue to lilac, and (in 'Ruby Giant') reddish purple. The bolder *C. vernus* comes in the same color range, including brighter shades, but also in golden yellow ('Dutch Yellow'), and with feathered forms (as in 'Joan of Arc') or stripes ('Winston Churchill'). These usually flower in mid-spring, as does *Crocus angustifolius* or cloth of gold, which has yellow flowers that are bronze-stained on the outside, with a delicate fragrance. The corms soon spread, forming small clumps. Robust forms are good for naturalizing in grass.
ht to 10cm/4in
sp 2.5cm/1in
Soil and position
Well-drained soil and a sunny situation, where they will not be disturbed.

Cyclamen coum
CYCLAMEN

This winter-flowering native of northern Turkey will flourish in the shelter of trees and shrubs. Flared-back flowers come in white and shades of pink and purple, and the flat, heart-shaped leaves are very dark green and usually attractively marbled in silver. Flowers continue until mid-spring. Must be bought from a licensed source to insure that illegally imported, wild corms are not used.
ht 10cm/4in
sp to 15cm/6in
Soil and position
Well-drained, humus-rich soil that does not dry out in summer; sun or partial shade.
CAUTION: ALL PARTS OF THE PLANT CAN CAUSE SEVERE STOMACH UPSET IF EATEN.

◄ Eranthis hyemalis, *winter aconite,* flowers in late winter.

Erythronium dens-canis
DOG'S TOOTH VIOLET

With their backward-flaring petals and marbled leaves these little plants look similar to cyclamen and flower in spring. The leaves are broad and pointed, with purplish brown splodges, and the flowers are in white, pink, or lilac, depending on the variety. 'Lilac Wonder', 'Pink Perfection', 'Snowflake', 'White Splendour', and 'Purple King' all live up to their names. Erythroniums look pretty growing under trees or shrubs, in rockeries, or naturalized in the lawn, and they spread to form small clumps.

ht and sp 10–15cm/4–6in
Soil and position
Well-drained, humus-rich soil that does not dry out in summer, in lightly dappled shade.

Fritillaria imperialis
CROWN IMPERIAL

This is a large and striking member of the fritillary family, flowering in late spring. Whorls of spiky, pale green leaves top the orange, bell-shaped flowers clustered at the tops of strong brown stems. The variety *F. i.* 'Lutea Maxima' has lemon-yellow flowers.

ht to 1.5m/3–5ft
sp to 90cm/12in
Soil and position
Fertile, well-drained soil in sun or partial shade.

Galtonia
SUMMER HYACINTH

True to the family they come from, galtonias look like loose-flowered hyacinths. The closely packed buds toward the tops of the stems open into pendent, bell-like flowers and the plants form clumps with wide, strap-shaped, slightly arching leaves.

Dahlia
DAHLIA

Dahlias jolly up the garden in late summer and last until the first frosts. Apart from the cheerful pompom-headed and multipetaled cactus types there are elegant single flowering dahlias for those who like restraint and dwarf-dahlias that don't need staking (as the others generally do). 'Bishop of Llandaff' is a peony-flowered form with brilliant red flowers and stunning reddish black foliage; 'Easter Sunday' is a white, single form with a 'collerette' of small petals around the central yellow disc; 'Moor Place' is a pompon dahlia in a rich clerical red'; 'Hamari Gold' is a multi-petaled decorative dahlia in a bright, warm golden orange, and 'Princess Marie Jose' is a single-flowered dahlia in soft pink.

ht 60 cm–1m/2–3ft
sp 45–60cm/18–24in

Soil and position
Fairly heavy, fertile soil and a sunny position.

Eranthis hyemalis
WINTER ACONITE

Bright yellow, buttercup flowers surrounded by green ruffs open on short stems in late winter, at the same time as the snowdrops, advising us that we'll soon be getting into our gardening boots again. In summer the plants disappear, to put out leaf again the following winter. Over the course of the years, provided they are at home, they will spread to form large clumps.

ht and sp 8–10cm/3–4in
Soil and situation
A well-drained, moist soil that doesn't dry out in summer and a sunny or semishaded position.

► Dahlia *'Bishop of Llandaff'* has brilliant red flowers and black foliage.

Galtonia candicans, the fragrant, white-flowered form, is the one most usually grown but there is also a more unusual galtonia with pale green flowers, *G. viridiflora*. They flower in late summer. Mulch the plants for winter protection in all but the mildest areas.
ht 1m/3ft
sp 20cm/8in
Soil and position
Well-drained soil that remains slightly moist in summer and a sunny, fairly sheltered position.

Iris
IRIS
Broadly, irises divide into two types: bulbous (grown from bulbs, and usually quite small) and rhizomatous (grown from rhizomes, and including the larger irises as well as some dwarf ones). Many of the rhizomatous kind are bearded, with rough crests on the three large, dropping outer petals or "falls" characteristic of all irises.

Bulbous irises include Spanish, English, and Dutch. Dutch flower in white, yellow, and blue in early summer, with the English (white, purple, and blue), and Spanish (white, purple, blue, and yellow), flowering later. Another bulbous type is the small and lovely winter-flowering *Iris reticulata* (with flowers in blue or purple).

Beardless, moisture-loving rhizomatous irises include the mid-summer-flowering *I. pseudacorus*, the yellow flag or water iris, a must for streams and pondside, and *I. sibirica* or Siberian flag, with blue or purple early summer flowers.

Bearded rhizomatous irises come in all sizes, from dwarf to tall. Two good, fragrant ones are *I. pallida* 'Variegata' with lilac blue flowers and green and yellow striped leaves, and the lovely winter-flowering *Iris*

▶ Iris reticulata, *a bulbous iris.*

unguicularis, almost hiding its low-growing lavender, blue, and lilac flowers among its leaves. Other favorites include 'Langport Smoke' in a clear, soft blue; 'Langport Song', with ruffled, lemon-yellow petals; 'Black Knight', dark purple; 'Bronze Cloud', copper and lavender blue, and 'Dante', golden bronze and raspberry red.
ht and sp 5–100cm/2–39in
Soil and position
Bulbous irises need well-drained soil and an open, sunny, sheltered position. Rhizomatous irises generally like warm, alkaline soil and a sunny, sheltered position, but the beardless, pondside ones like moist soil and semishade, and yellow flag will grow in water at the pond edge.
CAUTION: CAN CAUSE STOMACH UPSET IF EATEN.

Leucojum aestivum 'Gravetye'
SUMMER SNOWFLAKE OR LODDON LILY
Leucojum plants look like enlarged snowdrops. Small, flaring, bell-like flowers, in white, with green spots on the pointed tepal (a kind of petal) tips, hang prettily from the stem tops, just above the narrow, straplike leaves. *Leucojum aestivum* 'Gravetye' is a reliable variety which flowers in late spring. The lower-growing *L. vernum* flowers in early spring.
ht to 60cm/2ft (Leucojum aestivum); 20cm/8in (L. vernum)
sp 10cm/4in
Soil and position
Moist soil and, dappled shade.

Lilium
LILY
Lilies are a firm gardening favorite. They offer a huge choice, and the following are just a few favorites among lilies that

are undemanding and fairly easy to obtain. *Lilium candidum*, the madonna lily (white, very fragrant, midsummer flowering, and one of the few to need alkaline soil); *L. longiflorum*, the Easter lily (actually flowering in midsummer, very fragrant, lime-tolerant); *L. regale*, the regal lily (fragrant, white, with deep pink streaks on the outside, midsummer flowering); *L. mackliniae* (pink, unscented, midsummer flowering), *L. monadelphum* (fragrant, creamy yellow, purple-spotted inside, flowering early summer, tolerates lime); *L.* 'Enchantment' (rich orange, flowering early summer, not scented). *L.* 'Star Gazer' has beautiful reddish-pink flowers with darker spots; it is midsummer flowering.
ht to 1m/3ft or more; to 60cm/2ft (L. mackliniae)
sp 15–20cm/6–8in

◀ Nerine bowdenii, *nerine.*

ht 10–15cm/4–8in
sp 5cm/2in
Soil and position
Almost any reasonably well-drained soil in a sunny position.

Narcissus
DAFFODIL AND JONQUIL

There are far too many narcissi to begin to select—from short for rockeries and pots to tall for borders and from early to late flowerers. Among the smaller ones 'Tête a Tête' is a dwarf in cheerful yellow for early spring, 'Minnow' is a pale dwarf for mid-spring, *N. cyclamineus* is an early-flowering species with backward flaring perianths and long, narrow trumpets, and *N. cantabricus* is an enchanting white hooped petticoat daffodil with wide funnel-shaped trumpets and tiny pointed perianths. Late in the season *N. poeticus*, a tall species, produces fragrant white flowers with tiny orange cups instead of trumpets. The many hybrids include: 'Actaea' (white with orange centers); 'Cassata' (soft yellow); 'February Gold' (bright yellow); 'Ice Follies' (one of the best and most beautiful white varieties); 'St Keverne' (sturdy, with bright yellow flowers); 'Minnow' a dainty dwarf, with cream of yellow flowers); 'Suzy' (rich yellow with red cups); and 'Rainbow' (white and pink). Sturdy hybrids are useful for naturalizing in grass.
ht 20–50cm/8–20in, sp16cm/6in (hybrids and N. poeticus);
ht 15–20cm/6–8in,
sp 5–8cm/2–3in (the rest)
Soil and position
Ordinary garden soil and a sunny, light position.

Nerine bowdenii
NERINE

Nerines have wavy, loosely grouped lily-like flowers on tall, narrow stems, and strap-shaped, rather grass-like leaves; they flower from late summer and right through the fall, making them even more appreciated. While most species are not suitable for growing outdoors in a cold climate *Nerine bowdenii*, with its light raspberry pink flowers, is hardy and robust. *N. b.* 'Mark Fenwick' (aka 'Fenwick's Variety') is a stronger and taller variety, with deeper pink flowers, and *N. b.* f. *alba* has white or palest pink flowers.
ht 50cm/20in
sp 8cm/3in
Soil and position
Well-drained soil in a sunny and sheltered position, for example by a house wall.

Tulipa
TULIP

You can buy mixed tulips in unspecified colors and they will flower cheerfully in later spring, but sometimes only a special tulip will do. Among the many stunning varieties are 'Angelique' (double, pale pink); 'Golden Apeldorn' (bright yellow with black base), 'Queen of Night' (very dark, almost black); 'Spring Green' (white flowers with green feathering); 'White Parrot', and 'Black Parrot' (with twisting, fringed petals in white/almost black). Finally the small, early flowering water-lily tulip *T. kaufmanniana* has wide-open, scented flowers in cream or yellow, sometimes with contrasting centers.
ht 30cm/12in ('Angelique');
60cm/2ft ('Golden Apeldorn' and 'Queen of Night');
40cm/16in ('Spring Green');
55cm/22in ('White Parrot', and 'Black Parrot'); 20cm/8in (T. kaufmanniana)
sp 8–15cm/3–6in
Soil and position
Well-drained soil in a sunny, fairly sheltered position.

Soil and situation
Unless otherwise stated lilies require well-drained neutral or acid soil enriched with compost or leaf mold and a position in sun or lightly dappled shade.

Muscari
GRAPE HYACINTH

Grape hyacinths produce blue flowers arranged like miniature grapes on upright stems in spring, surrounded by a mass of somewhat untidy arching, grassy leaves. Unnamed varieties are generally available but it's worth looking out for *Muscari neglectum* (syn. *M. racemosum*), which has white-rimmed flowers in very deep blue, and *M. aucheri*, whose pale blue, almost drumhead flowers are again white rimmed and whose leaves are a pleasant grayish green.

PERENNIALS

Perennials form the mainstay of most garden planting, lasting from year to year and normally flowering annually. We have included in this section not only herbaceous perennials that die back over winter and grow up again in spring, but also some of the smaller shrubs. The plants listed here include some that flower in winter and fall as well as spring and summer.

Alchemilla mollis
LADY'S MANTLE

This is a "must-have" for almost any type of garden, at home in a formal or informal setting. Bundles of tiny, greenish yellow flowers weigh down the light stems for the whole summer and the downy, lobed leaves catch drops of rain or dew at the center. The plant lolls gracefully at the front of a border, forms large clumps, and self-seeds. Grows prettily in gravel or between the paving stones too.
ht 60cm/2ft
sp 75cm/30in
Soil and position
Prefers a fairly moist, rich soil but tolerates dry, fairly poor soils too. Thrives equally well in sun or semishade.
SLUGS AND SNAILS CAN ATTACK YOUNG LEAVES.

Anemone × *hybrida*
(syn. *A. japonica*)
JAPANESE ANEMONE

A tall and lovely plant for later summer, with flowers of white or shades of moody pink on upright, branching stems. The simple flowers, wide open and with a central boss of orange-yellow stamens are mainly single, as in the white 'Honorine Jobert', but 'Whirlwind' (white) and 'Queen Charlotte' (pink) are semidouble. The deeply toothed leaves cluster beautifully round the stem axils.
ht 1.2m/4ft
sp 60cm/2ft
Soil and position
Needs moist but well-drained, rich soil in sun or semishade.

Aquilegia
AQUILEGIA

Aquilegia, also known as columbine, granny's bonnets and old maid's bonnets, is a well-loved, old-fashioned garden plant and there are many hybrids, named and unnamed. Its flower bonnets with their distinctive spurs nod down from graceful stems which rise up from a mass of lobed leaves, often a grayish green. Flowering in early summer, this is a pretty plant for a cottage garden or meadow garden. Not long-lived, but generally self-seeding it will often colonize an area when it feels at home.

Types to choose include *A. vulgaris* hybrids, including the neatly frilled 'Nora Barlow'; *A.* Mrs Scott Elliott Hybrids, often bicolored with very long spurs; *A. longissima*, pale yellow flowers with very long spurs; *A. flabellata*, soft blue.
ht 90cm/3ft
sp 60cm/2ft
Soil and position
Likes well-drained soil and cool conditions.

Campanula persicifolia,
BELLFLOWER/CAMPANULA

There are many garden campanulas, including low-growing alpine varieties, most having flaring tube- or bell-shaped flowers in shades of blue, with white, some cream, and the occasional pink. *Campanula persicifolia* is tall and spiry, with slender stems sporting delicate-looking, harebell-like flowers of sky blue. *C. p. alba* is a similar white-flowered version. Slightly more uncommon, the smaller *C. alliariifolia* has stems of downward-facing, narrow, white flowers and *C.* 'Elizabeth' has extremely narrow, pink-flushed flowers, offset by deep-toothed foliage. All flower from mid- to late summer, especially if the stems are cut after flowering. Beware of tiny slugs and snails, which can ravage the flowers.
ht 90cm/3ft (C. persicifolia);
45cm/18in (C. alliariifolia); to
40cm/16in (C. 'Elizabeth')
sp 30cm/12in (C. persicifolia);
45cm/18in (C. alliariifolia); to
40cm/16in (C. 'Elizabeth')
Soil and position
Like moist but well-drained soil and partial shade.

Crambe cordifolia
COLEWORT

Tall, spreading and airy, this plant from the cabbage family has

▲ Anemone *x* hybrida *(syn. A. japonica), Japanese anemone.*

many-branching stems and a froth of tiny white flowers against enormous veined and crinkled leaves. The flowers are fragrant, and attractive to bees. *Crambe maritima* or sea kale is similar but low-growing and with thick, bluish leaves; it grows well in maritime conditions. Both plants flower in early summer. The stems of sea kale can be blanched in winter for spring eating.
ht 1.8m/6ft (C. cordifolia);
75cm/ 30in (C. maritima)
sp 1.8m/6ft (C. cordifolia);
60cm/2ft (C. maritima)
Soil and position
Need a sunny position, sheltered from wind, in well-drained, alkaline soil.

Dicentra spectabilis
BLEEDING HEART

In late spring and early summer the fleshy, dark pink stems of graceful *Dicentra spectabilis* (called by country people "ladies in the bath") are bowed with pink lockets hanging along their length. In the form *Dicentra spectabilis* 'Alba' the flowers are white and the stems green and more wiry. The plants form feathery-leaved clumps. *Dicentra formosa* is a similar but much lower growing plant.

ht 75cm/30in (Dicentra spectabilis); to 45cm/18in (Dicentra formosa)

sp 45cm/18in (Dicentra spectabilis); to 45cm/18in (Dicentra formosa)

Soil and position

Moist but well-drained, compost-rich soil in a sheltered, shady spot. Likes alkaline conditions.

Echinops
GLOBE THISTLE

Strong and sturdy, these plants have round drumheads of blue, thistle-like flowers and spiny, down-backed, gray-green leaves. The flowers, produced toward the end of the summer, are very attractive to bees, and dry well for dried flower arrangements. *E. bannaticus* 'Blue Globe' and the slightly more compact *E. ritro* 'Veitch's Blue' both have particularly well-colored flowers.

ht to 1m/3ft

sp 45–60cm/18–24in

Soil and position

Although at their best in full sun and poor, fairly dry, well-drained soil, globe thistles will grow in almost any position.

Epimedium
BARRENWORT

Sometimes known as bishop's miter or bishop's hat from the shape of their leaves, these are excellent ground-cover plants, especially for growing under trees and shrubs. There are many types available, and although they are grown mainly for their leaves many have attractive small flowers in yellow, orange, red, or pink. Choice varieties include *E. × rubrum*, with crimson flowers and red and reddish brown leaves that are particularly striking in winter; *E. × versicolor* 'Cupreum', which is very tolerant and has coppery leaves and pink flowers; and *E. × v.* 'Sulphureum', with coppery leaves and yellow flowers. Check other species when you buy, as some are fussy and some die down in winter.

ht to 30cm/12 in

sp indefinite

Soil and position

Woodland conditions with semishade to full shade, and moist, humus-rich soil.

Eryngium
SEA HOLLY

The overall effect of these architectural plants, with their holly-like leaves and cone-shaped flowers surrounded by arresting, spiny bracts, is of spiky shapes and gray-blue or metallic blue coloring. *Eryngium × oliverianum* is a good long-lived variety with silvery blue coloring that ages to purple-blue, while *E. × tripartitum*, also long-lived, is slightly taller, lighter in form, and more dainty, with violet-blue coloring. All flower until the fall and are good for cutting and drying.

ht 60 cm–1m/2–3ft

sp50–60cm/20–24 in

Soil and position

Needs a sunny position and very well-drained, ordinary soil that does not get waterlogged during the winter months.

Euphorbia
SPURGE, MILKWEED

Great favorites with knowledgeable gardeners, spurges provide a wide choice of bushy plants, generally evergreen, with strong, sappy stems, often a leaning habit, and flowers of yellowish green. *E. nicaeensis*★ has domes of lime-yellow, green-bracted flowers in spring and blue-green, curling leaves growing all the way down the strong stems. *E. characias*★ is tall and erect with densely flowered stems. Its flowers have purple nectar glands, though the subspecies known as *E.c. wulfenii* has greenish yellow flowers. The much smaller *E. polychroma* is very lime-yellow, starry flowering and mound forming. Other spurges to consider are *E. amygdaloides*★★, *E. cyparissias*★, *E. myrsinites*★, *E. griffithii* 'Dixter'★★ and *E. g.* 'Fireglow'★★.

ht 80cm/32in; sp 45cm/18in (E. nicaeensis)

ht and sp 1.2m/4ft (E. characias)

ht 40cm/16in; sp 60cm/2ft (E. polychroma)

ht 75cm/30in; sp 30cm/12in (E. amygdaloides)

ht 20–40cm/8–16in; sp indefinite (E. cyparissias)

ht 10cm/4in; sp to 30cm/12in (E. myrsinites)

ht 75cm/30in; sp 90cm/3ft (E. griffithii)

Soil and position

Those marked ★ like a sunny spot in well-drained soil; those marked ★★ need light, dappled shade and a moist soil with plenty of humus. *E. polychroma* adapts to sun or partial shade.

CAUTION: THE MILKY WHITE LIQUID IN THE STEMS IS POISONOUS IF INGESTED AND CAUSTIC TO THE TOUCH.

Geranium
CRANESBILL, GERANIUM

You can become addicted to geraniums and their modest charms. These are hardy, and, given conditions they like, very long-lasting plants, with flowers in shades of pale pink to magenta, white, and light sky blue. They have lobed or deeply cut leaves and simple, wide-open flowers, often delicately veined or deeply stained at the center, and they vary from small and compact to large clump-forming. Among the best are the very reliable G. 'Johnson's Blue', with warm blue flowers; G. *sanguineum* 'Album' (white), G. s. 'Shepherd's Warning' (deep pink), and G. s. var. *striatum* (pale pink, delicately marked with deeper pink). G. *renardii*, which flourishes in poor soil, has velvety leaves and dark-veined pale lavender flowers. The meadow cranesbill, G. *pratense*, is blue, with white varieties, and

flourishes in meadow-type conditions with rich, moist soil. The large G. *maderense*, (evergreen leaves, red stems, light magenta flowers) is short-lived in gardens but easily grown annually from seed.
ht to 45cm/18in, sp to 75cm/30in (G. 'Johnson's Blue')
ht 30cm/12in, sp 40cm/16in (G. sanguineum 'Album')
ht and sp 15cm/6in (G. s. 'Shepherd's Warning')
ht and sp 10cm/4in (G. s. var. striatum)
ht and sp 30cm/12in (G. renardii)
ht to 90cm/3ft sp 60cm/2ft (G. pratense)
ht and sp to 1.5m/5ft (G. maderense)
Soil and position
Unless stated above geraniums are happy in ordinary, well-drained garden soil, in sun or partial shade. The smallest species need very good drainage, with added grit or sharp sand.

Helleborus argutifolius
(syn. *H. corsicus*)
CORSICAN HELLEBORE

This large, shrubby-looking hellebore has bunches of small,

pale creamy green flowers for a long period from late winter and interesting, tooth-edged, leathery leaves throughout the year. The shorter *Helleborus foetidus* is very similar, also tough and shrubby looking, but with lime-green flowers, rimmed with crimson and lasting well into spring.

Shorter hellebores, best grown in groups, are the pure white *Helleborus niger* or Christmas rose and *Helleborus orientalis*, the lenten rose. Both have large and tender-looking, cup-like flowers, the first in late winter, the second in early spring. 'Potter's Wheel' is a good variety of the Christmas rose, generous with its pure white flowers. Lenten roses have plum colored flowers and there are many subtly shaded hybrids, named and unnamed.
ht 90cm/3ft, sp to 1.2m/4ft (Helleborus argutifolius)
ht 60cm/2ft, sp 45cm/18in (Helleborus foetidus)
ht and sp 30cm/12in (Helleborus niger)
ht and sp 45cm/18in (Helleborus orientalis)
Soil and position
Fertile, well-drained but moist, limy soil; shade or partial shade.
CAUTION: THE PLANTS ARE POISONOUS IF EATEN AND THE SAP CAN CAUSE IRRITATION.

Hemerocallis
DAY LILY

Members of the lily family, day lilies have sword-shaped leaves and twisting stems. They bear their flowers for only a day, but continue to produce new flowers during the whole of the summer. Many varieties have now been bred and there is a wide choice of colors and flower shapes, from spidery to double and triangular. The plants form large clumps. Among those to

choose are 'Berlin Red' and 'Red Precious' (red), 'Cartwheels' (orange), 'Lemon Bells', and Marion Vaughn', (shades of yellow), and 'Pink Damask' (pink). Shorter, so-called dwarf varieties such as 'Golden Chimes' and 'Stella de Oro' (yellow) are also available.
ht to 1.3m/4ft
sp to 90cm/3ft
Soil and position
A sunny position in fertile, moist, rather heavy but well-drained soil. Will also tolerate partial shade.

Heuchera
HEUCHERA OR CORAL FLOWER

A member of the saxifrage family, heuchera can be grown as ground cover in light shade, or in clumps in borders, where the flowers will attract bees. The plants make mounds of foliage out of which spring panicles of tiny flowers on tall stems. Most of the named varieties are red or coral pink but the species H. *cylindrica* offers green-flowered varieties such as 'Greenfinch', which can be used to much more subtle effect. Good red varieties include 'Red Spangles' and 'Coral Cloud'. If you want to use heuchera as a foliage plant try 'Palace Purple' (chocolate), 'Pewter Moon' (gray) or 'Snow Storm' (flecked white).
ht to 90cm/3ft, sp 60cm/2ft ('Greenfinch')
ht 50cm/20in, sp 25cm/10in ('Red Spangles')
ht 75cm/30in, sp 30cm/12in ('Coral Cloud')
ht and sp to 60cm/2ft ('Palace Purple')
ht to 40cm/16in, sp 30cm/12in ('Pewter Moon')
ht and sp 30cm/12in ('Snow Storm')
Soil and position
Moist but well-drained, preferably neutral soil in partial to full shade.

◄ Geranium, *cranesbill or geranium.*

Kniphofia
RED-HOT POKER

Red-hot poker is certainly a striking plant, in height, form and color, and it can be just what's needed to make bright points of color or as a foil for softer plants. Torches of red or orange flowers rise erect from the bundles of strap-like leaves in a show-stopping way in summer, with exact flowering times depending on the cultivar. Among the tall and reds you might choose the brilliant *K.* 'Atlanta' (red and yellow, flowering early summer), or the massive *K.* 'Prince Igor' (pure, brilliant red for the end of the summer). *K. caulescens* is a very hardy red-hot poker with more muted colors (dull purple red topping light yellow), flowering from late summer into the fall; the lower growing variety *K.* 'Bees Sunset' has warm light orange flowers throughout the summer, and for a yellow poker of modest height there is *K.* 'Sunningdale Yellow', which flowers from mid- to late summer.
ht 1.2m/4ft, sp 75cm/30in
('Atlanta')
ht 1.8m/6ft sp 90cm/3ft ('Prince Igor')
ht to 1.2m/4ft, sp 60cm/2ft (K. caulescens)
ht 90cm/3ft, sp 60cm/2ft ('Bees Sunset')
ht 90cm/3ft, sp 45cm/18in ('Sunningdale Yellow')
Soil and position
Fertile, sandy or well-drained soil in a sunny position. Tolerates light shade.

Lamium maculatum
LAMIUM OR DEAD NETTLE

Lamium is a ground-cover plant for shaded places, grown mainly for its tooth-edged white- and silver- mottled leaves. *Lamium maculatum* f. *album* has pure white flowers throughout the spring and early summer, as well as white-patterned leaves; *L. m.* 'Roseum' is its pink-flowered partner. *L. m.* 'White Nancy' has green-edged, silver leaves and white flowers, and *L. m.* 'Aureum' has yellow and white leaves, although (unusually for plants with golden variegation) like the rest, it must have semi-shade. The plants spread quickly and are hardy, keeping their leaves throughout the winter as long as it's not too wet.
ht 23–30cm/9–12in
sp to 60cm/2ft
Soil and position
Thrives in shade and semishade in ordinary soil. *L. m.* 'Aureum' needs more moisture and a more fertile soil than the others.

Lavandula
LAVENDER

Lavender (really a shrub) needs no introduction as a well-loved garden and herb garden plant for warm and well-drained sites. The flowers can be dried and used in pot pourri and for scenting linen. The bushy plants, with their gray-green leaves, look good even when not covered in the fragrant flower spikes. *Lavandula angustifolia* is the old English lavender, also know as *L. officinalis* or *L spica*. The variety 'Hidcote' is a true deep lavender blue; the more compact 'Munstead' is purple blue. 'Hidcote Pink' is (as its name suggests) a pink-flowered form, while 'Nana Alba' is small and neat and white-flowering. A less hardy and more unusual lavender is French lavender, *L. stoechas*, with flaring purple bracts above the flowers.
ht 60cm/2ft, sp 75cm/30in ('Hidcote' and 'Hidcote Pink')
ht 45cm/18in, sp 60cm/2ft ('Munstead')
ht and sp 30cm/12in ('Nana Alba')
ht and sp 60cm/2ft (L. stoechas)

Soil and position
Very well-drained soil, and a position in full sun.

Papaver orientale
ORIENTAL POPPY

Gardens need poppies. *Papaver orientale* is the brilliant orange-red poppy commonly seen in established gardens, but there are many hybrids, known by their own names, giving a wide choice of color and patterning. 'Black and White' is a luscious double creamy white poppy with black stamens; 'Bonfire Red' speaks for itself; 'Cedric Morris' has full-blown petals in soft pink, with black blotches at the center; 'Beauty of Livermore' is a clear poppy red, and 'Mrs Perry' is black-blotched salmon pink. (See also *P. somniferum*, page 232)
ht to 90cm/3ft
sp 60–90cm/2–3ft
Soil and position
Fertile soil, including heavy soil

▲ Kniphofia, *red-hot poker.*

as long as it is well-drained, and a sunny position.

Penstemon cultivars
PENSTEMON

With their profusion of foxglove bells and their tall but bushy growth these are lovely, though not very hardy or long-lived border plants, which flower well into the fall. In recent years more and more hybrids have been developed to widen the range of colors and improve hardiness. Colors vary from strong to pastel, mainly pinks, magenta and purples, but also blue and white. Give frost protection where winters are cold, and protect from slugs and snails, which are partial to this dish. All the following are hardy: 'Alice Hindley' (lilac blue), 'Apple Blossom' (apple blossom pink), 'Blackbird' (deep purple),

'Garnet' (garnet red), 'Hidcote Pink' (pale pink), 'Mother of Pearl' (pearly lilac and pink), 'White Bedder' (white).
ht and sp 10–60cm/4–24in
Soil and position
Penstemons need fertile soil with good drainage, especially during winter, and a warm, sheltered position in sun or partial shade.

Perovskia atriplicifolia
RUSSIAN SHADE

More people should grow this tolerant, shrubby plant for its tiny lilac blue flowers and gray-green, sage-scented leaves on wiry stems. The flowers are produced toward the end of the summer but, with its mass of tall and upward-branching grayish stems and narrow, tooth-edged leaves, the plant looks good all summer. *P.* 'Blue Spire' is very generous with its deep violet-

blue flowers. *P.* 'Hybrida' has lavender-blue flowers and is a little less tall.
ht 90 cm–1.5m/3–5ft
sp to 90cm/3ft
Soil and position
Needs a sunny position in freely draining soil but will grow in poor, dry, or chalky soil. May not survive winter in cold, damp conditions, but may revive if cut back in spring.

Phlox paniculata
GARDEN PHLOX

With their evocative, slightly woody scent and heads of simple, open flowers, these are good, long-lived herbaceous border plants. They flower in full summer, mostly in the pink, white and dusky purple color range, and often with a contrasting eye. Good specimens include 'Alba Grandiflora'

◀ Lamium maculatum, *Lamium or dead nettle.*

▶ Penstemon *cultivars*, penstemon.

(white), 'Amethyst' (violet), 'Blue Ice' (blue-tinged white with contrasting eye), 'Eva Callum' (deep pink with contrasting eye), 'Eventide' (lavender blue), 'Prince of Orange' (orange-red), 'Prospero' (pale lilac, edged), and 'White Admiral' (pure white). Plants may need staking in windy spots and frequent watering in dry weather.
ht 80 cm–1.2m/32in–4ft
sp 60–90cm/2–3ft
Soil and position
Fertile, heavy, moist but well-drained soil and a position in sun or partial shade.

Potentilla
POTENTILLA

There is a huge range of potentillas for the garden. They are in fact shrubs, but many make nice, well-rounded little bushes, small enough to blend well with perennials and border plants. They have attractive small leaves, sometimes deeply cut or silvery, and are incredibly floriferous, usually covered with small and delicate buttercup-like flowers from early summer until late fall.

Flowers are in white and all shades of yellow, orange, red, or pink. Among the many small garden hybrids are *Potentilla* 'Gibson's Scarlet' (blood-red flowers with dark centers), 'William Rollinson' (semi-double, flowers in red flecked with yellow) and *P. nepalensis* 'Miss Willmott' (raspberry pink with carmine markings). *P. recta* (pale lemon-yellow) and *P. fruticosa* 'Abbotswood' (delicate white flowers) are a little larger.
ht 30–45cm/12–18in, sp 60cm/2ft
('Gibson's Scarlet', 'William Rollinson', 'Miss Willmott')

ht 60cm/2ft, sp 45cm/18in
(P. recta)
ht 75cm/30in, sp 1.2m/4ft
(P. fruticosa 'Abbotswood')
Soil and position
Must have very well-drained soil, which need not be too fertile. Flower best in full sun.

Pulmonaria
PULMONARIA OR LUNGWORT

Also known as "soldiers and sailors," this is a lovely low-growing plant for early spring, one of the first to flower, and growing bigger and better as the season continues. When the flowers are over the white-blotched leaves come to the fore, and remain decoratively in the garden all summer and fall. The flowers are a beautiful blue, or in

some varieties varicolored pink and blue. Choice white varieties are also available, and a few are pink or red. Good blue varieties include *Pulmonaria* 'Mawson's Blue' (deep blue), *P. officinalis* 'Royal Blue' and *P. o.* 'Blue Mist'. *P. o.* 'Sissinghurst White' is the white to go for.
ht and sp 30cm/12in
Soil and position
Moist, fertile soil and a position in partial shade. Lungwort grows well beneath deciduous trees and shrubs.

Sedum spectabile
ICE PLANT
There is something cactus-like about this plant, with its fleshy, gray-green stems and leaves, and its densely packed flat flower heads of starry pink flowers attracting butterflies in late

◄ Sedum spectabile, ice plant, 'Mawson's Blue' variety.

summer. The plant has a rounded, compact shape and dry flower heads are an attraction throughout the winter. *Sedum spectabile* 'Autumn Joy' and *S. s.* 'Brilliant' are good varieties.
ht and sp 45cm/18in
Soil and position
Grows best in well-drained slightly alkaline soil, in full sun.

Stachys byzantina
LAMB'S EARS OR WOOLY BETONY
Soft, silver-gray and felted leaves are the main feature of this plant for dry places, although in summer it also has taller spikes of small purplish pink flowers set in whorls among tiny gray leaves and rising above the lamb's ear leaves. However, the main part of the plant is low-growing and it also spreads well and is

▲ Pulmonaria, *pulmonaria or lungwort.*

evergreen—or evergray—except that a damp winter can end its life.
ht to 45cm/18in
sp 60cm/2ft
Soil and position
Must have very well-drained soil (though will tolerate poor soil), and an open, fairly sunny position.

Verbascum
VERBASCUM OR MULLEIN
An elegant, tall, spiry plant with gray, felted leaves, verbascum is sometimes short-lived but is easily grown from seed. The flower spike ascends from a rosette of leaves in summer and some varieties are very tall. *Verbascum bombyciferum* with its immense height and sulfur-yellow flowers is an accent plant and a half. Many named garden varieties are available for those who want something a little less lofty or more subtly colored. *V.* 'Cotswold Beauty' has purple-centered yellow flowers; the flowers of 'Gainsborough' are

chalky yellow, and 'Pink Domino' has rosy or purple pink flowers. *V. phoeniceum* (purple mullein) hybrids give pink, white, and purple flowers.
ht 1.2m/4ft; to 1.6m/6ft (Verbascum bombyciferum)
sp 30–60cm/1–2ft
Soil and position
Alkaline, well-drained to dry soil, including poor soils. Does best in sun.

Verbena bonariensis
VERBENA
Tall, wiry, branching stems produce many small heads of bright purple flowers throughout the summer and early fall at varying heights. The stems are spruce green and pleasantly rough. Sometimes grown as an annual bedding plant, verbena survives the winter if protected from frost.
ht to 1.2m/4ft
sp 45cm/18in
Soil and position
Well-drained soil and full sun.

TREES AND SPECIMEN SHRUBS

Trees and shrubs give shape and form to the garden and can act as strong focal points. They need to be chosen and positioned with care as they make a permanent feature that can take up a lot of room, and make areas of shade, but they compensate by adding height and substance and helping to bring structure to the plot. The plants selected here are all suitable for smaller gardens and many have something of interest to offer for more than one season.

Acer
MAPLE

There are several ornamental maples whose height keeps to within ordinary garden limits, and they usually have bark appeal as well as leaf appeal and fall color. *Acer griseum* is a paper bark maple with peeling, orange-brown bark and broad, flat, three-lobed leaves which turn orange to red and scarlet in the fall. An advantage is that it can be grown as a single- or multistemmed tree. *Acer henryi* is a smallish, shapely maple which colors bright orange-red in the fall and *Acer rufinerve* (red vein maple) is a taller but less spreading maple with green and white striped bark, and red and orange leaves in fall.
ht and sp 5–10m / 16–32ft
Soil and position
Fertile, well-drained (but not dry) soil, in a light position.
(*Acer* 'Rubrum', page 135)

Amelanchier lamarckii
AMELANCHIER
OR SNOWY MESPILUS
Bronze unfolding leaves almost disappear as small white starry flowers smother the branches of the plant in spring. Amelanchier becomes less interesting as the

flowers die and leaves turn green, but in later summer coral pink fruits develop and then the leaves turn bright red. If the birds leave the fruits to ripen they eventually turn black. Can be grown as a single or

▲ Acer palmatum, *Japanese maple 'Dissectum Atropurpureum'.*

multistemmed plant.
ht 3m / 10ft
sp to 3m / 10ft
Soil and position

Moist, preferably neutral or acid soil in a light position.

Berberis sieboldii
BERBERIS OR BARBERRY
A spiny shrub with shiny reddish stems and clusters of small yellow flowers in late spring. In the fall these develop into red shining berries and the pointed leaves turn a magnificent vivid red in a display that lasts over a long period. The plant can be grown in a wide range of soils.
ht and sp 90–120cm / 3–4ft
Soil and position
Likes soils from sandy to almost boggy and a position in full sun.
CAUTION: TAKE CARE WHEN HANDLING BERBERIS BECAUSE OF ITS SPINES. ALL PARTS OF THE PLANT CAN CAUSE STOMACH UPSETS IF EATEN.

Buddleja davidii
BUDDLEJA
OR BUTTERFLY BUSH
Most people know buddleja, with its arching branches of honey-scented flowers that attract butterflies to the garden in late summer. Growing in densely covered plumes, the flowers are normally in shades of purple, from light soft bluish purple to deepest royal purple, though they also come in white. *Buddleja davidii* 'Black Knight' has the darkest flowers, 'Empire Blue' has lavender blue flowers, 'Harlequin' is cerise and has cream-margined leaves, and 'White Profusion' has very long tails of white flowers. The species *B. alternifolia*, with more delicate, clustered flowers and willow-like leaves, is a more unusual alternative that flowers earlier in the year.
ht to 3m / 10ft
sp to 4.5m / 15ft
Soil and position
Ordinary, well-drained garden soil in full sun.

◀ Buddleja davidii, *buddleja or butterfly bush 'Black Knight'.*

Ceanothus 'Gloire de Versailles'
CEANOTHUS OR CALIFORNIA LILAC

From ground-level upward, pale blue powderpuffs of flowers enliven this hardy California lilac all summer. Ceanothus makes a lovely plant for a warm, sheltered spot and grows well against a wall; many forms are to be found. 'Gloire de Versailles' is deciduous but in the late-spring-flowering 'Cascade' the little leaves are evergreen and the flowers a brighter blue.
ht and sp 1.5m/5ft or more ('Gloire de Versailles'); up to 3.6m/12ft ('Cascade')
Soil and position

These shrubs need good drainage and like poor, sandy soil. They must have warmth, and shelter from cold winds.

Cornus kousa var. chinensis
KOUSA DOGWOOD

This is a neat, upright shrub or small tree with minute green flowers surrounded by showy white bracts. In hot summers the flowers sometimes develop strawberry-like fruits and the tapered oval leaves are a bright crimson red in the fall.
ht to 7m/23ft
sp 4.5m/15ft
Soil and position
Almost any soil, as long as well-drained, and a position in sun or partial shade.

Cornus officinalis
DOGWOOD

This very hardy multistemmed dogwood is grown for its gray, brown and orange winter bark and purple-red fall leaves. Tolerant of most soils, it is very vigorous. Other dogwoods with colorful stems include C. stolonifera (dark red), C. stolonifera 'Flaviramea' (yellow-green), and C. alba (red). All look good growing near water, or where the winter light can filter through the stems.
ht and sp 3m/10ft (C. alba); ht and sp to 4.5m/15ft (C. officinalis); ht 1.8m/6ft, sp 3.6m/12ft (C. stolonifera)
Soil and position
Ordinary garden soil in an open, sunny position.

Cotinus
SMOKE BUSH

The smoke bush has leaves that color brightly in the fall and flowers that create the impression of plumes of smoke in summer. Cotinus 'Grace' has red and orange leaves in the fall; Cotinus coggygria 'Royal Purple' has smoky pink plumes of flower and purple foliage which provides a foil for many garden flowers and which colors bright red in the fall.
ht and sp 5m/16ft
Soil and position
Ordinary garden soil and a sunny position to bring out the best foliage color.

Cotoneaster
COTONEASTER

Cotoneasters are a family of very obliging shrubs which produce a wealth of red berries to attract the birds in the fall and generally keep their leaves throughout the winter. The leaves are dark green and often color up to red during the winter. In late spring plants bear a mass of small white flowers. The handsome, tree-like Cotoneaster 'Cornubia' has broad, semievergreen leaves and bright bunches of clear red fruits which weigh down the stems in the fall and often last all winter. C. 'Exburiensis' has yellow fruits.
ht and sp 6m/20ft ('Cornubia'); 4.5m/15ft ('Exburiensis')
Soil and position
Ordinary well-drained, or even dry, soil in sun or partial shade.

Elaeagnus pungens
ELAEAGNUS

This is a strong evergreen shrub with glossy green leaves, making it particularly useful in winter. In the variety 'Maculata' the leaves are gold outlined with deep green, and 'Dicksonii' has yellow-edged leaves. Elaeagnus has small but extremely fragrant cream-colored tubular flowers in the fall.
ht and sp to 4m/13ft or more but can be kept trimmed
Soil and position
Puts up with most soils and situations, including by the sea.

Eucalyptus gunnii
EUCALYPTUS OR CIDER GUM

This is a fast-growing Tasmanian tree that flourishes in European climates. The rounded young leaves, like the peeling bark, are a silvery gray, and the plant may produce more than one trunk. The leaves are evergreen and the young leaves are the prettiest, so the stems are best cut back each year in early spring to encourage new growth. The tree produces creamy white flowers in late summer to early fall.
ht 14m/46ft
sp 4.5m/15ft or more
Can be grown as a shrub trimmed to

ht 1.8m/6ft, sp 1.2m/4ft
Soil and position
Fertile, slightly acid, moist soil
and a sunny position with shelter
from cold winds.

Fothergilla major
FOTHERGILLA

Scented, cream-colored fuzzy
flowers in spring before the
leaves appear and radiant yellow
or yellow and scarlet leaves in
the fall make this a shrub for two
seasons. It spreads broadly and is
fairly low-growing. *Fothergilla
gardenii* is similar but smaller and
more compact and with crimson
fall leaves.
ht to 2.5m/8ft, sp to 1.8m/6ft
(Fothergilla major); ht 90cm/3ft, sp
to 1.2m/4ft (F. gardenii)
Soil and position
Needs light, acid soil and will
flourish in any position from full
sun to semishade.

Genista aetnensis
MOUNT ETNA BROOM

Graceful and arching, brooms
make fountains of golden flowers
in the summer months. Mount
Etna broom makes a rounded
small tree, the stems completely
hidden by flowers in full
summer. *G. cineria* is a lower-
growing multistemmed shrub,
billowing with sweetly scented
flowers in early summer.
ht to 6m/20ft, sp to 5.5m/18ft
(Genista aetnensis); ht to 3m/10ft,
sp to 2.5m/8ft (G. cineria)
Soil and position
Light, well-drained soil,
including poor soil, and a warm,
sunny position.

Hamamelis mollis
HAMAMELIS OR CHINESE
WITCH HAZEL

Witch hazel is a must for anyone
who wants winter fragrance. The
wispy yellow flowers on the bare
twigs actually benefit from cold,
which prolongs the flowering
period; the rounded leaves turn a

▶ *Cotinus*, smoke bush, requires a
sunny position for best color.

soft warm yellow in the fall.
H. × intermedia 'Pallida' (syn *H. m.*
'Pallida') has red-centered, pale
yellow flowers. Plant hamamelis
near the house or the front path,
so that you can sniff it when you
walk by.
ht and sp to 2.5m/8ft
Soil and position
Needs a fairly rich, moist soil
that is neutral to acid and a
sheltered spot in full sun or
semishade.

Hebe
HEBE

Hebes are staunch plants,
keeping their small, leathery
leaves all year and flowering for a
long period, as well as forming
neat, compact bushes that
generally grow well in
containers. In some varieties the
leaves are variegated, while the
numerous small flowers are
usually in shades of bluish
purple, with some pink- or
white-flowering varieties.
H. 'Autumn Glory' has flowers
in a warm purple blue, while
H. 'Midsummer Beauty' has lilac
colored flowers fading to
white, and both flower from
mid-summer until late fall.
H. speciosa 'Sapphire' is covered
in flowers of a warm, soft blue.
ht to 1.5m/5ft
sp 1.2–1.5m/ 4–5ft
Soil and position
Almost any soil, including chalk,
as long as it's well-drained, and a
sunny position. Hebes dislike real
cold, but withstand salt-laden
winds well.

Kolkwitzia amabilis
BEAUTY BUSH

A mass of delicate silvery pink
flowers gives rise to the name
beauty bush. The shrub can be
difficult to get started, but it
rewards persistence, producing its

lightly-scented foxglove-like
flowers on arching branches in
late spring and early summer.
ht to 3.6m/12ft
sp to 3m/10ft
Can be pruned to keep it smaller.
Soil and position
Ordinary, well-drained soil in a
sunny position. Flowers best in a
soil that is not too rich.

Lonicera periclymenum
HONEYSUCKLE

Honeysuckle climbs by twining
and can be grown on trellis or
fencing or over a large shrub.
A lovely plant for a scented arbor
or to grow against the house
wall, round the door, or over a
garden shed. All varieties of
Lonicera periclymenum have the

heady honeysuckle scent.
Here are some excellent choices:
L. p. 'Belgica' (purplish red and
yellowish cream) flowers in late
spring and early summer;
L. p. 'Graham Thomas' (white,
becoming yellow) flowers
through from midsummer until
the fall; and *L. p.* 'Serotina'
(creamy white inside, purple-red
outside) flowers from midsummer until late fall.
ht and sp 3.6–6m/12–20ft
Can be trimmed to suit the space.
Soil and situation
Ordinary, well-drained soil with
added compost or manure.
Flourishes in partial shade but
will do well in sun if the roots
are shaded.

◀ Lonicera periclymenum, *honeysuckle.*

Malus
CRAB APPLE

Crab apple trees are grown for their fragrant spring apple blossom and small and ornamental apple-like fruits that generally last from fall and into the next spring. Good and fairly compact specimens include *Malus* 'Crittenden', profusely covered in apple-blossom pink flowers followed by small bunches of bright red berries; *M.* 'Golden Hornet', with white flowers and warm yellow crab apples, and *Malus × arnoldiana*, which has pink flowers opening from pinky red buds and fading to white, followed by red-flushed yellow fruits.

ht 4.5–5.5m/15–18ft
sp to 6m/20ft
Soil and position
Ordinary to rich garden soil

which is well-drained, can take sun or partial shade.

Pieris japonica
PIERIS

This is a large and spreading evergreen shrub with cascades of little vase-shaped, waxy flowers in spring and copper red new leaves. The variety 'Debutante' is slow-growing and very hardy, and in mid-spring its leaves are almost hidden by a mass of creamy white flowers. Unlike most other forms of pieris this one is a dwarf, making it ideal for smaller gardens, roof gardens or patios.

ht and sp to 3m/10ft
Soil and position
Must have lime-free, well-drained soil; flowers best in full sun. Provide shelter from cold winds to prevent frost damage.

Potentilla
POTENTILLA

Potentillas come in all sizes and the small ones can be thought of as belonging with perennials. As a larger shrub, *Potentilla fruticosa* var. *arbuscula*) (syn. *P. arbuscula*) comes in many varieties, with flower colors in all shades of yellow and orange, as well as white, pink, and red. The buttercup-like flowers occur over a very long period from late spring onward. All have pretty leaves, some finely dissected.

ht 90 cm–1.5m/3–5ft
sp to 1.5m/5ft
Soil and position
Light, or even poor soil, as long as it is well-drained; a light, sunny position for best flowering is required.
(See also page 243)

Prunus
PRUNUS OR
FLOWERING CHERRY

The term 'prunus' covers a huge range of flowering cherries, plums and almond trees, many grown only for their clouds of spring flowers and not bearing fruit. Among these one of the loveliest is *Prunus* 'Shirotae', a Japanese cherry (syn. *P.* 'Mount Fuji'). This is a spreading tree with large, white, fragrant flowers, and stunning orange-red fall foliage.

ht 6m/20ft
sp 7.5m/25ft
Soil and position
Ordinary, fairly well-drained soil, preferably alkaline. May need support in exposed, windy areas.

Rhus typhina
STAGSHORN SUMAC

Stagshorn sumac produces spectacular orange-red leaf color in the fall, and has velvety twigs with smooth bark. It throws up suckers to form a multistemmed

tree or bush and takes happily to being pruned to size.

ht 3–4.5m/10–15ft
sp 3–4.5m/10–15ft
Can be cut to the ground each year in spring to produce vigorous new shoots and best foliage.
Soil and position
Will thrive in any soil that is not waterlogged. Best in a sunny position.
CAUTION: THE SAP CAN CAUSE SKIN BLISTERS.

Robinia pseudoacacia 'Frisia'
GOLDEN ACACIA
OR ROBINIA

A most ornamental foliage tree that makes a lovely backcloth for other garden plants, this acacia lookalike has stalks of small, paired leaflets, golden green in color, which ripple in the breeze. Older trees have white pea-flowers which hang down in clusters in early summer. Robinias can be trained to grow against a wall and trimmed to size or grown as free-standing trees. Eventually, it must be admitted, they can grow rather large.

ht 7.3m/24ft and eventually more
sp 3–4.5m/10–15ft
Soil and position
Any soil that does not get waterlogged, including alkaline soils, and full sun to light shade, as long as the tree is not exposed to harsh winds.

Sambucus racemosa 'Sutherland Gold'
GARDEN ELDER

This is an ornamental garden version of the common country elder and has upright, cone-shaped panicles of tiny white-ish cream flowers in early summer, followed in late summer by heads of small, bright red berries. The abundant golden leaves have finely cut edges.

ht and sp 3m/10ft but can be

trimmed to size
Soil and position
Almost any soil in dappled shade.

Sorbus aria 'Lutescens'
WHITEBEAM

This is a shapely, smallish
whitebeam with silver–gray
young foliage, later turning gray–
green. The leaves flutter white in
the breeze because of the dense
white felt on their undersides.
In late spring the tree has light
and airy corymbs of small,
creamy white, fuzzy flowers
ht 9m/30ft
sp 7.5m/25ft
Soil and position
Ordinary, well-drained garden
soil in an open, sunny position.

Sorbus commixta
MOUNTAIN ASH

The mountain ash or rowan
makes a good specimen tree
with its pinnate leaves and white
spring flowers which develop
into firm round fruits in late
summer. Most also have good fall
leaf color. 'Embley' has plentiful
flowers followed by bright red
fruits. The glossy, dark green
leaves are particularly well–
shaped and put on a fall
show of red and orange.
ht 10m/32ft
sp 7m/23ft
Soil and position
Well-drained but moist garden
soil and a position in sun or
semishade.
CAUTION: ALTHOUGH THE
FRUITS CAN BE USED FOR JELLY
THEY CAUSE STOMACH UPSETS
IF EATEN RAW.

Spirea 'Arguta'
FOAM OF MAY
OR BRIDAL WREATH

This is a pretty and graceful
shrub; abundant white flowers
clothe the arching stems in late
spring and the stems themselves
have an appealing reddish tint
when bare from fall to early

spring. S. thunbergii is rather
similar, and there are many other
spireas to choose, including the
(usually) pink-flowered S. japonica
which flowers in summer.
ht and sp to 2.5m/8ft; S. japonica
and S. thunbergii are smaller
Soil and position
Well-drained but reasonably
moist soil in sun or partial shade.

Symphoricarpos albus 'Laevigatus'
SNOWBERRY

Snowberries have to be chosen
carefully as they can colonize an
area, producing scrappy stems
and little fruit. However a good
snowberry is well worth
growing, especially for its effects
in winter. This one, with its large
white winter berries on delicate
stems is a good choice.
ht and sp 1.8m/6ft but can be kept
trimmed
Soil and position
Tolerates any soil except wet,
and any position from full sun to
shade.
CAUTION: THE BERRIES CAUSE
STOMACH UPSET IF EATEN AND
SOME PEOPLE FIND THEIR JUICE
IRRITATING TO THE SKIN.

Viburnum
VIBURNUM

There are so many viburnums
for the garden that this species
deserves several entries.
   Winter-flowering species,
with very fragrant pinkish white
flowers in small clusters on bare,
twiggy stems, are Viburnum farreri
(syn. V. fragrans), V. grandiflorum,
and V. × bodnantense 'Dawn', an
offspring of the two.
ht to 3m/10ft, sp to 2.5m/8ft
(Viburnum farreri);
ht and sp 1.8m/6ft (V.
grandiflorum);
ht 3m/10ft, sp 2m/6ft 6in
(V. × bodnantense 'Dawn')
   Viburnum × burkwoodii has
rounded balls of clustered
fragrant, white, tubular flowers

▲ Sambucus racemosa 'Sutherland Gold'.

in spring.
ht and sp 2.5m/8ft
   Viburnum tinus is a robust,
evergreen viburnum that bears
white flowers, sometimes almost
continuously, from late fall till
late spring.
ht to 3m/10ft, sp 1.8m/6ft
   Viburnum opulus, the guelder
rose, is a deciduous viburnum
with hydrangea-like heads of
creamy white flowers in late

spring, followed by jelly-red
berries in the fall.
ht to 3m/10ft
Soil and position
Fertile, fairly moist garden soil in
sun or semishade.
CAUTION: THE FRUITS OF
VIBURNUM OPULUS CAN CAUSE
STOMACH UPSETS IF EATEN.

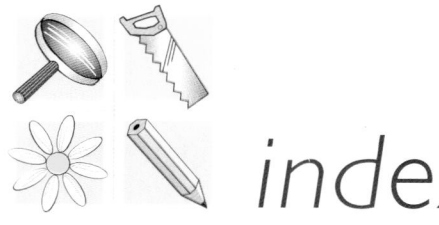

index

*Note: **bold** figures indicate plant profiles; roman figures indicate illustrations*

A

acacias **248**
Acer *(maple)* 220, 245, **245**
    A. henryi 245
    A. palmatum *(Japanese maple)* **135**, 245
    A. rufinerve 245
acers 135, 220, 245
Adam's needle 70
Adiantum capillus-veneris *(maidenhair fern)* 29
agapanthus 70, 178, **234**
Agapanthus africanus *(African lily)* 234, 235
    'Blue Giant' 70
Ajuga reptans *(bugle)* 115, 115
Alcea rosea *(hollyhock)* 41, **228**, 228
    'Chater's Double' 228
    'Majorette' 228
Alchemilla mollis *(lady's mantle)* **239**
alchemillas 55, **239**
algae 19
Allium christophii *(allium)* 234, **234**
    A. flavum 188
    A. sativum *(garlic)* 93
    A. schoenoprasum *(chives)* 93
    A. sphaerocephalon 104
    A. ursinum *(wild garlic)* 105
alliums 105, 178, 188, **234**
alpines 166
alum root 61
Amelanchier lamarckii *(snowy mespilus)* **245**
amelanchiers **245**
Ameria maritima *(sea thrift)* 199
Anemone blanda *(windflower)* **234**
A. x hybrida *(Japanese anemone)* 239, **239**
    'Queen Charlotte' 239

'Whirlwind' 239
Anethum graveolens *(dill)* 93
angelica 92
Angelica archangelica *(angelica)* 92
annuals 35, 40, 41, 54, 86, 93, 166, 210, 228–33
aphids 51
aquatic plants 13, 18–19
Aquilegia *(aquilegia)* 41, **211**, **239**
    'Nora Barlow' 41, 239
aquilegias 41, 104, 205, 211, **211**, **239**
Arbutus unedo *(strawberry tree)* 206, 211, **211**, 220
arches 44, 44, 49
aromatics 119, 162, 166
Artemisia absinthium *(wormwood)* 178
    A. dranunculus *(French tarragon)* 93
Arum italicum *(lords and ladies/cuckoopint)* **234**
    'Marmoratum' 234
    'Pictum' 234
arum lily 29
Arundinaria simonii *(bamboo)* 135
Asplenium scolopendrium 'Crispum' 28, 29
Aster novi-belgii *(michaelmas daisy)* **40–1**
Astilbe *(astilbe)* 29
    'Fanal' 115
astilbes 29, 105, 114, **115**
Athyrium filix-fermina 58
Aucuba japonica 'Salicifolia' 58
auriculas 125
autumn crocus see *colchicum*
azaleas 125, 225

B

bamboo curtains 90
bamboos 64, 134–5, 135, 156–7, 188
banana plant 70
barbecue equipment 193
barberry see *berberis*

barrenwort 115, **240**
basil 86, 93, 93
Bassia scoparia *(summer cypress)* **228**
    'Evergreen' **228**
batchelor's button 82, **228**
bay 86, 93, 215
beauty bush **247**
bedding plants 54, 205, 210
beds 48, 77
    marking out 226
    vegetable 80
beech fern 29
bees 118
beetroot 76
bellflower **239**
Bellis perennis *(batchelor's button)* 82, **228**
    'Carpet Mixed' 228
bells of Ireland 232
berberis **245**
Berberis sieboldii *(berberis/barberry)* **245**
bergamot 92
Beta vulgaris *(Swiss chard)* 83
betony 105
Betula spp. *(silver birch)* 220
    B. nigra *(black birch)* 115, **115**
biennials 35, 41, 205, 211, 228–33
birds 40, 215, 216, 220
bird's foot trefoil 104
black birch 115, **115**
black medick 104
blackfly 51
blackthorn 35
bleeding heart 29, **240**
bluebells 105
bog gardens 12–21
borage 82, 82–3, 92
Borago officinalis *(borage)* 82–3, 92
borders: designing/planting 48, 54–63
boulders 129, 132
boundaries for roofs 186
box 44, 71, 112–13, 122, 166, 215, 220, **221**
Brachyscome iberidifolia *(Swan River daisy)* **228**, 229

brassicas 76, 77
bridal wreath see *foam of May*
Briza media *(quaking grass)* 104, 105
Brompton stocks 125, **145**
broom 178, **247**
buddlejas 40, 188, 225, **245**, 246
Buddleja davidii *(buddleja/butterfly bush)* 40, 188, **245**, 246
    B. alternifolia 245
bugle 105, **115**
bulbs 40, 54, 105, 109, 205, 227, **234–8**
burning bush see *summer cypress*
busy lizzies 210
butterflies 40, 118
butterfly bush see *buddleja*
Buxus sempervirens *(box)* 71, 112–13, 123, **221**
buying plants 186

C

cacti 178
calendula 41, 61, 211, **229**
Calendula *(calendula)* **229**
    C. officinalis 41
    C. 'Pacific Beauty' 61
    'Yellow Queen' 229
California lilac 246
Californian poppies **105**, 166, 179, 179
Camellia japonica *(camellia)* **135**
camellias 110, **135**, 215, 219, 225
Campanula persicifolia *(bellflower/campanula)* **239**
    C. p. alba 239
    'Elizabeth' 239
campanulas 45, 225, 239
    see also *bellflower*
campion 102, 104
candytuft 166
cape hyacinths 61
cardoons 178, 179
carnations 61, 125, 145, 225
carrots 76
"catch crops" 76
catmint 41, 45
Ceanothus 'Gloire de Versailles'

(ceanothus/California lilac) **246**
celandine 105
Centaurea cyanus (cornflower)
41, 229, **229**
Centranthus ruber (valerian) 41
Chamaemelum nobile
(chamomile) 92
chamomile 92, 122
chard 83, **83**
cherry pie plant see heliotrope
children
gardens 150–9
and safety 22, 23, 151
Chilean bamboo 135
Chilean potato vine 71
Chimonanthus praecox
(wintersweet) 220
Chinese witch hazel see
hamamelis
Chionodoxa (glory of the snow)
235
'Pink Giant' 235
chives 82, 93
Choisya ternata (Mexican orange
blossom) 125, 198, **198–9**, 225
Christmas rose 241
chrysanthemums 61
Chusquea culeou (Chilean
bamboo) 135
cider gum see eucalyptus
Clarkia (clarkia/godetia) 41, **229**
clearing crops 104
clematis 45, **61**, 198, 225
Clematis armandii 71
'Etoile Violette' 61
C. montana 71
C. sieboldii 68
C. vitalba 61
climbers 35, 38, 55, 71, 90, 114,
122, 123, 166
climbing hydrangea 114
clover 105
Colchicum (colchicum/autumn
crocus) **235**
colchicums 235
colewort **239**
color in garden design 8, 9, 8–9,
55, 58, 118, 129, 144, 173
seasonal variations 206, 210,
214–15
columbines 211
comfrey 92, 105
common daisy 104
common laurel 220
companion planting 45

compost/composting 40, 79,
80–81, 187, 205
conifers 220
Consolida ajacis (larkspur) **229**
containers 65, 71, 160, 161, 183,
184, 185, 187, 205, 215
planting 19, 70, 82, 166, 208–9
Convallaria majalis (lily-of-the-
valley) 125
convolvulus 105
coral flower see hencheras
corms 234–8
corn marigold 105
corncockle 105
cornflowers 41, 98, 102, **229**
Cornus (dogwood) 220
C. kousa var. chinensis (Kousa
dogwood) **246**
C. officinalis (dogwood) **246**
Corsican hellibore 241
Cortaderia selloana (pampas
grass) 157
C. 'Gold Band' 199
cosmos 41, **229**
Cosmos bipinnatus
(cosmos/cosmea) **229**
'Sensation Mixed' 41, 229
Cotinus (smoke bush) **246**, 247
Cotoneaster (cotoneaster) **246**
cotoneasters **246**
cottage gardens 34–43
cotton lavender 188
courtyards 64–73
cow parsley 104
cowslip 102, 104, 105
crab apple 248
Crambe cordifolia (colewort) **239**
C. maritima (sea kale) 188,
239
cranesbill 41, 241, **241**
Crinum x Powellii (crinum) **235**
crinums 235
crocosmia 178, 211
Crocosmia 'Lucifer' 210, **211**
Crocus (crocus) **235**
'Dutch Yellow' 235
'Joan of Arc' 235
'Ruby Giant' 235
'Winston Churchill' 235
crocuses 105, **235**
crop rotation 77, 80
crown imperial **236**
cuckoopint see lords and ladies
currant bushes 41
Cyclamen coum (cyclamen) **235**

cyclamen **235**
Cynara cardunculus (cardoon)
178, **179**
Cytisus scoparius (common
broom) 178

D

daffodils 105, **238**
Dahlia (dahlia) 236, **236**
'Bishop of Llandaff' 236, 236
'Easter Sunday' 236
'Hamari Gold' 236
'Moor Place' 236
'Princess Marie Jose' 236
dahlias 61, 236, **236**
daisy bush 178, 179
dame's violet 125
dandelion 104
Daphne mezereum 125
D. odora 220
daphnes 125, 220
day lilies **241**
deadheading 50, 61
deadnettle see lamium
decking 174, 176, 182, 186, 194,
196–7
delphiniums 45, 59, 61
designs see garden design
Dianthus spp. (pinks) 41, 61,
125
D. barbatus (sweet william) 41,
211, **229–30**
'Mrs Sinkins' 145, **145**
Dicentra formosa 240
D. spectabilis (bleeding heart)
29, **240**
'Alba' **240**
digging 226
Digitalis purpurea (foxglove) 41,
230
dill 93
dog's tooth violet 236
dogwood 215, 220, **246**
drainage 71
Dryopteris affinis (golden-scaled
male fern) 29
D. erythrosora 29
D. filix-mas (male fern) 29, 112
Dutch hoes 38

E

Easter lily 237
easy-reach gardens 160–169
echinops 61, 240
Echinops (globe thistle) **240**

'Blue Globe' 240
'Veitch's Blue' 240
edging 48
elaeagnus 178, 179, **246**
Elaeagnus pungens (elaeagnus)
178, **246**
elecampane 92
electrical installations 26, 139,
140, 142
Ensete ventricosum 70
Epimedium (barrenwort) 58, **240**
E. x versicolor 'Cupreum' 240
E. x. v. 'Sulphuream' 240
epimediums 58, 115, 166, 240
Eranthis hyemalis (winter aconite)
236, **236**
Erica carnea (winter heather)
219, 220, **221**
ericas see heathers
Eruca sativa (rocket) 93
Eryngium x oliverianum (sea
holly) 188, **189**, 240, 240
eryngiums 61, 184, 189, 240, **240**
Erysimum cheiri (wallflower)
41, 125, **230**
'Blood Red' 230
'Bowles Mauve' 230
'Cloth of Gold' 230
'Persian Carpet' 230
Erysimum x allionii (Siberian
wallflower) 124, **124**
Erythronium dens-canis
(dog's tooth violet) **236**
'Lilac Wonder' 236
'Pink Perfection' 236
'Purple King' 236
'Snowflake' 236
'White Splendour' 236
Escallonia spp. 178
Eschscholzia (Californian poppy)
166, **179**
Eucalyptus gunnii
(eucalyptus/cider gum) **246**
eucalyptus **246**
Euonymus fortunei 'Silver
Queen' 112
E. japonica aureovariagatus 112
Euphorbia (spurge/milkweed) **240**
E. characias 199
E. marginata (ghost weed) **230**
E. griffithii 'Dixter' 240
'Fireglow' 240
E. polychroma 61
euphorbias 61, 108, 112, 199,
230, 240

evening primroses 105
evergreens 35, 54, 71, 109, 112, 178, 198, 206, 215, 216
    hedges 112–13
    for winter gardens 215, 220–1
exposed sites 172–81, 182–91

F
Fallopia aubertii *(Russian vine)* 114
Fargesia murielias *(umbrella bamboo)* 135
farmyard manure 40, 61
Fatsia japonica *(Japanese aralia)* **157**
fencing 65, 151, 173, 176–7, 194, 196, 215
fennel 41, 41, 86, 93
ferns **28–29**, 109, 112, 198
fertilizers 105
feverfew 92
Filipendula *(meadowsweet)* 29
fish 13, 219
flax 105
flowering cherry **221, 248**
foam flower 115
foam of May **249**
Foeniculum vulgare *(fennel)* 93
    'Rubra' **41**
forget-me-not 100, 104, 105
Fothergilla major *(fothergilla)* 125, **247**
fothergillas **247**
fountain grass 157
fountains 23, 24, 26
foxgloves 35, 41, 45, 92, 105, 109, 198, 226, **230**
fragrant plants 119, 162, 220
French roses 41
French beans 83, **83**
French tarragon 93
Fritillaria imperialis *(crown imperial)* **236**
fritillaries 236
fruit trees/bushes 40, **41**
Fuschsia magellanica *(hardy fuschsia)* 178

G
Galanthus nivalis *(snowdrop)* 220
Galtonia *(summer hyacinth)* 61, **236–7**
    G. candicans 237
    G. veridiflora 237
garden elder 125, **248**, 249

garden furniture 193
    see also *seating*
garden phlox 125, **243**
garlic 93
Genista aetnensis *(Mount Etna broom)* **247**
    G.hispanica *(Spanish gorse)* 178
Geranium *(cranesbill/geranium)* 41, 225, 241, **241**
    'Johnson's Blue' 241
    G. maderense 241
    G. pratense *(meadow cranesbill)* 105, 241
    G. sanguineum 'Album' 241
    G.s. 'Shepherd's Warning' 241
geraniums 45, 166, 225, 241
    see also *cranesbill*
geums 61
ghost weed **230**
globe amaranths **230**
globe thistles 61, **240**
glory of the snow **235**
goat's beard 104
godetias see *clarkias*
Gomphrena globosa *(globe amaranth)* **230**
gorse 178, 187
grape hyacinths 105, **238**
grasses 18, 19, 98, 100, 105, 109, 156–7, 184, 188–9, 199, 216, 219
gravel 129, 132
greenfly 51
Gunnera manicata *(gunnera)* 156

H
Hakonechloa macra 'Aureola' 70
Hamamelis mollis *(witch hazel)* 220, **247**
hamamelis **247**
harebells 102, 105
hart's tongue fern 29
hawkbit 105
hawthorn 35
heathers 215, 219, **221**, 225
Hebe *(hebe)* **247**
hebes 166, **247**
Hedera helix *(ivy)* 71, 114
    'Gold Heart' 71
    'Maple Leaf' 71
hedging 34–5, 44, 45, 55, 65, 71, 110, 123, 166, 173, 215, 220
    planting box 112–13

Helianthus annuus *(annual sunflower)* 41, 230, **230**
    'Music Box' 41, 230
    'Pacino' 230
    'Teddy Bear' 230
Heliotropium arborescens *(heliotrope/cherry pie plant)* 125
heliotropes 125
Helleborus argutifolius *(Corsican hellebore)* **241**
    H. niger *(Christmas rose)* 241
    H. x ballardiae 29
hellebores 29, 198, 221, 225, **241**
Helleborus orientalis *(lenten rose)* 28, 41, 221, 241
Hemerocallis *(day lily)* 241
    'Berlin Red' 241
    'Cartwheels' 241
    'Golden Chimes' 241
    'Lemon Bells' 241
    'Marion Vaughn' 241
    'Pink Damask' 241
    'Red Precious' 241
    'Stella de Oro' 241
herb robert 105
herbal remedies 86, 91
herbs 45, 82, 166
    gardens 6, 86–95
Hesperis matronalis *(dame's violet/sweet rocket)* 125
Heuchera *(heuchera/coral flower)* **241**
    'Coral Cloud' 241
    'Greenfinch' 41, **61**, 241
    'Palace Purple' 241
    'Pewter Moon' 241
    'Red Spangles' 241
    'Snow Storm' 241
heucheras 41, 166, 241
hoeing 38, 61, 80, 82
hollies 35, 199
hollyfern 29
hollyhocks 41, 61, **228**
honesty **231**
honeysuckles 35, 71, 166, 220, **247**, 248
hop plant 114
Hosta crispula 58
    H. 'Tokudama' 29
    H. 'Whirlwind' 60
hostas 29, 29, 60, 61, 108, **115**, 195, 198
houseleeks 178
Humulus lupulus *(hop plant)*114
hyacinths 118, 125

Hyacinthus cultivars 125
Hydrangea petiolaris *(climbing hydrangea)* 114
hyssop 92

I
Iberis *(candytuft)* 166
ice plant 188, 244, **244**
Ilex aquifolium *(holly)* 199, **199**
impatiens (busy lizzies) 210
insecticides 51
insects 82, 98
Ipomea *(morning glory)* **231**
Iris *(iris)* **237**
    'Black Knight' 237
    'Bronze Cloud' 237
    'Dante' 237
    'Langport Smoke' 237
    'Langport Song' 237
    I. pallida, 'Variegata' 237
    I. reticulata 220, 237, 237
    I. sibirica 19, 237
    I. unguicularis 237
Iris *(water iris)* **19**
    I. pseudoacorus *(yellow flag iris)* 19, 19
irises 19, 61, 220, **237**
ivies 71, 114

J
Japanese anemone 61, **239**, 239
Japanese aralia 156, **157**
Japanese maple 134, **135**
jasmine 119, 122, 166, **167**, 198
Jasminum officinale *(jasmine)* 166, **167**
jonquils **125**
    see also *daffodils*
junipers 178, 220
Juniperus communis *(juniper)* 178

K
kidney vetch 104
kitchen gardens 76–85
knapweed 104, 105
Kniphofia *(red hot poker)* 188, 242, **242**
    'Bees Sunset' **157**
    K. caulescens 199, 242
Kochia scoparia *(summer cypress)* 112
Kolkwitzia amabilis *(beauty bush)* **247**
Kousa dogwood **246**

L

lady's bedstraw 104
lady's mantle 198, **239**
lady's smock 105
lamb's ears **244**
Lamium maculatum
  (lamium/dead nettle) 115, 167,
  167, **242**, 243
  lamiums 115, 167, 242, 243
larkspur **229**
Lathyrus odoratus (sweet pea)
  41, 125, 231, **231**
  'Jet Set Mixed' 231
  'Knee High' 231
Laurus nobilis (bay) 93
Lavandula (lavender) 125, 199,
  242
  L. augustifolia 'Hidcote' 242
  L. augustifolia 'Munstead' 242
  L. stoechas 242
lavatera 211, **231**
Lavatera trimestris (annual
  garden mallow) **231**
  'Mont Blanc' 231
  'Silver Cup' 231
lavenders 35, 44, 45, 45, 71, 92,
  125, 166, 188, 199, **242**
lawns 55, 105, 120, 205
leeks 76
legumes 76, 77
lemon balm 86, 92
lenten rose 241
lettuces 77
Leucanthemum vulgare (ox-eye
  daisy) 105
Leucojum aestivum (summer
  snowflake/Loddon lily) **237**
  'Gravetye' 237
  L. vernum 237
lighting 138–139, 140, 142–3,
  193
Ligustrum ovalifolium (privet)
  220
lilacs 125, 144–5, 225
lilies 45, 92, 119, 125, 225, **237**
Lilium (lily) **237**
  L. candidum ('madonna lily')
  237
  'Enchantment' 237
  L. longiflorum ('Easter lily') 237
  L. mackliniae 237
  L. monadelphum 237
  L. regale ('regal lily') 125, 237
  'Star Gazer' 237
lily-of-the-valley 105, 125

Limnanthes douglasii (poached
  egg plant) **231**
liners: pond 14, 16–17, 18–19
Loddon lily see summer snowflake
log rolls 48
Lonicera (honeysuckle) 166
  L. fragrantissima 220
  L. nitida 71
  L.n. 'Baggesen's Gold' 71
  L. periclymenum 114, **247**, 248
  L.p. 'Serotina' 71
lords and ladies **234**
love in a mist 41, 98, 232, **232**
Lunaria annua (honesty/money
  plant) **231**
  'Alba Variegata' 231
  'Variegata' 231
lungwort 244
  see also pulmonaria
lupins 41, 61, 98, 105
Lupinus polyphyllus (lupins) 41

M

madonna lily 237
magnolias **61**, 125
Magnolia grandiflora 125
  M. stellata (star magnolia) **61**,
  125
Mahonia x media 'Charity'
  (mahonia) 199, **199**, 220
  mahonias 199, 220
  maidenhair fern 29
maintenance 35, 38, 50–1, 61,
  87, 91, 98–9
  end of season 205
  for easy-reach gardens 160
  feeding 61, 80
  pest/disease control 61, 77
  soil improvement 225–6
mallows **231**
Malus (crab apple) **248**
maples 134, 135, 220, 245, **245**
marigolds 35, 41, 105, 211
marjoram 93
materials 45, 206
  for bog gardens 14
  for brick paths/patios 218–19
  for compost making 80–1
  for easy-reach gardens 160–1,
  165
  landscaping 7, 9, 68
  light fittings 142
  for planters 123
  for ponds 13
  for water features 22

for windbreaks 187
for Zen gardens 132–3
Matthiola bicornis (night-scented
  stock) 125
M. incana (Brompton stock) 125,
  145, **145**
meadow clary 104, 105
meadow cranesbill 104, 105
meadow gardens 98–107
meadowsweet 29, 105
Meconopsis cambrica (Welsh
  poppy) 41, **232**, 233
Melissa officinalis (lemon balm) 92
Mentha spicata (mint) 93
Mexican orange blossom 125,
  198–9, 225
michaelmas daisies **40–1**, 61
milkweed see spurge
mimulus 105
mint 93
miscanthus **19**, 157
Miscanthus sinensis **19**, 157
  'Gracillimus' 18, 19, 19, 157
mock orange **124**, 225
Moluccella laevis (bells of
  Ireland) **232**
montbretia 61, 211
morning glory **231**
Mount Etna broom **247**
mountain ash **249**
mulching 40, 50, 61, 110, 226
mullein 105
  see also verbascum
Musa basjoo (banana plant) 70
Muscari (grape hyacinth) **238**
myosotis see forget-me-not

N

Narcissus (daffodil/jonquil) **238**
  N. Cantabricus 238
  N. cyclamineus 238
  N. jonquilla (jonquil) 125
  'Minnow' **238**
  N. poeticus 238
  N. pseudonarcissus (daffodil)
  105
  N. 'Tête à Tête' **238**
nasturtiums 82, 92, 93, **93**, 166,
  198, **233**
Nemophila menziesii
  (nemophila) **232**
  'Baby Blue Eyes' 232
  'Penny Black' 232
  'Snowstorm' 232
nepeta 41, 45

see also catmint
Nepeta (catmint) 41
Nerine bowdenii (nerine) 238,
  238
  'Mark Fenwick' **238**
nerines 238
New Zealand flax 70–1
Nicotiana (tobacco plant) 125,
  231, **232**
Nigella damascena (nigella/love
  in a mist) 41, 232, **232**
  'Miss Jekyll' 232
night gardens 138–47
night-scented stock 119, 125
Nymphaea (water lilies) 29

O

Ocimum basilicum (basil) 93
Olearia cheesmanii (daisy bush)
  178
  O. x haastii 178
  olearias 178, 179
onions 76
opium poppies 41, 61, 211
oriental poppies 45, **242**
Origanum vulgare (marjoram) 93
ox-eye daisies 102, 104, 105

P

Paeonia officinalis (cottage garden
  peony) 41
  'Sarah Bernhardt' 125
pampas grass 157
Papaver (poppy) 41, **232**
  P. orientale (oriental poppy)
  45, **242**
  P. rhoeas (shirley poppy) 41
  P. somniferum (opium poppy)
  41, 61, 211
parrot tulips 71
parsley 82, 93
Passiflora caaerulea (passion
  flower) 71
passion flowers 71
paths 48, 55, 109, 162
  laying **39**, 79
  marking out 226
patios 24, 142, 192–201,
  205
Pelargonium crispum
  (pelargoniums) 125
pelargoniums 125, 184, 198,
  205, 211
Pennisetum alopecuroides
  (fountain grass) 157, 189, **189**

pennyroyal 92
Penstemon cultivars **242**, 243
penstemons 242
peonies 41, 45, 59, 61
perennials 40, 41, 54, 86, 93,
   166, 216, 219, 239–44
pergolas 114, 215
periwinkle 71, 115, 166
Perovskia atriplicifolia
   (perovskia) **243**
pests/diseases 51, 61, 82, 98
   control 61, 77
Petasites fragrans (winter
   heliotrope) 220
Petroselinum crispum (parsley) 93
Petunia hybrids 125
petunias 125, 210
pH measurement 224–5
Phaseolus vulgaris (pole bean)
   83
pheasant's tail grass **156**, 157
Phegopteris connectilis (beech
   fern) 29
philadelphus 61, **124**, 225
   Philadelphus 'Belle Etoile' 124,
   124
phlox 41, 61, 125, **243**
Phlox paniculata (phlox) 41,
   125, 243
Phormium spp. **189**, 199
P. tenax (New Zealand flax) 58,
   70–1, 189, **199**
phormiums 58, 70–1, 179, 184, 189
Phyllostachys nigra 135
   P. viridiglaucescens 135
pieris **248**
Pieris japonica (pieris) **248**
pinks 41, 61, 105, 125, 145,
   166, 225
planning see design
planters 123, 160
plants/planting 50–1, 112–13,
   166, 218, 227
   acid/alkaline soils 225
   borders 58, 60–1
   children's gardens 156–7
   cottage gardens 34–5, **40–1**
   courtyards 70–1
   herb gardens 92–3
   kitchen gardens 82–3
   low-maintenance 166–7, 174,
   188
   meadow gardens 100, 104–5
   patios 194–5, 198–9
   roof gardens 188–9
   scented gardens 118–19, 124–5

seaside gardens 178–9
shade/woodland gardens
   108–9, 114–15
summer gardens 205, 206,
   210–11
water gardens 18–19, 24, 28–9
winter gardens 214–15, 220–1
Zen gardens 134–5
play areas 152
Pleioblastus (bamboo)
   P. auricomus 135
   P. pygmaeus 188
   P. simonii 135
   P. variegatus 135
poached egg plant **231**
pole beans 83
pollinators 118
polyantha roses 166
Polystichum setiferum (soft
   shield fern) 29
ponds 23, 219
   designing 12–13, 17
   planting 17, 18–19
   pond and bog gardens 12–21
poppies 35, 41, 61, 166, **232**,
   242
pot marigolds 35, 41
potatoes 77, 104
Potentilla (potentilla) **243**, 248
   P. fruticosa 'Abbotswood' 243
   P. nepalensis 'Miss Willmott' 243
potentillas 166, 225, **243**, 248
Poterium sansquisorba 93
pots 55, 205
preparation
   beds 80
   soil 50, **76–7**, 224–5
primroses 102, 104, 125
Primula auricula (auricula) 125
   P. secundiflora 18
   P. vulgaris (primrose) 125
primulas 16, 16, 29, 41
privet hedging 220
projects
   bog gardens 16–17
   borders 58
   box hedge planting 112–13
   brick paths 219
   compost making 80–1
   cottage garden 38–9
   enclosures 68
   garden lighting 142–3
   raised beds 164–5
   sand pit 155
   scented seats 122–3
   sowing meadow seed 102–3

timber arch 48–9
trellis battening 90–1
water features 26–7
windbreaks 177, 186–7
Zen elements 132–3
propagation 40, 61, 112
   see also seedlings; seeds
pruning 50
prunus 220, **221**, **248**
Prunus laurocerasus (common
   laurel) 220
   P. serrula (flowering cherry)
   221
   P. 'Shirotae' **248**
Pseudosana japonica (arrow
   bamboo) 135
Pulmonaria
   (pulmonaria/lungwort) **243–4**,
   244
   P. officinalis 244
pulmonarias **243–4**, 244
pumps 26
purple loosestrife 105
pyracantha 40

Q

quaking grass 105

R

radishes 76
ragged robin 104
raised beds 48, 71, 76, 80, 91,
   161
red hot pokers 151, **157**, 188,
   199, 225, 242, **242**
regal lily 125, 237
Rhododendron luteum (Ghent
   azalea) 125
rhododendrons 125, 224, 225
Rhus typhina (stagshorn sumach)
   248
robinia see acacia
Robinia pseudoacacia (golden
   acacia/robinia) **248**
rocket 93
rocks 129
roof gardens 182–191
rose gardens 44–53
Rosa
   'Banksiae' 71
   centifolia 'Robert le Diable' 125
   R. damascena (damask rose)
   125
   R. gallica (French/Provins
   rose) 40, **41**, **125**
   'Cardinal Richelieu' 125

'Suffolk' 50, **51**
'Margaret Merrill' 125
'Mme Pierre Oger' (bourbon
   rose) 125
R. moschata (musk rose) 125
'Penelope' 125
R. rugosa 125
'Gertrude Jeckyll' 51, **51**
'Wedding Day' **51**
'William Lobb' 125
'Zéphirine Drouhin' 125
rosemary 44, 82, 92, **93**, 188
roses 35, 40, 41, 45, 51, 71, 92,
   114, 118–19, 122, 125
   gardens 44–53
   miniature 166
   planting 50–1
   polyanthas 166
Rosmarinus officinalis
   (rosemary) **93**, 123
Rudbeckia hirta (rudbeckia)
   232–3
   'Becky Mixed' 233
   'Goldilocks' 232
   'Marmalade' 233
   'Rustic Dwarfs' 232
rue 91, 179, **179**
rugosa roses 35
Russell lupius 41
Russian sage 243
Russian vine 114
Ruta graveolens (Common rue)
   179, **179**

S

sage 45, 93, **93**, 166
St John's wort 105
Salad burnet 93
Salix (dogwood) 220
   S. britzensis 221
Salvia officinalis (sage) 93
S. splendens (salvia) 230, **233**
   'Blaze of Fire' 233
   'Phoenix Mixed' 233
   'Phoenix Purple' 233
   'Sizzler Mixed' 233
Sambucus (garden elder) 125
   S. racemosa 'Sutherland Gold'
   248, 249
sand pits 151, **155**
sand raking 132
sandy soils 104
santolina 45, 188, 199
Santolina chamaecyparissus
   (cotton lavender) 188
Sasa veitchii 135

Saxifraga hirsuta *58*
Scabiosa *(scabious) 41*
　S. atropurpurea *(sweet scabious)* **233**
　'Double Mixed' **233**
scabious 41, 98, 104
scented plants 45, 118–19, 124–5, 144–5
screening 65, 71, 173, 178–9, 182, 186
sculptures 66, 67, 140
sea hollies 61, 189, 240, **240**
sea thrift 199
seakale 184, 188, 239
seaside gardens 172-181
seating 35, 44, 119, 122–3, 161, 205
Sedum spectabile *(ice plant) 188, 199, 244,* **244**
sedums 61, 178, 184, 188, 199, **244**
seedlings 35, 102
seeds 80, 102–3, 205
self-heal 104
Semiarundinaria fastuosa *(Narihira bamboo) 135*
Sempervivum *spp. 178*
shade gardens 108-117
shade-loving plants 45, 55, 105, 109, 114–15, 198
shirley poppies 41
shrub roses 35
shrubs 40, 54, 109, 245–9
　low-maintenance 166
　scented 125
　wind-resistant 178–9
Siberian wallflower **124**
silver birch 140, 215
sites/siting 226
　for kitchen gardens 78
　for ponds 13
slugs/snails 61
smoke bush **246**, *247*
snapdragons 210
snowberry **249**
snowdrops 105, 220
snowy mespilus see amelanchier
soft shield fern 29
soil types 100, 104, 105
　acid/alkaline 224–5
　dry/well-drained 76, 105
Solanum crispum *(Chilean potato vine) 71, 71*
Sorbus aria *'Lutescens'*

(whitebeam) **249**
　S. commixta *(mountain ash)* **249**
Spirea *'Arguta' (foam of May/bridal wreath)* **249**
spleenwort 29
spraying 50
spurge **240**
Stachys byzantina *(lamb's ear/wooly betony)* **244**
stagshorn sumach **248**
staking 38, **59**, *61, 218*
Stipa arundinacea *(pheasant's tail grass)* **156**, *157*
　S. gigantea *(golden oats) 157, 188*
　S. splendens *157*
stone 132, 160
strawberry tree 206, 211, **211**, *220*
succulents 178
summer cypress 112, **228**
summer hyacinth **236–7**
summer snowflake **237**
sunflowers 41, 230, **230**
supports
　plant 45, 59, 65
　see also *wigwams*
Swan River daisy **228**
sweet peas 41, 125, **231**
sweet rocket 125
sweet scabious **233**
sweet williams 41, 211, **229–30**
Symphytum officinale *(comfrey) 92*
Symphoricarpos albus *'Laevigatus' (snowberry)* **249**
Syringa *(lilac) 125, 225*
　S. vulgaris *144,* **144–5**

T
Tanacetum parthenium *(feverfew) 92*
tansy 92
tarragon 86
Taxus baccata *(yew) 71*
terraces 24
Thalictrum rochebruneanum *58*
thymes 82, 86, 93, 93, 166, 167, **167**, *188*
Thymus *spp. 167,* **167**
　T. vulgaris *93*
Tiarella cordifolia *(foam flower) 115*

toadflax 105
tobacco plants 119, 125, 210, **232**
tools 38, 225
Trachelospermum asiaticum *114*
　T. jasminoides *166*
tree houses 151, 154
trees 40, 54, 109, 245–9
　planting 218
　scented 125
trellis 55, 65, 66, 68, 80, 123, 173, 183, 198, 215
　against a wall 90-91
Trillium grandiflorum *58*
trollius 105
Tropaeolum *(nasturtium) 92,* **93**, *166,* **233**
trumpet lilies 45
tubers 234–8
Tulipa *(tulip)* **238**
　'Angelique' 238
　'Black Parrot' 238
　'Golden Apeldorn' 238
　T. kaufmanniana *238*
　'Queen of the Night' 238
　'Spring Green' 238
　T. sylvestris *(wood tulip) 105*
　'White Parrot' 238
tulips 70, 71, 105, **238**
turnips 76

U
umbrella bamboo 135
underplanting 45, 109, 198

V
valerian 41
vegetables 76–7
Verbascum *(verbascum/mullein) 244*
　V. phoeniceum **244**
verbascums 205, 211, **244**
Verbena bonariensis *41,* **244**
verbenas **244**
vetch 105
viburnums 58, 60, 125, 220, **249**
Viburnum *(viburnam)* **249**
　cultivars 125
　V. farreri *220*
　V. *'Opulus roseum' 60*
　V. tinus *58*
Vinca major *(periwinkle) 115, 166*
　V. minor *112*
vines 71, 114
Viola odorata *(English/sweet violet) 58,* **124**

violas 45, 58
violets 124
Vitis coignetiae *(vine) 71, 114*

W
wallflowers 41, 118, 125, 205, **230**
walls 65, 71, 162, 165, 173, 198, 215
water features 13, 22–7, 161
　and child safety 23, 151
water gardens 12–21, 22–31
water iris **19**
water lilies 19, **29**
watering 61, 65, 161, 183
weeds 82, 104
　control 104, 219
Welsh poppies 41, **232**, *233*
wheelchair access 164
whitebeam **249**
white lilac **144-5**
wigwams 38, **39**, *45*
wild garlic 105
wildlife 13, 14, 40, 98
windbreaks 173, **176–7**, *182, 184, 186–7*
windflower **234**
windproof plants 188–9
winter aconite 236, **236**
winter heliotrope 220
wintersweet 220
wisteria 114
Wisteria sinensis *(wisteria) 114*
witch hazel 220, **247**
wood anemone 105
wood tulips 105
woodland plants/gardens 105, 109
Woodsia polystichoides *(hollyfern) 29*

Y
yarrow 104, 105
yew 44, 71, 215, 220
Yucca filamentosa *(Adam's needle) 70, 70, 71, 199*
yuccas 70, 71, 199
Yushania anceps *(anceps bamboo) 135*

Z
Zantedeschia aethiopica *(arum lily) 29*
Zen gardens 128–137, 130–31
Zen bridges 132–133

Acknowledgements

Bridgewater Book Company would like to thank Sue Hook for her garden schemes and designs, Barry Robson and Vanessa Luff for their Illustrations, and Liz Eddison for her photography. Bridgewater would also like to extend their gratitude to Roger Benjamin, Georgina Steeds and Smith's Nurseries, New Denham, Middlesex, UK.